LOLITA

Major Literary Characters

**THE ANCIENT WORLD THROUGH
THE SEVENTEENTH CENTURY**

ACHILLES
Homer, *Iliad*

CALIBAN
William Shakespeare, *The Tempest*
Robert Browning, *Caliban upon Setebos*

CLEOPATRA
William Shakespeare, *Antony and
    Cleopatra*
John Dryden, *All for Love*
George Bernard Shaw, *Caesar and
    Cleopatra*

DON QUIXOTE
Miguel de Cervantes, *Don Quixote*
Franz Kafka, *Parables*

FALSTAFF
William Shakespeare, *Henry IV, Part I,
    Henry IV, Part II, The Merry Wives
    of Windsor*

FAUST
Christopher Marlowe, *Doctor Faustus*
Johann Wolfgang von Goethe, *Faust*
Thomas Mann, *Doctor Faustus*

HAMLET
William Shakespeare, *Hamlet*

IAGO
William Shakespeare, *Othello*

JULIUS CAESAR
William Shakespeare, *Julius Caesar*
George Bernard Shaw, *Caesar and
    Cleopatra*

KING LEAR
William Shakespeare, *King Lear*

MACBETH
William Shakespeare, *Macbeth*

ODYSSEUS/ULYSSES
Homer, *Odyssey*
James Joyce, *Ulysses*

OEDIPUS
Sophocles, *Oedipus Rex, Oedipus
    at Colonus*

OTHELLO
William Shakespeare, *Othello*

ROSALIND
William Shakespeare, *As You Like It*

SANCHO PANZA
Miguel de Cervantes, *Don Quixote*
Franz Kafka, *Parables*

SATAN
The Book of Job
John Milton, *Paradise Lost*

SHYLOCK
William Shakespeare, *The Merchant
    of Venice*

THE WIFE OF BATH
Geoffrey Chaucer, *The Canterbury
    Tales*

**THE EIGHTEENTH AND
NINETEENTH CENTURIES**

AHAB
Herman Melville, *Moby-Dick*

ISABEL ARCHER
Henry James, *Portrait of a Lady*

EMMA BOVARY
Gustave Flaubert, *Madame Bovary*

DOROTHEA BROOKE
George Eliot, *Middlemarch*

CHELSEA HOUSE PUBLISHERS

Major Literary Characters

DAVID COPPERFIELD
Charles Dickens, *David Copperfield*

ROBINSON CRUSOE
Daniel Defoe, *Robinson Crusoe*

DON JUAN
Molière, *Don Juan*
Lord Byron, *Don Juan*

HUCK FINN
Mark Twain, *The Adventures of Tom Sawyer, Adventures of Huckleberry Finn*

CLARISSA HARLOWE
Samuel Richardson, *Clarissa*

HEATHCLIFF
Emily Brontë, *Wuthering Heights*

ANNA KARENINA
Leo Tolstoy, *Anna Karenina*

MR. PICKWICK
Charles Dickens, *The Pickwick Papers*

HESTER PRYNNE
Nathaniel Hawthorne, *The Scarlet Letter*

BECKY SHARP
William Makepeace Thackeray, *Vanity Fair*

LAMBERT STRETHER
Henry James, *The Ambassadors*

EUSTACIA VYE
Thomas Hardy, *The Return of the Native*

TWENTIETH CENTURY

ÁNTONIA
Willa Cather, *My Ántonia*

BRETT ASHLEY
Ernest Hemingway, *The Sun Also Rises*

HANS CASTORP
Thomas Mann, *The Magic Mountain*

HOLDEN CAULFIELD
J. D. Salinger, *The Catcher in the Rye*

CADDY COMPSON
William Faulkner, *The Sound and the Fury*

JANIE CRAWFORD
Zora Neale Hurston, *Their Eyes Were Watching God*

CLARISSA DALLOWAY
Virginia Woolf, *Mrs. Dalloway*

DILSEY
William Faulkner, *The Sound and the Fury*

GATSBY
F. Scott Fitzgerald, *The Great Gatsby*

HERZOG
Saul Bellow, *Herzog*

JOAN OF ARC
William Shakespeare, *Henry VI*
George Bernard Shaw, *Saint Joan*

LOLITA
Vladimir Nabokov, *Lolita*

WILLY LOMAN
Arthur Miller, *Death of a Salesman*

MARLOW
Joseph Conrad, *Lord Jim, Heart of Darkness, Youth, Chance*

PORTNOY
Philip Roth, *Portnoy's Complaint*

BIGGER THOMAS
Richard Wright, *Native Son*

CHELSEA HOUSE PUBLISHERS

Major Literary Characters

L O L I T A

Edited and with an introduction by
HAROLD BLOOM

CHELSEA HOUSE PUBLISHERS
New York ◇ Philadelphia

Jacket illustration: Sue Lyon as Lolita in the film adaptation of *Lolita* (1962)
(Performing Arts Research Center, the New York Public Library
at Lincoln Center, Astor, Lenox and Tilden Foundations). *Inset:* Title page
of the first edition of *Lolita* (Paris: Olympia Press, 1955)
(Department of Rare Books, Cornell University Library).

Chelsea House Publishers

Editor-in-Chief   Richard S. Papale
Managing Editor   Karyn Gullen Browne
Picture Editor   Adrian G. Allen
Art Director   Maria Epes
Manufacturing Director   Gerald Levine

Major Literary Characters

Senior Editor   S. T. Joshi
Copy Chief   Philip Koslow
Designer   Maria Epes

Staff for LOLITA

Picture Researcher   Ellen Barrett
Assistant Art Director   Howard Brotman
Production Manager   Joseph Romano
Production Coordinator   Marie Claire Cebrián

Printed and bound in the United States of America

First Printing

1   3   5   7   9   8   6   4   2

Library of Congress Cataloging-in-Publication Data

Lolita / edited and with an introduction by Harold Bloom.
p.   cm.—(Major literary characters)
Includes bibliographical references and index.
ISBN 0-7910-0961-0.—ISBN 0-7910-1016-3 (pbk.)
1. Nabokov, Vladimir Vladimirovich, 1899–1977. Lolita.
I. Bloom, Harold.   II. Series.
PS3527.A15L6327   1992
813.'54—dc20
92-3508
CIP

CONTENTS

THE ANALYSIS OF CHARACTER   ix

EDITOR'S NOTE   xv

INTRODUCTION   I
Harold Bloom

CRITICAL EXTRACTS
Vladimir Nabokov 5   Dorothy Parker 9   Lionel Trilling 10
Thomas Molnar 11   Frank S. Meyer 12   Allan Brick 14
Diana Butler 16   Wayne C. Booth 18   Denis de Rougemont 18
Nona Balakian 21   Vladimir Nabokov and Alvin Toffler 22
Leslie A. Fiedler 23   David L. Jones 24   Julian Moynahan 29
Garry Wills 32   James Twitchell 34   Robert T. Levine 39
Susan Elizabeth Sweeney 45   Katherine Tiernan O'Connor 49

CRITICAL ESSAYS

LOLITA: PARODY AND THE PURSUIT OF BEAUTY   53
Gabriel Josipovici

FOLK CHARACTERIZATION IN LOLITA   68
Steven Swann Jones

NECROPHILIA IN LOLITA   79
Lucy B. Maddox

HUMBERT THE CHARACTER, HUMBERT THE WRITER   90
Richard H. Bullock

NABOKOV AND THE VIENNESE WITCH DOCTOR   105
Jeffrey Berman

THE AMERICANIZATION OF HUMBERT HUMBERT   120
John Haegert

''LO'' AND BEHOLD: SOLVING THE LOLITA RIDDLE   134
Trevor McNeely

FRAMING LOLITA: IS THERE A WOMAN IN THE TEXT?   149
Linda Kauffman

LOLITA   169
Vladimir E. Alexandrov

CONTENTS

CONTRIBUTORS 195
BIBLIOGRAPHY 197
ACKNOWLEDGMENTS 201
INDEX 203

THE ANALYSIS OF CHARACTER

Harold Bloom

"Character," according to our dictionaries, still has as a primary meaning a graphic symbol, such as a letter of the alphabet. This meaning reflects the word's apparent origin in the ancient Greek *charactēr,* a sharp stylus. *Charactēr* also meant the mark of the stylus' incisions. Recent fashions in literary criticism have reduced "character" in literature to a matter of marks upon a page. But our word "character" also has a very different meaning, matching that of the ancient Greek *ēthos,* "habitual way of life." Shall we say then that literary character is an imitation of human character, or is it just a grouping of marks? The issue is between a critic like Dr. Samuel Johnson, for whom words were as much like people as like things, and a critic like the late Roland Barthes, who told us that "the fact can only exist linguistically, as a term of discourse." Who is closer to our experience of reading literature, Johnson or Barthes? What difference does it make, if we side with one critic rather than the other?

Barthes is famous, like Foucault and other recent French theorists, for having added to Nietzsche's proclamation of the death of God a subsidiary demise, that of the literary author. If there are no authors, then there are no fictional personages, presumably because literature does not refer to a world outside language. Words indeed necessarily refer to other words in the first place, but the impact of words ultimately is drawn from a universe of fact. Stories, poems, and plays are recognizable as such because they are human utterances within traditions of utterances, and traditions, by achieving authority, become a kind of fact, or at least the sense of a fact. Our sense that literary characters, within the context of a fictive cosmos, indeed are fictional personages is also a kind of fact. The meaning and value of every character in a successful work of literary representation depend upon our ideas of persons in the factual reality of our lives.

Literary character is always an invention, and inventions generally are indebted to prior inventions. Shakespeare is the inventor of literary character as we know it; he reformed the universal human expectations for the verbal imitation of personality, and the reformation appears now to be permanent and uncannily inevitable. Remarkable as the Bible and Homer are at representing personages, their characters are relatively unchanging. They age within their stories, but their habitual modes of being do not develop. Jacob and Achilles unfold before us, but without metamorphoses. Lear and Macbeth, Hamlet and Othello severely modify themselves not only by their actions, but by their utterances, and most of all through *overhearing themselves,* whether they speak to themselves or to others. Pondering what they themselves have said, they will to change, and actually do change, sometimes extravagantly yet always persuasively. Or else they suffer change, without willing it, but in reaction not so much to their language as to their relation to that language.

I do not think it useful to say that Shakespeare successfully imitated elements in our characters. Rather, it could be argued that he compelled aspects of character to appear that previously were concealed, or not available to representation. This is not to say that Shakespeare is God, but to remind us that language is not God either. The mimesis of character in Shakespeare's dramas now seems to us normative, and indeed became the accepted mode almost immediately, as Ben Jonson shrewdly and somewhat grudgingly implied. And yet, Shakespearean representation has surprisingly little in common with the imitation of reality in Jonson or in Christopher Marlowe. The origins of Shakespeare's originality in the portrayal of men and women are to be found in the *Canterbury Tales* of Geoffrey Chaucer, insofar as they can be located anywhere before Shakespeare himself. Chaucer's savage and superb Pardoner overhears his own tale-telling, as well as his mocking rehearsal of his own spiel, and through this overhearing he is emboldened to forget himself, and enthusiastically urges all his fellow-pilgrims to come forward to be fleeced by him. His self-awareness, and apocalyptically rancid sense of spiritual fall, are preludes to the even grander abysses of the perverted will in Iago and in Edmund. What might be called the character trait of a negative charisma may be Chaucer's invention, but came to its perfection in Shakespearean mimesis.

The analysis of character is as much Shakespeare's invention as the representation of character is, since Iago and Edmund are adepts at analyzing both themselves and their victims. Hamlet, whose overwhelming charisma has many negative components, is certainly the most comprehensive of all literary characters, and so necessarily prophesies the labyrinthine complexities of the will in Iago and Edmund. Charisma, according to Max Weber, its first codifier, is primarily a natural endowment, and implies a primordial and idiosyncratic power over nature, and so finally over death. Hamlet's uncanniness is at its most suggestive in the scene of his long dying, where the audience, through the mediation of Horatio, itself is compelled to meditate upon suicide, if only because outliving the prince of Denmark scarcely seems an option.

Shakespearean representation has usurped not only our sense of literary character, but our sense of ourselves as characters, with Hamlet playing the part of the largest of these usurpations. Insofar as we have an idea of human disinterestedness, we tend to derive it from the Hamlet of Act V, whose quietism has about it a ghostly authority. Oscar Wilde, in his profound and profoundly witty dialogue, "The Decay of Lying," expressed a permanent insight when he insisted that art shaped every era, far more than any age formed art. Life imitates art, we imitate Shakespeare, because without Shakespeare we would perish for lack of images. Wilde's grandest audacity demystifies Shakespearean mimesis with a Shakespearean vivaciousness: "This unfortunate aphorism about art holding the mirror up to Nature is deliberately said by Hamlet in order to convince the bystanders of his absolute insanity in all art-matters." Of *Hamlet*'s influence upon the ages Wilde remarked that: "The world has grown sad because a puppet was once melancholy." "Puppet" is Wilde's own deconstruction, a brilliant reminder that Shakespeare's artistry of illusion has so mastered reality as to have changed reality, evidently forever.

The analysis of character, as a critical pursuit, seems to me as much a Shakespearean invention as literary character was, since much of what we know about how to analyze character necessarily follows Shakespearean procedures. His hero-villains, from Richard III through Iago, Edmund, and Macbeth, are shrewd and endless questers into their own self-motivations. If we could bear to see Hamlet, in his unwearied negations, as another hero-villain, then we would judge him the supreme analyst of the darker recalcitrances in the selfhood. Freud followed the pre-Socratic Empedocles, in arguing that character is fate, a frightening doctrine that maintains the fear that there are no accidents, that overdetermination rules us all of our lives. Hamlet assumes the same, yet adds to this argument the terrible passivity he manifests in Act V. Throughout Shakespeare's tragedies, the most interesting personages seem doom-eager, reminding us again that a Shakespearean reading of Freud would be more illuminating than a Freudian exegesis of Shakespeare. We learn more when we discover Hamlet in the Freudian Death Drive, than when we read *Beyond the Pleasure Principle* into *Hamlet.*

In Shakespearean comedy, character achieves its true literary apotheosis, which is the representation of the inner freedom that can be created by great wit alone. Rosalind and Falstaff, perhaps alone among Shakespeare's personages, match Hamlet in wit, though hardly in the metaphysics of consciousness. Whether in the comic or the modern mode, Shakespeare has set the standard of measurement in the balance between character and passion.

In Shakespeare the self is more dramatized than theatricalized, which is why a Shakespearean reading of Freud works out so well. Character-formation after the passing of the Oedipal stage takes the place of fetishistic fragmentings of the self. Critics who now call literary character into question, and who proclaim also the death of the author, invariably also regard all notions, literary and human, of a stable character as being mere reductions of deeper pre-Oedipal desires. It becomes clear that the fortunes of literary character rise and fall with the prestige of normative conceptions of the ego. Shakespeare's Iago, who wars against being, may be the first deconstructionist of the self, with his proclamation of "I am not what I am." This constitutes the necessary prologue to any view that would regard a fixed ego as a virtual abnormality. But deconstructions of the self are no more modern than Modernism is. Like literary modernism, the decentered ego came out of the Hellenistic culture of ancient Alexandria. The Gnostic heretics believed that the psyche, like the body, was a fallen entity, mechanically fashioned by the Demiurge or false creator. They held however that each of us possessed also a spark or pneuma, which was a fragment of the original Abyss or true, alien God. The soul or psyche within every one of us was thus at war with the self or pneuma, and only that sparklike self could be saved.

Shakespeare, following after Chaucer in this respect, was the first and remains still the greatest master of representing character both as a stable soul and a wavering self. There is a substance that endures in Shakespeare's figures, and there is also a quicksilver rendition of the unsettling sparks. Racine and Tolstoy, Balzac and Dickens, follow in Shakespeare's wake by giving us some sense of pre-Oedipal sparks or drives, and considerably more sense of post-Oedipal character and personality, stabilizations or sublimations of the fetish-seeking drives. Critics like Leo Bersani and René Girard argue eloquently against our taking this mimesis as the only proper work of literature. I would suggest that strong fictions of the self, from the Bible through Samuel Beckett, necessarily participate in both modes, the sublimation of desire, and the persistence of a primordial desire. The mystery of Hamlet or of Lear is intimately invested in the tangled mixture of the two modes of representation.

Psychic mobility is proposed by Bersani as the ideal to which deconstructions of the literary self may yet guide us. The ideal has its pathos, but the realities of literary representation seem to me very different, perhaps destructively so. When a novelist like D. H. Lawrence sought to reduce his characters to Eros and the Death Drive, he still had to persuade us of his authority at mimesis by lavishing upon the figures of *The Rainbow* and *Women in Love* all of the vivid stigmata of normative personality. Birkin and Ursula may represent antithetical and uncanny drives, but they develop and change as characters pondering their own pronouncements and reactions to self and others. The cost of a non-Shakespearean representation is enormous. Pynchon, in *The Crying of Lot 49* and *Gravity's Rainbow*, evades the burden of the normative by resorting to something like Christopher Marlowe's art of caricature in *The Jew of Malta*. Marlowe's Barabas is a marvelous rhetorician, yet he is a cartoon alongside the troublingly equivocal Shylock. Pynchon's personages are deliberate cartoons also, as flat as comic strips. Marlowe's achievement, and Pynchon's, are beyond dispute, yet they are like the prelude and the postlude to Shakespearean reality. They do not wish to engage with our hunger for the empirical world and so they enter the problematic cosmos of literary fantasy.

No writer, not even Shakespeare or Proust, alters the available stock that we agree to call reality, but Shakespeare, more than any other, does show us how much of reality we could encounter if only we retained adequate desire. The strong literary representation of character is already an analysis of character, and is part of the healing work of a literary culture, which implicitly seeks to cure violence through a normative mimesis of ego, *as if it were stable,* whether in actuality it is or is not. I do not believe that this is a social quest taken on by literary culture, but rather that we confront here the aesthetic essence of what makes a culture *literary,* rather than metaphysical or ethical or religious. A culture becomes literary when its conceptual modes have failed it, which means when religion, philosophy, and science have begun to lose their authority. If they cannot heal violence, then literature attempts to do so, which may be only a turning inside out of the critical arguments of Girard and Bersani.

I conclude by offering a particular instance or special case as a paradigm for the healing enterprise that is at once the representation and the analysis of literary character. Let us call it the aesthetics of being outraged, or rather of successfully representing the state of being outraged. W. C. Fields was one modern master of such representation, and Nathanael West was another, as was Faulkner before him. Here also the greatest master remains Shakespeare, whose Macbeth, himself a bloody outrage, yet retains our imaginative sympathy precisely because he grows increasingly outraged as he experiences the equivocation of the fiend that lies like truth. The double-natured promises and the prophecies of the weird sisters finally induce in Macbeth an apocalyptic version of the stage actor's anxiety at missing cues, the horror of a phantasmagoric stage fright of missing one's time, of always reacting too late. Macbeth, a veritable monster of solipsistic inwardness but no intellectual, counters his dilemma by fresh murders, that prolong him in time yet provoke him only to a perpetually freshened sense of being outraged, as all his expectations become still worse confounded. We are moved by Macbeth, however estrangedly, because his terrible inwardness is a paradigm for our own solipsism, but also because none of us can resist a strong and successful representation of the human in a state of being outraged.

The ultimate outrage is the necessity of dying, an outrage concealed in a multitude of masks, including the tyrannical ambitions of Macbeth. I suspect that our outrage at being outraged is the most difficult of all our affects for us to represent to ourselves, which is why we are so inclined to imaginative sympathy for a character who strongly conveys that affect to us. The Shrike of West's *Miss Lonelyhearts* or Faulkner's Joe Christmas of *Light in August* are crucial modern instances, but such figures can be located in many other works, since the ability to represent this extreme emotion is one of the tests that strong writers are driven to set for themselves.

However a reader seeks to reduce literary character to a question of marks on a page, she will come at last to the impasse constituted by the thought of death, her death, and before that to all the stations of being outraged that memorialize her own drive towards death. In reading, she quests for evidences that are strong representations, whether of her desire or her despair. Such questings constitute the necessary basis for the analysis of literary character, an enterprise that always will survive every vagary of critical fashion.

EDITOR'S NOTE

This volume brings together a representative selection of the best criticism that has been devoted to Nabokov's Lolita, considered as a literary character. The critical extracts and the essays each are represented here in the chronological order of their original publication. I am grateful to Richard Fumosa and S. T. Joshi for their assistance in editing this book.

My introduction seeks to chart the ambiguities that result from the curious balance of ironic parody and moral pathos in Nabokov's portrait of Lolita.

The critical extracts begin with early observations by Nabokov himself, Dorothy Parker, and Lionel Trilling. Subsequently there are meditations upon Lolita by such well-known figures as Wayne C. Booth, Leslie A. Fiedler, and Garry Wills, as well as part of a Nabokov interview.

The critical essays commence with Gabriel Josipovici's pioneering analysis of Lolita-as-parody. Folklore is emphasized by Stephen Swann Jones, while Lucy B. Maddox explores the Poe-like element of necrophilia in Lolita's aura.

Richard H. Bullock achieves a useful perspective upon Lolita by exploring the contrast between her representations by Humbert as lover, and Humbert as author of the narrative. Nabokov's hostility toward Freud, and its effect upon our sense of Lolita, is analyzed by Jeffrey Berman.

The American qualities of Lolita emerge in John Haegert's account of the involuntary Americanization of Humbert. Lolita-as-riddle, or the enigma of her thwarted personality, is placed by Trevor McNeely in the context of Nabokov's endless trickiness.

A fierce feminist view of Lolita as the victim of male lust and bodily exploitation is propounded by Linda Kauffman, after which Vladimir E. Alexandrov concludes this volume by a comprehensive overview of Nabokov's most memorable and controversial literary character.

INTRODUCTION

Nabokov's Lolita has only one thing in common with Faulkner's Caddy Compson, the heroine of *The Sound and the Fury:* both characters are available to us only as mediated by others (Caddy's three brothers, and Dilsey) or by a single other: the outrageous Humbert Humbert. No consideration of Lolita apart from Humbert is therefore possible; only in their final scene together does Lolita appear to stand apart from Humbert's obsessive love for her. Even that is one of Nabokov's incessant ironies; Lolita becomes a person, rather than a caricature, for us at precisely the moment when Humbert's love breaks through (apparently) his own perversion of nympholepsy. The Lolita he vainly urges to return to him is no longer a preadolescent nymphet but a seventeen-year-old, prematurely worn down and pregnant with another man's child. Whether we are to read the transformation of Humbert's passion as another Nabokovian ironic parody, or as an authentic pathos, is perhaps not decidable, but either way it alters our vision of Lolita as well as our feeling for Humbert:

> ... and there she was with her ruined looks and her adult, rope-veined narrow hands and her goose-flesh white arms, and her shallow ears, and her unkempt armpits, there she was (my Lolita!), hopelessly worn at seventeen, with that baby, dreaming already in her of becoming a big shot and retiring around 2020 A.D.—and I looked and looked at her, and knew as clearly as I know I am to die, that I loved her more than anything I had ever seen or imagined on earth, or hoped for anywhere else. She was only the faint violet whiff and dead leaf echo of the nymphet I had rolled myself upon with such cries in the past; an echo on the brink of a russet ravine, with a far wood under a white sky, and brown leaves choking the brook, and one last cricket in the crisp weeds ... but thank God it was not that echo alone that I worshiped.

Yet until now we have known, not Lolita, but an echo alone, the aftershock of Humbert's compulsions. If Humbert indeed has been cured of his nympholepsy, but not of his love, the cure itself (or belated maturation) has no more to do with Lolita's personality than the earlier obsession did. For Humbert, and perhaps even for Nabokov, Lolita is one of the poems of our climate, the American girl as love-object, rival to Caddy Compson. A great (and ignorant, in this) hater of Sigmund Freud, Nabokov would not have appreciated being told that, on Freudian grounds, or reality's, Humbert's transcendence of a lifetime's perversion is just not persuasive. "This is the cure by love, which he prefers to analysis," would have been Freud's mordant comment upon Humbert, and upon Nabokov. "The overestimation of the object" was Freud's grim reduction of romantic love. Still a nympholept, an actual Humbert, in Freud's view, would have driven away from the faded, pregnant seventeen-year-old, in order to fall in love instead with the next available twelve-year-old charmer, who alone could have provided the material basis for overestimation.

But it is Nabokov's book, rather than Freud's, at least in its more vital first half, and so we must accept both Humbert's Lolita and Nabokov's Lolita, even when they do not quite coincide. Certainly Lolita is considerably more interesting as Humbert's erotic projection than she is as the wasted realist who refuses Humbert's final proposals. Falling out of love, according to Iris Murdoch, is one of the great human experiences, but Nabokov denies it to his Humbert. We do not envision Humbert, like Proust's Swann mourning: "And to think I went through all this for a woman who did not really suit me, who was not even my style!" Nor can one imagine a Humbert who would say, in the mode of Robert Penn Warren's Burden in *All the King's Men:* "Goodbye Lolita, and I forgive you for everything I ever did to you." Style, to Humbert the aesthete, is a secondary consideration in erotic matters, and precisely what Humbert cannot do is to forgive Lolita for everything he ever did to her. The Freudian wisdom of erotic mobility would urge Humbert away from the lost Lolita to the nearest American street-corner, where the European follower of Edgar Allan Poe could jangle the change in his pockets, while eying a procession of black-leather-miniskirted nymphets as they march by. But Nabokov, whether in his loving parody of Romanticism, or as another belated last Romantic himself, would not allow Humbert any option except dying of, and murdering for, his obsessive-compulsive passion.

Humbert then does not change, indeed cannot change, unless you accept Nabokov's metamorphosis of the overdetermined nympholept into the constant lover of the novel's conclusion. Yet Lolita evidently does change, as her abandonment of Humbert for Quilty, and final adherence to her own husband, would seem to indicate. Her character, both enigmatic and simplistic, leads one critic to speak of her "shortcomings as a human being" (compared to Humbert's!), and another to remark upon "the warm humanity of the person." The conventional twelve-year-old, having suffered Humbert, and his dark double, Quilty, is at seventeen something more than a conventional realist. Her wonderful freedom from bitterness, rightly remarked by many critics, astonishes us, and would astonish horrible Humbert more than it does if he ever truly could break through his solipsistic ecstasy, whether of bliss or of loss.

Nabokov was too shrewd a moralist, despite his professed aestheticism, not to see that he had permitted Lolita to escape the prison of parody at the book's close. Refusing Freud, Nabokov still offers us his own Romantic moralism, and shows us a Lolita who has begun to overcome some of the brutalizing consequences of her victimization by the possessed Humbert. She muses upon the *strangeness* of her lost girlhood, rather than upon the indubitable crime committed against her own development, and in that moment of almost-detached contemplation she achieves a moral freedom that her lover Humbert could never attain. Humbert has lived a life of parody, of failed art, and will die into a parody of immortality, a self-professed Dante adoring a Beatrice. Lolita, as a literary character, achieves authentic pathos, the pathos of a victim of masculine Romantic solipsism, who nevertheless turns away from bitterness to find whatever life is still available to her.

—H. B.

CRITICAL EXTRACTS

VLADIMIR NABOKOV

After doing my impersonation of suave John Ray, the character in *Lolita* who pens the Foreword, any comments coming straight from me may strike one—may strike me, in fact—as an impersonation of Vladimir Nabokov talking about his own book. A few points, however, have to be discussed; and the autobiographic device may induce mimic and model to blend.

Teachers of Literature are apt to think up such problems as "What is the author's purpose?" or still worse "What is the guy trying to say?" Now, I happen to be the kind of author who in starting to work on a book has no other purpose than to get rid of that book and who, when asked to explain its origin and growth, has to rely on such ancient terms as Interreaction of Inspiration and Combination—which, I admit, sounds like a conjurer explaining one trick by performing another.

The first little throb of *Lolita* went through me late in 1939 or early in 1940, in Paris, at a time when I was laid up with a severe attack of intercostal neuralgia. As far as I can recall, the initial shiver of inspiration was somehow prompted by a newspaper story about an ape in the Jardin des Plantes who, after months of coaxing by a scientist, produced the first drawing ever charcoaled by an animal: this sketch showed the bars of the poor creature's cage. The impulse I record had no textual connection with the ensuing train of thought, which resulted, however, in a prototype of my present novel, a short story some thirty pages long. I wrote it in Russian, the language in which I had been writing novels since 1924 (the best of these are not translated into English, and all are prohibited for political reasons in Russia). The man was a Central European, the anonymous nymphet was French, and the loci were Paris and Provence. I had him marry the little girl's sick mother who soon died, and after a thwarted attempt to take advantage of the orphan in a hotel room, Arthur (for that was his name) threw himself under the wheels of a truck. I read the story one blue-papered wartime night to a group of friends—Mark Aldanov, two social revolutionaries, and a woman doctor; but I was not pleased with the thing and destroyed it sometime after moving to America in 1940.

5

Around 1949, in Ithaca, upstate New York, the throbbing, which had never quite ceased, began to plague me again. Combination joined inspiration with fresh zest and involved me in a new treatment of the theme, this time in English—the language of my first governess in St. Petersburg, circa 1903, a Miss Rachel Home. The nymphet, now with a dash of Irish blood, was really much the same lass, and the basic marrying-her-mother idea also subsisted; but otherwise the thing was new and had grown in secret the claws and wings of a novel.

The book developed slowly, with many interruptions and asides. It had taken me some forty years to invent Russia and Western Europe, and now I was faced by the task of inventing America. The obtaining of such local ingredients as would allow me to inject a modicum of average "reality" (one of the few words which mean nothing without quotes) into the brew of individual fancy, proved at fifty a much more difficult process than it had been in the Europe of my youth when receptiveness and retention were at their automatic best. Other books intervened. Once or twice I was on the point of burning the unfinished draft and had carried my Juanita Dark as far as the shadow of the leaning incinerator on the innocent lawn, when I was stopped by the thought that the ghost of the destroyed book would haunt my files for the rest of my life.

Every summer my wife and I go butterfly hunting. The specimens are deposited at scientific institutions, such as the Museum of Comparative Zoology at Harvard or the Cornell University collection. The locality labels pinned under these butterflies will be a boon to some twenty-first-century scholar with a taste for recondite biography. It was at such of our headquarters as Telluride, Colorado; Afton, Wyoming; Portal, Arizona; and Ashland, Oregon, that Lolita was energetically resumed in the evenings or on cloudy days. I finished copying the thing out in longhand in the spring of 1954, and at once began casting around for a publisher.

At first, on the advice of a wary old friend, I was meek enough to stipulate that the book be brought out anonymously. I doubt that I shall ever regret that soon afterwards, realizing how likely a mask was to betray my own cause, I decided to sign Lolita. The four American publishers W, X, Y, Z, who in turn were offered the typescript and had their readers glance at it, were shocked by Lolita to a degree that even my wary old friend F.P. had not expected.

While it is true that in ancient Europe, and well into the eighteenth century (obvious examples come from France), deliberate lewdness was not inconsistent with flashes of comedy, or vigorous satire, or even the verve of a fine poet in a wanton mood, it is also true that in modern times the term "pornography" connotes mediocrity, commercialism, and certain strict rules of narration. Obscenity must be mated with banality because every kind of aesthetic enjoyment has to be entirely replaced by simple sexual stimulation which demands the traditional word for direct action upon the patient. Old rigid rules must be followed by the pornographer in order to have his patient feel the same security of satisfaction as, for example, fans of detective stories feel—stories where, if you do not watch out, the real murderer may turn out to be, to the fan's disgust, artistic originality (who for instance would want a detective story without a single dialogue in it?). Thus, in pornographic novels, action has to be limited to the copulation of clichés. Style, structure, imagery should never distract the reader from his tepid lust. The novel must consist of an alternation of sexual scenes. The passages in between must be reduced to sutures of sense, logical bridges of the simplest design, brief expositions and explanations, which the reader will probably skip but must know they exist in order not to feel cheated (a mentality stemming from the routine of "true" fairy tales in childhood). Moreover, the sexual scenes in the book must follow a crescendo line, with new variations, new combinations, new sexes, and a steady increase in the number of participants (in a Sade play they call the gardener in), and therefore the end of the book must be more replete with lewd lore than the first chapters.

Certain techniques in the beginning of *Lolita* (Humbert's Journal, for example) misled some of my first readers into assuming that this was going to be a lewd book. They expected the rising succession of erotic scenes; when these stopped, the readers stopped, too, and felt bored and let down. This, I suspect, is one of the reasons why not all the four firms read the typescript to the end. Whether they found it pornographic or not did not interest me. Their refusal to buy the book was based not on my treatment of the theme but on the theme itself, for there are at least three themes which are utterly taboo as far as most American publishers are concerned. The two others are: a Negro-White marriage which is a complete and glorious success resulting in lots of children and grandchildren; and the total atheist who lives a happy and useful life, and dies in his sleep at the age of 106.

Some of the reactions were very amusing: one reader suggested that his firm might consider publication if I turned my Lolita into a twelve-year-old lad and had him seduced by Humbert, a farmer, in a barn, amidst gaunt and arid surroundings, all this set forth in short, strong, "realistic" sentences ("He acts crazy. We all act crazy, I guess. I guess God acts crazy." Etc.). Although everybody should know that I detest symbols and allegories (which is due partly to my old feud with Freudian voodooism and partly to my loathing of generalizations devised by literary mythists and sociologists), an otherwise intelligent reader who flipped through the first part described *Lolita* as "Old Europe debauching young America," while another flipper saw in it "Young America debauching old Europe." Publisher X, whose advisers got so bored with Humbert that they never got beyond page 188, had the naïveté to write me that Part Two was too long. Publisher Y, on the other hand, regretted there were no good people in the book. Publisher Z said if he printed *Lolita*, he and I would go to jail.

No writer in a free country should be expected to bother about the exact demarcation between the sensuous and the sensual; this is preposterous; I can only admire but cannot emulate the accuracy of judgment of those who pose the fair young mammals photographed in magazines where the general neckline is just low enough to provoke a past master's chuckle and just high enough not to make a postmaster frown. I presume there exist readers who find titillating the display of mural words in those hopelessly banal and enormous novels which are typed out by the thumbs of tense mediocrities and called "powerful" and "stark" by the reviewing hack. There are gentle souls who would pronounce *Lolita* meaningless because it does not teach them anything. I am neither a reader nor a writer of didactic fiction, and, despite John Ray's assertion, *Lolita* has no moral in tow. For me a work of fiction exists only insofar as it affords me what I shall bluntly call aesthetic bliss, that is a sense of being somehow, somewhere, connected with other states of being where art (curiosity, tenderness, kindness, ecstasy) is the norm. There are not many such books. All the rest is either topical trash or what some call the Literature of Ideas, which very often is topical trash coming in huge blocks of plaster that are carefully transmitted from age to age until somebody comes along with a hammer and takes a good crack at Balzac, at Gorki, at Mann.

Another charge which some readers have made is that *Lolita* is anti-American. This is something that pains me considerably more than the idiotic accusation of immorality. Considerations of depth and perspective (a suburban lawn, a mountain meadow) led me to build a number of North American sets. I needed a certain exhilarating milieu. Nothing is more exhilarating than philistine vulgarity. But in regard to philistine vulgarity there is no intrinsic difference between Palearctic manners and Nearctic manners. Any proletarian from Chicago can be as bourgeois (in the Flaubertian sense) as a duke. I chose American motels instead of Swiss hotels or English inns only because I am trying to be an American writer and claim only the same rights that other American writers enjoy. On the other hand, my creature Humbert is a foreigner and an anarchist, and there are many things, besides nymphets, in which I disagree with him. And all my Russian readers know that my old worlds—Russian, British, German, French—are just as fantastic and personal as my new one is.

Lest the little statement I am making here seem an airing of grudges, I must hasten to add that besides the lambs who read the typescript of *Lolita* or its Olympia Press edition in a spirit of "Why did he have to write it?" or "Why should I read about maniacs?" there have been a number of wise, sensitive, and staunch people who understood my book much better than I can explain its mechanism here.

Every serious writer, I dare say, is aware of this or that published book of his as of a constant comforting presence. Its pilot light is steadily burning somewhere in the basement and a mere touch applied to one's private thermostat instantly results in a quiet little explosion of familiar warmth. This presence, this glow of the book in an ever accessible remoteness is a most companionable feeling, and the better the book has conformed to its prefigured contour and color the ampler and smoother it glows. But even so, there are certain points, byroads, favorite hollows that one evokes more eagerly and enjoys more tenderly than the rest of one's book. I have not reread *Lolita* since I went through the proofs in the winter of 1954 but I find it to be a delightful presence now that it quietly hangs about the house like a summer day which one knows to be bright behind the haze. And when I thus think of *Lolita*, I seem always to pick out for special delectation such images as Mr. Taxovich, or that class list of Ramsdale School, or Charlotte saying "waterproof," or Lolita in slow motion advancing towards Humbert's gifts, or the pictures decorating the stylized garret of Gaston Godin, or the Kasbeam barber (who cost me a month of work), or Lolita playing tennis, or the hospital at Elphinstone, or pale, pregnant, beloved, irretrievable Dolly Schiller dying in Gray Star (the capital town of the book), or the tinkling sounds of the valley town coming up the mountain trail (on which I caught the first known female of *Lycaeides sublivens* Nabokov). These are the nerves of the novel. These are the secret points, the subliminal co-ordinates by means of which the book is plotted—although I realize very clearly that these and other scenes will be skimmed over or not noticed, or never even reached, by those who begin reading the book under the impression that it is something on the lines of *Memoirs of a Woman of Pleasure* or *Les Amours de Milord Grosvit.* That my novel does contain various allusions to the physiological urges of a pervert is quite true. But after all we are not children, not illiterate juvenile delinquents, not English public school boys who after a night of homosexual romps have to endure the paradox of reading the Ancients in expurgated versions.

It is childish to study a work of fiction in order to gain information about a country or about a social class or about the author. And yet one of my very few intimate friends, after reading *Lolita,* was sincerely worried that I (I!) should be living "among such depressing people"—when the only discomfort I really experienced was to live in my workshop among discarded limbs and unfinished torsos.

After Olympia Press, in Paris, published the book, an American critic suggested that *Lolita* was the record of my love affair with the romantic novel. The substitution "English language" for "romantic novel" would make this elegant formula more correct. But here I feel my voice rising to a much too strident pitch. None of my American friends have read my Russian books and thus every appraisal on the strength of my English ones is bound to be out of focus. My private tragedy, which cannot, and indeed should not, be anybody's concern, is that I had to abandon my natural idiom, my untrammeled, rich, and infinitely docile Russian tongue for a second-rate brand of English, devoid of any of those apparatuses—the baffling mirror, the black velvet backdrop, the implied associations and traditions—which the native illusionist, frac-tails flying, can magically use to transcend the heritage in his own way.

—VLADIMIR NABOKOV, "On a Book Entitled *Lolita,*" *Anchor Review* 2 (1957): 105–12

DOROTHY PARKER

I do not think that *Lolita* is a filthy book. I cannot regard it as pornography, either sheer, unrestrained, or any other kind. It is the engrossing, anguished story of a man, a man of taste and culture, who can love only little girls. They must be between the ages of nine and fourteen, and he calls them nymphets. But not every child in the age group is a nymphet, nor is even the prettiest one. She must have that quality for which there is no one word, unless you want to call it "It," which I do not. In twelve-year-old Lolita, he finds his ideal nymphet.

She is a dreadful little creature, selfish, hard, vulgar, and foul-tempered. He knows that; he knows all of what she is. That the knowledge cannot turn away his obsession with her is his agony.

An anguished book, but sometimes wildly funny, as in the saga of his travel across and around the United States with her, in search of some place that might possibly please her; and in the account of that trek are descriptions of the American hinterlands that Sinclair Lewis could never touch. Lolita leaves him, of course, for a creature even worse than she is, but he is so riddled with his need of her that he follows the trail of her and her new lover, losing it and picking it up again, over and over. When he finds her, she is seventeen, haggard in the face and swollen with pregnancy, married to a poor, simple fool. He gives her all the money he has—she has a fondness for money—and starts on another weary quest: to find and kill the man who took her from him.

No. There is no good, I see at this late moment, to try to melt down the story. It is in its writing that Mr. Nabokov has made it the work of art that it is. Mr. Nabokov—the same man, you know, that wrote the delicate stories in *Pnin*—started writing in English long after his first youth. His command of the language is absolute, and his *Lolita* is a fine book, a distinguished book—all right, then—a great book.

—DOROTHY PARKER, "Sex—without the Asterisks," *Esquire* 50, No. 4
(October 1958): 103

LIONEL TRILLING

This, then, is the story of *Lolita* and it is indeed shocking. In a tone which is calculatedly not serious, it makes a prolonged assault on one of our unquestioned and unquestionably sexual prohibitions, the sexual inviolability of girls of a certain age (and compounds the impiousness with what amounts to incest).

It is all very well for us to remember that Juliet was fourteen when she was betrothed to Paris, and gave herself, with our full approval, to Romeo. It is all very well for us to find a wry idyllic charm in the story of the aged David and the little maid Abishag. And to gravely receive Dante's account of being struck to the heart by an eight-year-old Beatrice. And to say that distant cultures—H.H. gives a list of them to put his idiosyncracy in some moral perspective—and hot climates make a difference in ideas of the right age for female sexuality to begin. All very well for us to have long ago got over our first horror at what Freud told us about the sexuality of children; and to receive blandly what he has told us about the "family romance" and its part in the dynamics of the psyche. All very well for the family and society to take approving note of the little girl's developing sexual charms, to find a sweet comedy in her growing awareness of them and her learning to use them, and for her mother to be open and frank and delighted and ironic over the teacups about the clear signs of the explosive force of her sexual impulse. We have all become so nicely clear-eyed, so sensibly Coming-of-Age-in-Samoa. But let an adult male seriously think about the girl as a sexual object and all our sensibility is revolted.

The response is not reasoned but visceral. Within the range of possible heterosexual conduct, this is one of the few prohibitions which still seem to us to be confirmed by nature itself. Virginity once seemed so confirmed, as did the marital fidelity of women, but they do so no longer. No novelist would expect us to respond with any moral intensity to his representing an unmarried girl having a sexual experience, whether in love or curiosity; the infidelity of a wife may perhaps be a little more interesting, but not much. The most serious response the novelist would expect from us is that we should "understand," which he would count on us to do automatically.

But our response to the situation that Mr. Nabokov presents to us is that of shock. And we find ourselves the more shocked when we realise that, in the course of reading the novel, we have come virtually to condone the violation it presents. Charles Dickens, by no means a naïve man, was once required to meet a young woman who had lived for some years with a man out of wedlock; he was dreadfully agitated at the prospect, and when he met the girl he was appalled to discover that he was not confronting a piece of depravity but a principled, attractive young person, virtually a lady. It was a terrible blow to the certitude of his moral feelings. That we may experience the same loss of certitude about the sexual behavior that *Lolita* describes is perhaps suggested by the tone of my summary of the story—I was plainly not able to muster up the note of moral outrage. And it is likely that any reader of *Lolita* will discover that he comes to see the situation as less and less abstract and moral and horrible, and more and more as human and "understandable." Less and less, indeed, do we see a *situation;* what we become aware of is people. Humbert is perfectly willing to say that he is a monster; no doubt he is, but we find ourselves less and less eager to say so. Perhaps his depravity is the easier to accept when we learn that he deals with a Lolita who is not innocent, and who seems to have very few emotions to be violated; and I suppose we naturally incline to be lenient towards a rapist—legally and by intention H.H. is that—who eventually feels a deathless devotion to his victim!

But we have only to let the immediate influence of the book diminish a little with time, we have only to free ourselves from the rationalising effect of H.H.'s obsessive passion, we have only to move back into the real world where twelve-year-olds are being bored by Social Studies and plagued by orthodonture, to feel again the outrage at the violation of the sexual prohibition. And to feel this the more because we have been seduced into conniving in the violation, because we have permitted our fantasies to accept what we know to be revolting.

—LIONEL TRILLING "The Last Lover: Vladimir Nabokov's Lolita,"
Encounter 11, No. 4 (October 1958): 13–14

THOMAS MOLNAR

Humbert is a feather-weight intellectual, with his point of gravity situated below the belt; but he becomes a tragic—although at the same time comic—character in his pursuit of an impossible happiness for the morsels of which he pays an ever higher price of self-debasement, humiliation, and remorse. The depth of his personal inferno is aptly measured by two episodes: the moment when Lolita, still unaware of her mother's death, finds her new stepfather in her own bed, intent like a lover, fearful and humble like a dog waiting to be patted; then that other moment, this time one of painful reminiscence, when Humbert recalls the picture of himself, having just possessed Lolita and now adoring in her the suffering, debauched child, but with lust again rising in him, imperious, demanding submission.

The central question the reader ought to ask of himself is whether he feels pity for the girl. Our ethical ideal would require that we look at Lolita as a sacrificial limb, that we become, in imagination, her knight-protector. Yet this is impossible for two reasons. One is very simple: before yielding to Humbert, the girl had had a nasty little affair with a nasty little thirteen-year-old in an expensive summer camp. Besides, she is a spoiled sub-teenager with a foul mouth, a self-offered target for lechers, movie-magazine editors, and corrupt classmates. The second reason is that throughout their not-quite-sentimental journey, Lolita remains as unknown to us as to Humbert himself, seen only in bed or in the car, existing only through the lustful gaze of her stepfather. She remains an object, perhaps even to herself, and only at the very end, as a teen-age mother, married to a simpleton and comically serious in her vulgarity, does she become human, no longer a corrupt little animal, and no longer a nymphet.

Yet both she and Humbert, her mother and friends, the many people we pass by in the lust-and-anguish-driven car, form a fantastic, wonderful cavalcade of humanity, described, analyzed, judged with incomparable virtuosity. It has been said that this book has a high literary value; it has much more; a style, an individuality, a brilliance which may yet create a tradition in American letters.

—THOMAS MOLNAR, "Matter-of-Fact Confession of a Non-Penitent,"
Commonweal, 24 October 1958, p. 102

FRANK S. MEYER

Never has a society been more smugly proof against satire than ours. When one idea is as good as another and one institution is as good as another, when a dull equalizing relativism destroys all definitions and distinctions, satire is impotent. For the satiric genius works by shocking the reader into using the standards he implicitly holds but has failed to apply. It achieves its results by creating so savage a presentation of contemporary evil (exaggerated, caricatured, grotesque, but a true simulacrum of the essence of the social scene) that the bland and habitual surface of actuality is riven apart. But where there are no standards, satire has no ground from which to fight.

It is not on record that even the bitterest enemy of the Irish greeted Swift's *A Modest Proposal* with dithyrambs of praise for his great acuity and daring in breaking the bonds of conventional morality that had previously kept men from publicly espousing cannibalism. The smuggest of the eighteenth century recognized satire when it hit them in the face.

Today things are different. Vladimir Nabokov writes a novel, *Lolita.* With scarifying wit and masterly descriptive power, he excoriates the materialist monstrosities of our civilization—from progressive education to motel architecture, and back again through the middle-brow culture racket to the incredible vulgarity and moral nihilism in which our children of all classes are raised, and on to psychoanalysis and the literary scene. He stamps indelibly on every page of his book the revulsion and disgust with which he is inspired, by loathsomely dwelling upon a loathsome plot: a detailed unfolding of the long-continued captivity and sexual abuse of a twelve-year-old girl. To drive home the macabre grotesquerie of what he sees about him, he climaxes the novel with a murder that is at the same time horrible and ridiculous, poised between Grand Guignol and Punch and Judy.

What happens? The critics hail his "grace and delicacy" and his ability to understand and present "love" in the most unlikely circumstances. The modern devaluation of values seems to have deprived them of the ability to distinguish love from lust and rape. And first among them that dean of critics, Lionel Trilling, who compares *Lolita* to the legend of Tristan and Isolde!

This *succès d'estime* is matched only by its success of pocketbook, as it reaches the top of the best-seller list with a current sale of over 100,000 copies. Completely successful, and having completely missed the target at which he shot, one wonders what Mr. Nabokov thinks. It is as if Swift had been feted for his pamphlet by the King's Lord-Lieutenant of Ireland, or Juvenal banqueted by the degenerate Roman rich and powerful, and their more degenerate toadies, whom his satire celebrates.

Without exception, in all the reviews I have read—and they are many— nowhere has even the suspicion crept in that *Lolita* might be something totally different from the temptingly perverted surface it presents to the degenerate taste of the age. Not a whiff of a hint that it could be what it must be, if it is judged by the standards of good and beauty which once were undisputed in the West—and if it is, as the power of its writing shows it to be, more than a mere exercise in salaciousness.

Only the editors of the *New Republic,* speaking in their editorial columns (after the fact of their review, and against their reviewer, who had done the usual with *Lolita*), smelled a rat. But, as so often with the *New Republic* when it departs, as it sometimes does, from the safe paths of moderate Liberal conformism, it smelled the wrong rat and went dashing off in the wrong direction. The editors of the *New Republic,* to their credit, cannot stomach the idea advanced by the critical gentry that no moral judgment of the brutal and tawdry central theme of *Lolita* should be made. They accuse Mr. Nabokov of saying that the moral abomination he describes does not matter, since it is no worse than the tawdriness of our social scene—a view of the fruits of Liberalism that very much upsets them.

They have at least come close enough to the secret to suspect that Mr. Nabokov is implying some sort of relation between the horror of his plot and the social scene; but they reverse his meaning. Mr. Nabokov is not saying that what happens to Lolita is excusable because it is no worse than the general *mores* of our society. So insensitive a judgment would be impossible for a man who can write with his intense sensitivity. He is saying the opposite—and saying it clearly to all who have ears to hear. He is saying that Lolita's fate is indeed fearful and horrible; and that the world ravaged by relativism which he describes is just as horrible. He is not excusing outrage; he is painting a specific outrage as the symbol of an outrageous society.

The editors of the *New Republic,* with justice, attack the indecent blindness of Lionel Trilling who writes of the perverted protagonist of *Lolita*: "In recent fiction no lover has thought of his beloved with so much tenderness." They themselves, however, look with so much tenderness upon their world that they cannot recognize the terrible satire whose essence they have dimly perceived. *De te fabula narratur.* Satire couches its lance in vain.

And satire, I am sure, considering his ability and the quality of what he has written, was Mr. Nabokov's intention. Of course I may be wrong. He may simply be an immensely gifted writer with a perverted and salacious mind. But if the latter is true, it does not change the situation much. *Lolita,* in the context of the reception it has been given, remains nevertheless a savage indictment of an age that can see itself epitomized in such horror as beauty, delicacy, understanding. But I hope that this is not so, that Mr. Nabokov knew what he was doing. It is so much more exhilarating to the spirit if the evil that human beings have created is castigated by the conscious vigor of a human being, not by the mere accident of the mirror, the momentary unpurposeful reflection of evil back upon evil.

—FRANK S. MEYER, "A Lance into Cotton Wool," *National Review,* 22 November 1958, pp. 340–41

ALLAN BRICK

Consciously echoing Poe's ideal of a child-bride—from the marriage with Virginia Clemm and, more specifically, from "Annabel Lee"—Nabokov writes of a sex pervert, an incurable idealist, who destroys himself and those around him in a furious quest for a "nymphet," one of an imagined coterie of girl-children (aged nine to fourteen) who are mysteriously possessed of "the fey grace, the elusive, shifty, soul-shattering, insidious charm that separates ... [them] from such coevals ... as are incomparably dependent on the spatial world of synchronous phenomena that on that intangible island of entranced time where Lolita plays with her likes." The tragedy of Humbert Humbert lies in his romanticism—his idealist insistence upon a being which, seen within these girls by no one else, exists only on an island in the sea of his imagination: "You have to be an artist and a madman, a creature of infinite melancholy, ... in order to discern ... the little deadly demon among the wholesome [stereotype] children; *she* stands unrecognized by them and unconscious herself of her fantastic power." Humbert Humbert's fear throughout the story is that his creatures don't really exist: "What drives me insane is the twofold nature of this nymphet—of every nymphet, perhaps; this mixture in my Lolita of tender dreamy childishness and a kind of eerie vulgarity, stemming from the snubnosed cuteness of ads and magazine pictures."

So oppressed is Humbert by the picture of Spillane Woman forced upon his mind from without, the picture actually filled by his Lolita's (available) mother—"well-groomed and shapely ... [with] heavy hips, round knees, ripe bust ... and all the rest of that story and dull thing: a handsome woman"—that he cannot keep his vision free, cannot forget that *this* is Lolita's "big sister," the form awaiting her after adolescence. While the real-life child, Lolita, is destroyed by his frequent and furious possession, while she actually grows into the stereotyped woman he abhors, his ideal Lolita flees him, banished by his attempted incarnation. The real-life Lolita actually flees with a mad and celebrated playwright, Clare Quilty, who, coming into prominence only with Humbert's first physical possession of the girl, personifies for Humbert the lower, goatish part of his own nature—that part which seems increasingly to exclude any other. Most devastating of all is the final comment of the rediscovered, but now grownup and married, Lolita that she would sooner go back to Quilty than accept the offered chance to return to Humbert; for thus Humbert realizes that after that first intercourse it was exclusively Quilty she desired. Insofar as her mind had been taken over by the stereotypes, the girl had always wanted the slick, ersatz (lecher that he was, Quilty turns out to be impotent) sex of Hollywood. One remembers now with full force an early description of the wall over Lolita's bed:

> A full-page ad ripped out of a slick magazine was affixed to the wall above the bed, between a crooner's mug and the lashes of a movie actress. It represented a dark-haired young husband with a kind of drained look in his Irish eyes. He was modeling a robe by So-and-So and holding a bridgelike tray by So-and-So, with breakfast for two.... Lo had drawn a jocose arrow to the haggard lover's face and had put, in block letters: H.H. And indeed, despite a difference of a few years, the resemblance was striking. Under this was another picture, also a colored ad. A distinguished playwright was solemnly smoking a Drome. He always smoked Dromes. The resemblance was slight. Under his was Lo's chaste bed, littered with "comics."

The lower picture which only slightly resembled Humbert was—though unknown to him—that of Quilty, already inseparable from the stereotypes dominating his heroine. On the bed under these pictures were the comics which—unknown to, or at least unadmitted by, Humbert—are the essential terrain of Lolita's mind. That his supposed nymphet was *all along* just another one of the "wholesome children" who, even before adolescence, think and feel only in terms of outwardly imposed stereotypes becomes for Humbert the central horror.

—ALLAN BRICK, "The Madman in His Cell: Joyce, Beckett, Nabokov and the Stereotypes," *Massachusetts Review* 1, No. 1 (October 1959): 52–54

DIANA BUTLER

Humbert Humbert moralizes very little. His attitude is a scientific one, whether the science be nympholepsy or lepidoptery. Even the most "pornographic" passages of *Lolita* depict the heroine with scientific detachment, and her extraordinary charm is rendered by the use of minute specific details.

These specific details coincide with the markings of the most important butterfly of Nabokov's life. We are not subjected to raptures about Lolita's hair, breasts, or the usual barrage of femininity. Instead, Nabokov repeatedly mentions the golden-brown color of her arms and legs. The upperwings of the female of *Lycaeides sublivens* Nabokov are the color of a summer tan. Nabokov stresses the minute downy hairs on Lolita's arms and legs. The scales of a butterfly are modified hairs, and the word "pubescence," so often applied to Lo, means literally the soft down hairs on an insect, such as a butterfly. The whitish background of the underwings of *Lycaeides sublivens* recalls Lo's white shorts, white shirts, white socks, and the untanned white parts of her body. The small dark spots on this butterfly's underwings are seen in the asymmetrical freckles of her nose, her assorted bruises and moles.

Nabokov stresses the "reverse" side of his heroine, as if recalling the two sides of his butterfly, brown and white. He speaks of "Brown, naked, frail Lo, her narrow white buttocks to me" and of her "honey-brown body, with the white negative image of a rudimentary swimsuit patterned against her tan."

He tells us she is shameless in matters of leg show, but admires the "sudden smooth nether loveliness." Nabokov speaks of Lolita's arms and legs collectively, as one thinks of a butterfly's wings: "how I longed to enfold them, all your four limpid lovely limbs."

Lolita's eyes are wide-spaced and poor-sighted, like a butterfly's. Her smile seems hardly human: "While the tender, nectared, dimpled brightness played, it was never directed at the stranger in the room but hung in its own remote flowered void, so to speak, or wandered with myopic softness over chance objects."

Different butterflies have different characteristic resting positions. The Lycaenidae, to which family Nabokov's butterfly belongs, according to Klots's *Field Guide to the Butterflies,* upon alighting "hold the forewings together over the back, spread the hindwings slightly out at the sides, and then rub the hindwings forward and back alternating them with each other." Here is Lolita in an identical movement: "her feet gestured all the time: she would stand on her left instep with her right toe, remove it backward, cross her feet, rock slightly, sketch a few steps, and then start the series all over again."

Like butterflies, Lolita's favorite food is fruit. Even when, as an all-American girl, she drinks Cokes and eats sundaes, she prefers them with fruit syrup. The first sign Humbert sees of the heroine when he enters the Haze house is the brown core of an apple. Later on in Kasbeam, "I must say she was very sweet and languid, and craved for fresh fruits. . . . She became aware of the bananas. . . . Lo applied herself to the fruit."

Butterflies employ odors to attract a mate. In his autobiography Nabokov describes the "subtle perfume of butterfly wings on my fingers, a perfume which varies with the species—vanilla, or lemon, or musk, or a musty sweetish odor difficult to define."

Humbert prides himself on his well-developed sense of smell, and has even inherited a perfume business. He describes the scent of his first love, Annabel, as "a sweetish, lowly, musky perfume," and says Lolita "smelt almost exactly like the other one, the Riviera one, but more intensely so, with rougher overtones—a torrid odor that at once set my manhood astir." In helping one of Lo's fellow nymphets to play tennis, Humbert would "inhale her faint musky fragrance as I touched her forearm and held her knobby wrist, and push this way or that her cool thigh to show her the backhand stance."

Humbert's science of nympholepsy has much in common with lepidoptery. The notebook he keeps during his first days at the Haze house contains the essential data of a lepidopterist's field notebook: descriptions of locale and terrain, weather conditions, and vantage points, as well as the minute details of appearance already noted. For example, "*Thursday*. Very warm day. From a vantage point (bathroom window) saw Dolores taking things off a clothesline." Or, "*Sunday*. Heat ripple still with us; a most favonian week. This time I took up a strategic position . . ."

Humbert says he copied out his entries "with obvious abbreviations"; in referring to names of states, he also uses the standard abbreviations employed by butterfly collectors in identifying specimens. The Latin names of butterflies are written in italics, and Humbert tells us on his first night alone with Lolita "A breeze from wonderland had begun to affect my thoughts, and now they seemed couched in italics."

Humbert, buying clothes for Lolita, laboriously lists for us her "January measurements: hip girth, twenty-nine inches; thigh girth (just below the gluteal sulcus), seventeen; calf girth and neck circumference, eleven"; etc. Just such lists of precise measurements are included in scientific papers on butterflies.

Humbert says of his arctic expedition, "I felt curiously aloof from my own self. No temptations maddened me. . . . Nymphets do not occur in polar regions." Butterflies are only absent from the regions around the poles.

Humbert presents us with the scientific methods of nympholepsy. He tells us that not all girl-children are nymphets, but that only an expert can be sure of detecting the difference between a nymphet and an "ordinary, plumpish" little girl. "Neither are good looks any criterion." "You have to be an artist and a madman . . . in order to discern at once, by ineffable signs—the slightly feline outline of a cheekbone, the slenderness of a downy limb, and other indices which despair and shame and tears of tenderness forbid me to tabulate—the little deadly demon among the wholesome children. . . ." Humbert's distinctions between nymphets and non-nymphets echo the distinctions between moths and butterflies, which together comprise the order Lepidoptera. Although moths are big-bodied and butterflies are slender-bodied, some moths are more beautiful than butterflies, and only an expert can be sure of telling them apart.

—DIANA BUTLER, "Lolita Lepidoptera," *New World Writing* 16 (1960): 63–67

WAYNE C. BOOTH

Can we really be surprised that readers have overlooked Nabokov's ironies in *Lolita,* when Humbert Humbert is given full and unlimited control of the rhetorical resources? "I do not intend to convey the impression that I did not manage to be happy. Reader must understand that in the possession and thralldom of a nymphet the enchanted traveler stands, as it were, beyond happiness. For there is no other bliss on earth comparable to that of fondling a nymphet. It is *hors concours,* that bliss, it belongs to another class, another plane of sensitivity." This sounds very good, indeed. "Despite our tiffs, despite her nastiness, despite all the fuss and faces she made, and the vulgarity, and the danger, and the horrible hopelessness of it all, I still dwelled deep in my elected paradise—a paradise whose skies were the color of hell-flames—but still a 'paradise.'" All for love. Just like Antony and Cleopatra, or any of the other great lovers! We have already seen that Lionel Trilling cannot accept Humbert's later self-castigation as genuine after all this lively self-defense. And who is to blame him? The "paradise" is dramatized and described and praised at length; the repentance is merely expounded—though it is expounded power- fully: "Unless it can be proven to me—to me as I am now, today, with my heart and my beard, and my putrefaction—that in the infinite run it does not matter a jot that a North American girl-child named Dolores Haze has been deprived of her child- hood by a maniac, unless this can be proven (and if it can, then life is a joke), I see nothing for the treatment of my misery but the melancholy and very local palliative of articulate art." Nabokov means what he makes Humbert say here, and one can understand his feeling that he has done all that anyone but an "illiterate juvenile delinquent" could possibly need to prevent misunderstanding. But the laws of art are against him. His most skilful and mature readers, it is true, will have repudiated Humbert's blandishments from the beginning; the clues are numerous, the style is a dead giveaway throughout—*if* one happens to see it as such. One of the major delights of this delightful, profound book is that of watching Humbert *almost* make a case for himself. But Nabokov has insured that many, perhaps most, of his readers will be unsuccessful, in that they will identify Humbert with the author more than Nabokov intends. And for them, no amount of final recantation will cancel out the vividness of the earlier scenes.

—WAYNE C. BOOTH, "The Morality of Personal Narration," *The Rhetoric of Fiction* (Chicago: University of Chicago Press, 1961), pp. 390–91

DENIS DE ROUGEMONT

"Between the age limits of nine and fourteen there occur maidens who, to certain bewitched travelers, twice or many times older than they, reveal their true nature, which is not human, but nymphic (that is, demoniac); and these chosen creatures I propose to designate as 'nymphets.'" Lolita, twelve years and seven months old, has the disturbing charm, the innocent shamelessness, and the touch of vulgarity that characterize the nymphet. Humbert Humbert, a European in his late thirties, who has been in America only a short time, discovers her in a small town where he is taking his vacation. Love at first sight. Lunatic plot to possess the child, whose mother he marries first. This unfortunate creature soon dies, run over by an automobile. H.H. takes Lolita away with him to a hotel called The Enchanted Hunters. He gives her a sleeping pill, but dares not take advantage of her slumbers. In the morning, it is she who seduces him! Then begins the long flight of the stepfather and daughter, tracked by their secret guilt, across the entire expanse of the United States, until the day Lolita escapes, seduced by another middle-aged man whom Humbert will eventually kill. At seventeen, married to a brawny young mechanic, she dies in childbed, a few weeks after Humbert, who is spared capital punishment by a coronary thrombosis.

I do not mean to veil or to excuse the novel's scandalous character, for it appears to be essential, and the author misses no opportunity to underline and accentuate it, either by reproaching his hero in a preface attributed, moreover, to an American psychiatrist; or, more convincingly, by the cynical flippancy of Humbert Humbert's style. If loving nymphets was not, in our day and age, one of the last surviving sexual taboos (with incest), there would be neither true passion nor true novel, in the "Tristanian" sense of these terms. For the necessary obstacle would be missing between the two protagonists, the necessary *distance* by which the mutual attraction, instead of being mitigated or exhausted by sensual gratification, is metamorphosed into passion. It is first and foremost the evident scandal, the profaning character of H.H.'s love for Lolita that betrays the presence of the myth.

Let us leave aside for the moment the profound differences that separate this ironic and witty novel from the somber epic of a Béroul, so simple and immediate in its effects. We must not overlook the fact that the story of Tristan was no less shocking to the twelfth century than *Lolita* is today.

What habit and anachronistic illusion, assisted by Bédier's modern version, make us accept all too easily as the touching story of an almost chaste love that happened to be conceived out of wedlock, actually concealed revolutionary powers for readers of the period. The first versions of Tristan glorified a form of love not only opposed to marriage but unable to exist save outside it. They "justified" in the name of this new love a whole series of actions regarded as crimes: blasphemous stratagem of the rigged trial-by-ordeal, repeated violation of allegiances and sworn faith, profanation of the feudal oath and of the Catholic sacraments, witchcraft, black magic. All this against a background of heresy much more dangerous at the time than are modern youth's extravagances, ephemeral fashions that seem to profit press and cinema more than they prey on society.

On the other hand, passionate love for a still impubescent girl would not have seemed surprising in the Middle Ages. It is customary to venerate Dante's love for Beatrice, who was nine years old, and Petrarch's for Laura, who was twelve; these two examples establish a tradition of high European literature, which will be illustrated at closer range by Goethe creating the character of Mignon, Novalis dedicating his work to the love of Sophie von Kühn, who died at sixteen, Edgar Allan

Poe marrying a girl of fourteen, and especially by the inspired Lewis Carroll: *Alice in Wonderland* is the product of nymphet-love suppressed by the clergyman's conscience but avowed by some of his poems and betrayed by the often savage jokes in his letters to little girls.

Adultery today leads only to divorce or exhausts itself in commonplace liaisons. It no longer offers a serious support to what Freud once called the *élan mortel*, secret of Tristanian love. And the absence of the sacred dims the passions, which awareness of a profanation once caused to burn so brightly. We are left with two sexual taboos, strangely respected by our mores in rapid transition from a primitive sense of the sacred to a scientific hygiene: nymphet-love and incest. Are these two loves *contra naturam?* we find them widely practiced in the animal world and in the great majority of human societies, the Western bourgeoisie constituting the most notable exception. Such practices are less against nature than against civilization. "I found myself maturing amid a civilization which allows a man of twenty-five to court a girl of sixteen but not a girl of twelve." Humbert describes, at the beginning of his memoirs, the love he conceived at the age of thirteen for a child of twelve whom he called Annabel and who died soon after—an evocation of Poe. Thus the Eros of this adult, otherwise sexually normal male is fixated on the child-woman, rendered doubly inaccessible by the difference in age and by the idea of death. This is how the nymphet becomes the mainstay of passion—that is, of the infinite desire which escapes the natural rhythms and plays the role of an absolute preferable to life itself. The possession of this inaccessible object then becomes ecstasy, "the supreme joy," the *höchste Lust* of the dying Isolde.

Yet those who have read *Lolita* with more perverse amusement than emotion will be entitled to suspect the legitimacy of so solemn an interpretation.

Of course, from the initial *coup de foudre* to the death of the separated lovers—the consequence of a forbidden love that exiles them from the community and consumes without truly uniting them—the great moments of the Myth are easily identifiable. Has the author been aware of them? Certain episodes of the novel would suggest that this was the case, allusions to the most typical situations and peripeties of the Tristan legend. But it is curious to note that on each occasion a touch of irony accompanies the allusion. Thus the hero's mother dies very early (as in Tristan), but this is the tone of the narrative: "My very photogenic mother died in a freak accident (picnic, lightning) when I was three." (We remember the lugubrious tone of fate, the *alte Weise* that marks the mother's death in *Tristan!*) The name of the hotel where the seduction occurs, The Enchanted Hunters, obviously recalls the state of trance of the avowal scene in *Tristan,* but the entire description of the place aims precisely at disenchanting it. The episode of the love-philter is present, but made absurd by its failure: it is only a sleeping pill which H.H. makes Lolita take by a ruse, and which moreover turns out to be too weak, the doctor who provided it having erred as to its ingredients or having bilked his client. (A point-by-point and probably deliberate inversion of the account of Brangaene's "fatal" error.) As in *Tristan,* it is true, the attack on marriage in the name of passion animates the entire narrative. As in *Tristan,* we feel that the author is not interested by the sexual aspect of his story, but solely by the magic of Eros, and he says as much: "I am not concerned with so-called 'sex' at all. Anybody can imagine those elements of animality. A greater endeavor lures on: to fix once and for all the perilous magic of nymphets." As in *Tristan,* "the lovers flee the world, and the world them." Lastly, as in *Tristan,* they die within a short time of one another, separated. But their death is as sordid as the death of the legendary lovers was triumphant in the twelfth-century and Wagnerian versions.

This is because in reality H.H. and Lolita have never known what I call "un-happy reciprocal love." Lolita has never responded to the fierce and tender passion of her elder lover. Hence the failure of the Myth and the "savagely facetious" tone of the novel, its pitiless realism and its somewhat mad jokes saved (just barely, on occasion) from vulgarity by a dazzling verbal virtuosity. If Lolita had loved the narrator, if she had been his Iseult, the realistic novel would have given way to the poem, and the social satire to an inner lyricism. The hypothesis is not an arbitrary one, for this is precisely what happens in Musil's great book ⟨. . .⟩. But the absence, here very striking, not only of any kind of emotional impurity, but also of any spiritual horizon, reduces the novel to the dimensions of a genre-study of mores in the manner of Hogarth. We share the author's irritations, we acclaim his syntax and his vocabulary, we laugh often, we are never moved.

Such as it is, this perfect work remains, too, a *Tristan manqué.* And this is consonant with the immaturity of the very object of the passion described; yet without this immaturity there would be no obstacle, hence no passion. Perhaps the book, after all, is vicious only with regard to this circle.

> —DENIS DE ROUGEMONT, "*Lolita,* or Scandal," *Love Declared: Essays on the Myths of Love* [1961], tr. Richard Howard (New York: Pantheon, 1963), pp. 48–54

NONA BALAKIAN

Nabokov's stand is clear-cut. In the nymphet, Lolita, he has consolidated a neg-ative view of modern woman which in effect embraces much of the criticism implied by the other writers discussed. Nabokov's tour de force, the source of the book's real shock, is that he could make us believe in the suffering and ec-stasy of a pathological love, could engage our sympathy for the middle-aged Humbert Humbert who is thus afflicted. He was able to do this because he saw that the real aggressor, ironically, was not the abnormal Humbert but the seem-ingly normal Lolita. Thus, while Humbert languishes in the sweet transport and rapture of love, Lolita cynically and selfishly appropriates Humbert's passion— first in the spirit of voluptuous excitement, later with a design to bargain for material advantages.

Poor Humbert is unable to understand her indifference—"as if [her passion] were something she had sat upon and was too indolent to remove." For Lolita, at thirteen, amorous relations are a commonplace that she must face with boredom:

"All that noise about boys gags me," she protests. Used up physically before her deeper feelings have been aroused, she cannot grow to the real meaning of love. Her lust for life has no other object than creature comforts and infantile excitements. As our last glimpse of her suggests, she will grow old before having known what it is to be young and fulfilled.

—NONA BALAKIAN, "The Prophetic Voyage of the Anti-Heroine,"
Southwest Review 47, No. 1 (Winter 1962): 140–41

VLADIMIR NABOKOV AND ALVIN TOFFLER

PLAYBOY: Speaking of the very sick, you suggested in *Lolita* that Humbert Humbert's appetite for nymphets is the result of an unrequited childhood love affair; in *Invitation to a Beheading* you wrote about a 12-year-old girl, Emmie, who is erotically interested in a man twice her age; and in *Bend Sinister*, your protagonist dreams that he is "surreptitiously enjoying Mariette [his maid] while she sat, wincing a little, in his lap during the rehearsal of a play in which she was supposed to be his daughter." Some critics, in poring over your works for clues to your personality, have pointed to this recurrent theme as evidence of an unwholesome preoccupation on your part with the subject of sexual attraction between pubescent girls and middle-aged men. Do you feel that there may be some truth to this charge?

NABOKOV: I think it would be more correct to say that had I not written *Lolita*, readers would not have started finding nymphets in my other works and in their own households. I find it very amusing when a friendly, polite person says to me—probably just in order to be friendly and polite—"Mr. Naborkov," or "Mr. Nabahkov," or "Mr. Nabkov" or "Mr. Nabohkov," depending on his linguistic abilities, "I have a little daughter who is a regular Lolita." People tend to underestimate the power of my imagination and my capacity of evolving serial selves in my writings. And then, of course, there is that special type of critic, the ferrety, human-interest fiend, the jolly vulgarian. Someone, for instance, discovered tell-tale affinities between Humbert's boyhood romance on the Riviera and my own recollections about little Colette, with whom I built sand castles in Biarritz when I was 10. Somber Humbert was, of course, 13 and in the throes of a pretty extravagant sexual excitement, whereas my own romance with Colette had no trace of erotic desire and indeed was perfectly commonplace and normal. And, of course, at 9 and 10 years of age, in that set, in those times, we knew nothing whatsoever about the false facts of life that are imparted nowadays to infants by progressive parents.

PLAYBOY: Why false?

NABOKOV: Because the imagination of a small child—especially a town child—at once distorts, stylizes or otherwise alters the bizarre things he is told about the busy bee, which neither he nor his parents can distinguish from a bumblebee, anyway.

PLAYBOY: What one critic has termed your "almost obsessive attention to the phrasing, rhythm, cadence and connotation of words" is evident even in the selection of names for your own celebrated bee and bumblebee—Lolita and Humbert Humbert. How did they occur to you?

NABOKOV: For my nymphet I needed a diminutive with a lyrical lilt to it. One of the most limpid and luminous letters is "L." The suffix "-ita" has a lot of Latin tenderness, and this I required too. Hence: Lolita. However, it should not be pronounced as you and most Americans pronounce it: Low-lee-ta, with a heavy, clammy "L" and a long "o." No, the first syllable should be as in "lollipop," the "L" liquid and delicate, the "lee" not too sharp. Spaniards and Italians pronounce it, of course, with exactly the necessary note of archness and caress. Another consideration was the welcome murmur of its source name, the fountain name: those roses and tears in "Dolores." My little girl's heart-rending fate had to be taken into account together with the cuteness and limpidity. Dolores also provided her with another, plainer, more familiar and infantile diminutive: Dolly, which went nicely with the surname "Haze," where Irish mists blend with a German bunny—I mean a small German hare.

PLAYBOY: You're making a world-playful reference, of course, to a German term for rabbit—*Hase*. But what inspired you to dub Lolita's aging inamorato with such engaging redundancy?

NABOKOV: That, too, was easy. The double rumble is, I think, very nasty, very suggestive. It is a hateful name for a hateful person. It is also a kingly name, and I did need a royal vibration for Humbert the Fierce and Humbert the Humble. Lends itself also to a number of puns. And the execrable diminutive "Hum" is on a par, socially and emotionally, with "Lo," as her mother calls her.

—VLADIMIR NABOKOV AND ALVIN TOFFLER, "*Playboy* Interview: Vladimir Nabokov," *Playboy* 11, No. 1 (January 1964): 36–38

LESLIE A. FIEDLER

Nabokov's theme involves multiple ironies; for in his novel, it is the naïve child, the female, the American who corrupts the sophisticated adult, the male, the European. In a single work, Richardson, Mrs. Stowe, and Henry James are all controverted, all customary symbols for the encounter of innocence and experience stood on their heads. *Lolita, or the Confession of a White Widowed Male* is the international novel moved to America along with the émigré who is its male protagonist. As full as *The Marble Faun* or *The Ambassadors* of guidebook observations, it devotes them not to châteaux or museums or the Church of the Capuchins but to highways and motels and roadside cafés; its America comes out of the AAA Tourguide and

Duncan Hines, as surely as the Europe of Hawthorne out of the Baedeker. Nowhere in our recent literature is there so detailed and acute a picture of our landscape, topographical and moral, as in *Lolita*. But more profoundly than the scenery and the setting, Lolita herself is America—just as Daisy or Hilda or Maggie were America before her; and representing America to the mind of a European, she is even more Annabel Lee than Maggie Verver. Indeed, the book begins with an evocation of Poe's "Kingdom by the Sea"; and before it is through, the names of his girl-love and Nabokov's fade into each other, blur to a single entangled formula: "Annabel Haze, alias Dolores Lee, alias Loleeta. . . ." Annabel Lee as nymphomaniac, demonic rapist of the soul—such is the lithe, brown Campfire Girl, who loves her mummy but was devirginated at the age of twelve (like Justine before her, Nabokov reminds us)!

Into Lolita and her mummy, the bitch-girl and the semi-preserved suburban predator, the pure American female has been split and degraded; but the European confronts her in both her latter-day avatars as helplessly as when she was still whole and dazzling in her purity. Like Prince Amerigo in *The Golden Bowl,* Nabokov's Humbert Humbert is still engaged in the discovery of America through Poe and the American woman; but unlike the Prince he is not redeemed, merely fascinated, raped, driven to murder, and left to die of a heart attack in jail. At every turn of its complications, the perverse theme of *Lolita* parodies some myth of the Sentimental Love Religion and the cult of the child. And it is surely for this reason that the book was banned and then blessed with a popular success; for it is the final blasphemy against the mythical innocence of the woman and the child, more than sufficient unto a day haunted by the fear that there may, after all, have been such an innocence—that somewhere underground it may still persist.

—LESLIE A. FIEDLER, "The Revenge on Woman: From Lucy to Lolita,"
Love and Death in the American Novel (1960; rev. ed. New York:
Stein & Day, 1966), pp. 335–36

DAVID L. JONES

"The poor woman"—Charlotte Haze, mother of Dolores Haze, alias Lolita, chosen nymphet of the gay madman Humbert Humbert—

> busied herself with a number of things she had foregone long before or had never been much interested in, as if (to prolong these Proustian intonations) by my marrying the mother of the child I loved I had enabled my wife to regain an abundance of youth by proxy.

Vladimir Nabokov has Humbert express his amused disdain in what is indeed a capsule parody of Proust's analytic style, in a sentence which is briefer than most Proustian incantations, but which retains the Proustian love of intellectual exploration and syntactical qualification. Similarly, many of Nabokov's lyrical passages offer a light parody, or at least a reminiscence, of the verbal ecstasies of Proust's narrator.

The strongest Proustian imprint, however, appears not on Nabokov's style but on the narrative structure and content of *Lolita*. Humbert informs his readers:

> This book is about Lolita, and now that I have reached the part which (had I not been forestalled by another internal combustion martyr) might be called '*Dolorès Disparue*,' there would be little sense in analyzing the three empty years that followed.

The allusion to Proust's *Albertine disparue* suggests this imprint: *Lolita* often follows the Albertine episodes of *A la recherche du temps perdu* in the content and in some of the methods of narrative and characterization. Sometimes Nabokov uses parody and comic exaggeration, and sometimes he writes a straightforward Proustian story of love and jealousy.

Humbert Humbert's obsession with the nymphets of the world forms something of a parallel with the enchantment which Proust's narrator experiences for the young girls of Balbec, "les jeunes filles en fleurs"; and the younger Humbert's "princedom by the sea," where he loved the doomed young Annabel, is an echo of the Proustian seascape. Young Humbert's love for Annabel, like the love of Proust's young narrator for Albertine and her companions, is of course a normal love, free of the perversion which marks the love of middle-aged Humbert for twelve-year-old Lolita. But even Humbert's nympholepsy has its Proustian parallel, for Proust's narrator retains a marked (if technically chaste) interest in young girls as he grows older.

The important sexual perversion in Proust's story, however, is not the narrator's but Albertine's. The narrator first sees Albertine and her friends as rather loose and undisciplined girls whose nature is "hardie, frivole et dure," girls who are "incapables de subir un attrait d'ordre intellectuel ou moral." Soon, in a different setting, Albertine impresses him as a more cultivated young lady, though her vaguely suggestive smiles disturb him. Still later, he observes her "pronociation . . . charnelle et . . . douce," her "beau rire . . . voluptueux," "la riante expression causée par le désir qu'elle inspirait. He becomes skilled in detecting the slightest sign of her suppressed sensuality and lesbianism. His jealous fears perhaps magnify and distort such signs, much as the desires of Humbert Humbert sharpen his eye for detecting the nymphet in a young girl. But in both novels the reality of the heroines' sensuality remains: both Albertine and Lolita are marked by a demonic quality, a possessing or a being possessed by a dynamic sexual power. Even when Albertine consciously tries to repress her perverse tastes and remove all possible causes of jealously, the narrator is shocked by the unconscious betrayal in a word or a gesture. Humbert Humbert says that the nymphet is "demoniac," a "deadly little demon . . . unconscious herself of her fantastic power." Lolita throws off—for Humbert's eyes at least—a "special languorous glow," "a diabolical glow." The two young ladies differ sharply in one respect. Albertine, even when she first appears in Balbec, has a veneer of cultivation with which she can sometimes cover her adolescent brashness, and as she matures the narrator is subtly tortured by the contrast between the sensitive, intelligent young lady and the depraved sensualist. Humbert is also tortured, but ludicrously, comically, by the cheap and imitative sensuality of Lolita, "for all the world, like the cheapest of cheap cuties. For that is what nymphets imitate—while we moan and die."

Although Lolita's initial experiences, like Albertine's, are lesbian, her real "perversion" consists of nothing more than sexual precocity. But Lolita's precocious heterosexuality and Albertine's habitual lesbianism are alike in being furtive activities, frowned on by society. In the essential narratives of love and jealously, however, the furtiveness of both girls consists not in deceiving society at large but in deceiving their lovers. Humbert rues the day that he allowed young Lolita to study acting, for he "suffered her to cultivate deceit." Lolita's lying and deceit grow as her desire to leave Humbert for Clare Quilty grows. Proust's narrator believes that Albertine is "par nature ... menteuse," but her specific lies are often caused less by natural inclination than by her lover's criticism and by her desire to gain his respect. In fact the narrator is often impressed by Albertine's frankness, which seems (to the reader if not to the narrator) more natural than her fearful deceptions. In the younger Albertine, this frankness often takes the form of adolescent sarcasm and rudeness: during his first sojourn at Balbec the narrator observes Albertine's "ton rude et ses maniéres 'petite bande.'" Similarly, Humbert Humbert notes that a nymphet frequently possesses "vulgarity, or at least what a given community terms so," and on one occasion he observes that Lolita is "her usual sarcastic self." This ebullient youthful effrontery spills over into the speech of both girls. Lolita uses a slangy and (to Humbert's ears) vulgar vocabulary, and the younger Albertine sometimes employs "des termes d'argot ... voyous." Such speech is not an indicator of innate vulgarity, but simply a mode of adolescent conventionality. The brashly cynical and spirited Lolita is a rather intelligent lass, but her normally adolescent tastes and language lead Humbert to classify her as "a disgustingly conventional little girl." The older Albertine develops, under the narrator's guidance, a certain social and intellectual savoir faire which Humbert misses in his Lolita. Proust's narrator succeeds in playing the part of a third-rate Pygmalion, although he fails, tragically, to realize how well Albertine is filling the part he has created for her. But Nabokov sets out to create a comedy of unfulfilled desire and allows Humbert Humbert to squirm between the ecstasy of Lolita's physical maturity and the frustration of her emotional and intellectual childishness.

Both Proust's narrator and Humbert Humbert pursue an elusive ideal woman, but the essential narrative concerns their jealous efforts to capture and retain an actual woman. The tragic jealousy of Proust's narrator sometimes skirts the comic as he contemplates the complexities of guarding Albertine from the attentions of not one sex but two. Justifiable as his concern may be, his jealousy often runs to painful excesses: he is afraid to leave Albertine alone for even a minute during the Verdurins' evenings at la Raspelière, and he decides against taking her to an exhibit at the Louvre for fear some of the paintings might prove too suggestive. Humbert's jealousy, which becomes entangled "in the fine fabrics of nymphet falsity," proves justified, but his exquisitely comic suffering in his bizarre social and sexual situation caricatures the strange problem and the intense suffering of Proust's narrator.

The narrative pattern in both books might be outlined so: jealousy, incarceration, alternating submission and revolt, and flight. Proust's jealous narrator subjects Albertine to a virtual imprisonment in his parents' Paris apartment, and Humbert Humbert isolates Lolita in an endless chain of motels. Nabokov transmutes the gray and somber imprisonment of Albertine into a garish picaresque comedy of the American highway: the different settings reflect the contrast between Lolita's brash adolescence and Albertine's nascent maturity. Albertine usually remains passive and docile during her imprisonment, partly from love and partly from fear, but the narrator's unreasonable scrutiny of her slightest word or action sometimes drives her to revolt. Even after she has fled from Paris, she writes the narrator that she is willing to return—"si vous aviez besoin de moi." But the pathological tragedy of the narrator's pursuit of the elusive reality of Albertine continues after her flight, and even after her death. Lolita, during her imprisonment, is physically docile, regarding her sex life with Humbert first as a game and later as a boring duty, but emotionally she is indifferent and often rebellious. Lolita's flight with Clare Quilty involves Humbert in a hilarious cross-country pursuit of his wayward nymphet, but as his emotional involvement with Lolita grows the comedy begins to shade into a pathological tragedy which parallels more than it caricatures the tragedy of Proust's narrator.

Proust's narrator is aware of his great sensitivity, but he is ultimately incapable of recognizing how extreme his treatment of Albertine has been. Even after Albertine's death, he feels his own loss much more acutely than the torture he has inflicted on his mistress. Nabokov sets out to caricature the Proustian psychology by creating a character who is aware of his own psychopathic nature and glories in it. Humbert refers to his mental instability and his visits to sanatoria. He admits that he is a "naïve . . . pervert" and an "internal combustion martyr," and he speaks of his "Dostoevskian grin" and the "cesspool of rotting monsters behind his slow boyish smile." And yet Humbert is often driven by the intensity of his feeling to consider his internal, personal world of perversion as the real world, the normal world. "I have but followed nature," he says a bit flippantly. "I am nature's faithful hound."

Humbert's psychological tragedy springs from his perverted desire to establish a perfectly normal sexual relationship with a twelve-year-old girl, just as the tragedy of Proust's narrator results from a perverted desire to possess and to comprehend Albertine completely. Albertine's lesbianism is irrelevant here: the narrator would be psychopathically jealous even if he had only male rivals to contend with. Albertine submits to her lover's tortures as long as she believes she has a chance of winning his confidence. Then she leaves. Lolita plans Humbert's sexual games with "amused distaste" and sometimes with "plain repulsion." Humbert is at first amused, but he is saddened as he realizes that Lolita feels no real love for him, that she regards him simply as a habit to be escaped. As his love for Lolita grows and his suffering intensifies, the novel becomes less of a caricature and more of an imitation of Proustian psychological tragedy—though Nabokov deftly mixes the comic with the tragic. Humbert not only suffers for himself but comes more and more to realize what a ruin he has made of Lolita's life. "It had become gradually clear to my conventional Lolita during our singular and bestial cohabitation," Humbert writes, "that even the most miserable of family lives was better than the parody of incest, which, in the long run, was the best I could offer the waif." Nabokov's style here gives a subtly comic turn to Humbert's observations, but the tone becomes more somber when Humbert hears "the melody of children at play" and realizes "that the hopelessly poignant thing was not Lolita's absence from my side, but the absence of her voice from that concord."

Both Proust and Nabokov tread a fine line between a real world and an unreal world—Nabokov more consciously than Proust. The isolated world in which each narrator imprisons his mistress may have its own peculiar psychological reality, but it is cut off from the moral and social standards of the external world. Albertine, a supposedly respectable young lady, shares an apartment with her lover during his parents' absence; and Lolita, a twelve-year-old girl, shares the motel beds of forty-year-old Humbert. The situations are similar in their unreality, though Nabokov emphasizes the unreality—for comic purposes. Proust's narrator and Humbert both enjoy vivid erotic fantasies which they manage to realize at least partially in their ivory towers.

Humbert Humbert several times considers the matter of nymphets from a historical perspective, noting that what modern society calls a "perversion" has been accepted as normal in other cultures. Proust's narrator makes similar comments on homosexuality—"l'opprobre seul fait le crime." But he tries vainly to view Albertine's lesbianism as an ignorant amorality, and he is oppressed by a growing feeling that she is consciously and habitually immoral in her sexual life. Humbert Humbert remarks that he and Lolita live "in a world of total evil"; but Lolita, who "saw the stark act merely as part of a youngster's furtive world, unknown to adults," is simply living an undisciplined existence which has nothing to do with the moral standards of adult society. For Humbert, the whole affair with Lolita is a flight from discipline into fantasy, the sort of fantasy he had tried to escape years earlier by searching for a routine, ordered life in his marriage to Valeria. The problem of discipline is also treated by Proust: the narrator tries to order both his personal and artistic life, and Albertine pathetically tries to gain her lover's confidence by reining her natural impulses.

The task of depicting the inner world of a psychopathic narrator presents both Proust and Nabokov with a problem of artistic control. The intimacy of a first-person narrative elicits automatic sympathy from a reader, and the initial reaction of Proust's reader is apt to be an empathic immersion in the jealous narrator's intense suffering. Proust does focus on the narrator's psychological tragedy, but the richness of his world eventually compels the reader to move outside this focus. Proust constantly gives hints of Albertine's real and laudable motives, motives unseen or virtually ignored by the narrator, and the reader is led to wonder about the exact degree of her depravity and sensuality and to question the precision of the narrator's observations and interpretations. Proust has created his psychological world so fully that it sometimes eludes his control.

The problem is actually one of reality, of real and normal human action and sympathy, clashing with the abnormal psychological exaggeration of the narrator's partly realized dream world. Proust focuses on the dream world, but the shadowy world of the real, the human Albertine intrudes. Nabokov faces a similar problem, but his method of control is a comic one (depending partly on Proustian parody): he creates a world which is comic because of its difference from the normal world. But as the story moves on, and Humbert's suffering grows more intense, *Lolita* often becomes Proustian parallel more than Proustian parody. The very real sufferings—of both Humbert and Lolita—differ from the comic frustations and satisfactions which dominate the earlier parts of the book. The reader's emotional attitude toward Humbert Humbert, as towards Proust's narrator, is necessarily ambivalent. The strength of each novel lies not in the consistency of the writer's tragic or comic control, but in the richness of the psychological world he creates. In this sense, the very emotional ambivalence created by Proust and by Nabokov is a strength, not a weakness.

—DAVID L. JONES, "'Dolorès Disparue,'" *Symposium* 20, No. 2 (Summer 1966):
135–40

JULIAN MOYNAHAN

In terms of Nabokov's own work *Lolita* has a ⟨. . .⟩ centrality and prominence. In it he comes to final accommodation with the nymphet theme, which he had been echoing and reechoing in his work for decades, and links the theme lucidly to the master themes of nostalgia (or preterism) and of imagination which form the principal coordinates of his entire created world. Unlike Albinus in *Laughter in the Dark*, who never understands what he is doing, Humbert Humbert, conducting his own defense—"O ladies and gentlemen of the jury"—and, as critics often fail to note, his own prosecution, comes to know fully what he has done and is responsible for. He is in all of Nabokov's fiction the supremely conscious individualist, the wholly confident manipulator of the bewildering variety of his roles, and in this confidence reflects Nabokov's own masterly grasp of his most complex creation in character.

Nabokov has remarked of Humbert that although he went straight and properly to hell after the guards found him dead of a coronary in his cell, where he awaited trial for the slaying of Quilty, the man who had taken Lolita from him, Humbert may be allowed the privilege of returning to earth for one day each year. On that day one might expect him to haunt the environs of the little mining town in the American West, mentioned in the book's concluding pages, "that lay at my feet, in a fold of the valley," from which rose "the melody of children at play." Here it was that the bestial and enchanted hunter of nymphets rejoined the human race when he at last "knew that the hopelessly poignant thing was not Lolita's absence from my side, but the absence of her voice from that concord." And if we are inclined to suspect his sentiments here there is another late episode which indicates the same belated conversion. Lolita has written him after years of silence and absence to say she is married, pregnant, and in need of money. He finds her in a shack in "Coalmont," eight hundred miles from New York City, big-bellied, worn out at seventeen, and he wants to steal her away again or kill her if she will not come. But then he realizes that he loves her *as she is*, not merely as the echo or memory "of the nymphet I had rolled myself upon which cries in the past . . . Thank God it was not that echo alone that I worshiped." The "echo" of course points to the "eidolon" he had pursued lifelong, spying into "jewel-bright" windows and depraving little girls because the print of sexual characteristics was still so faintly impressed upon their childish bodies that he could pretend when savaging them that he was cleaving to a pure form and recapturing the lost Edenic time he had spent in childhood with "Annabel Lee." Lolita is spectacularly and maturely pregnant, no longer the "Idolores" of his original quest. He earns his overnight pass from hell by loving her and leaving her—several thousand dollars richer—going off to hunt down and kill the "rival devil," Quilty, whose taste for sexual frolics with children, as with dwarfs, is an ordinary piece of psychopathy lacking transcendental overtones.

But even at Coalmont Humbert does not relinquish his habit of imaginary role playing. He casts the scene as Don José's final confrontation with Carmen (*"Changeons de vie, ma Carmen,"* etc.) and says goodbye to his "American sweet immortal dead love," who has just made him understand for the first time that "the past was the past," under the aspect of a fat tenor from grand opera. One of the joys of *Lolita* is Humbert's role playing. Just as the book as a whole encapsulates and parodies every literary confession of a great sinner from St. Augustine to Sade, Rousseau, and Stavrogin, so do Humbert's roles introduce a rich variety of imaginative frames and thematic aspects through which the book's action may be viewed.

To touch very lightly on this matter, consider the following. When Lolita is Bee or Beatrice, Humbert is Dante and the evoked mode is an inversion of "divine comedy" (hellish comedy?). When she is "Dolorès Disparue," Humbert is Proust's Marcel lamenting the vanished Albertine and the mode is Proustian speculation about the enigmas of time and memory. When she is Vee (Virginia Clemm), Humbert is Edgar Allan Poe and the frame is artist's biography in the era of "romantic agony." When she merges with "Annabel" Humbert is the child narrator of Poe's famous poem. And when Humbert, fleeing the mysterious Aztec red convertible with Lolita through the American night, murmurs *"lente, lente, currite noctics equi,"* Humbert is Faustus, Lolita is both Helen and Gretchen, and the mode, if not the mood, is that of Marlowe's tragic morality play. Also there are Humbert's less literary roles, each played to the hilt: the spy and voyeur ("Humbert Humbert— two eyes burning in the dark"), the European gentleman with a "past," the family friend, the husband and mature lover, the "stepfather" concerned to guard his little charge safely through the toils of teendom, the private investigator, the madman, the devil slayer ("guilty of killing Quilty"), and, finally and throughout, the pleader- prosecutor at heaven's bar—"O winged gentlemen!"

Nabokov's own cryptic key to *Lolita* was given in a 1956 "Postscript" to the first American edition. There he said the idea came to him in Paris in 1938, during an attack of neuralgia and after reading a "pointless" newspaper story about a scientist who attempted to teach an ape to draw. The ape did produce a drawing, but it was only of the bars of its cage. Humbert, that greatly talented ape, attempts a break-out, an act of transcendence,through his mad and cruel pursuit of the eidolon, incarnate in little Dolores Haze, Lolita, but he merely succeeds in confirming his confinement in matter, in the grossly sensual self, in vice and in time. One can add to this very little, except perhaps—since *Lolita* is already an assured American classic—a suggestion of how the book reverberates through our specifically American historic culture.

The core element of Humbert's sexual perversity, arch-romanticism, and derangement is an attitude toward time which may remind us of other eccentric or deranged heroes of American fiction. Humbert is fixated on the past—on his childhood love affair with "Annabel Lee"—and his pursuit, seduction, and enslavement of Dolores Haze are an attempt to reinstate in the present and preserve into the future what was irretrievably lost in the past. The expensiveness of indulgence in this illusion is very great: it costs no less than the wrecking of a child's life, as Humbert finally admits after abandoning his corrupt rationalizations concerning the natural depravity and sexual precocity of American little girls. Humbert and his time problem are summed up on the final page of *The Great Gatsby*, ⟨...⟩ and in a number of other classic American texts.

But how can this vile European stand in for an archetypal American? There is really no problem. America, as a "brand new, mad new dream world where everything [is] permissible," is Europe's dream of itself according to the romantic error that past time is retrievable. Emerson, Whitman, and Hart Crane might have approved Humbert's thought, if not his exact words and their appalling application. We are all Europeans when we dream that dangerous, beguiling, ever-so-American dream.

These speculations can be pushed a bit further under the general rubric of fate, freedom, and America. *Lolita*, because it is heavy with fate, would seem to present a situation in which the margin of freedom which interests us in fictional characters, particularly in the characters appearing in modern books, has diminished virtually to nothing. For instance, Humbert is obsessed, Lolita is enslaved, Charlotte Haze is totally duped, and a character like Quilty is the slave of his sinister vices. And in fate as the "synchronizing phantom" arranging happenstance and coincidence upon wholly mysterious principles and freedom disappears altogether from the book. From another angle, there is freedom in *Lolita* of a rather awful sort. Humbert is free, unencumbered with compunction before his "conversion." Through most of the book he has the freedom of his viciousness, as does Quilty. Humbert's actions take place at a point in history when traditional sanctions have lapsed or at least loosened, and there would be very little consensus of judgment against his deeds from the "enlightened" sector of the community, apart from agreement that he is psychologically "disturbed." This in effect forgives and forgets by understanding or claiming to.

Dolores Haze also is free in a sense, in that the nature of contemporary American "suburban" culture ties her to nothing, asks nothing of her, presents her with nothing. What is she? A junior consumer, of comic books and bubble gum, a "starlet" with a thirst for cheap films and Coke. There is a great vacancy in and around her, a voidness and loneliness only partly created by Humbert's machinations. This vacancy is cultural in the first instance, American.

For Europe, as first de Toqueville and then D. H. Lawrence have expounded, America has figured as the place beyond cabined and confined traditions and sanctions. It has been the place where time itself might be redeemed, where the dream of a new Eden, of a second life, could be realized. Naturally, there has been a dark, pathological side to this. America has been the place indubitably attractive to great mischief makers, psychopaths, men on the run, unclubable and violent persons, con men. Humbert lives on the dark side of the American freedom I am describing. There is some truth in the statement that what drove Humbert to America was his vice and the hope of satisfying it in the land of opportunity. And there is also some truth in the idea that the history of Lolita, who died in childbed in a town of the "remotest Northwest" on her way to Alaska, the last American frontier, expresses the final decadence of that European myth which we call the American Dream.

—JULIAN MOYNAHAN, *Vladimir Nabokov* (Minneapolis: University of
Minnesota Press, 1971), pp. 32–36

GARRY WILLS

It begins when a match is struck on a darkened hotel porch, and a soft voice rasps "th' equivocations of the fiend."

"Where the devil did you get her?"

"I beg your pardon?"

"I said: the weather is getting better."

"Seems so."

"Who's the lassie?"

"My daughter."

"You lie—she's not."

"I beg your pardon?"

"I said: July was hot. Where's her mother?"

"Dead."

Humbert Humbert knew, without knowing it, that McFate would speak in time—"Aubrey McFate," the obscure thwarter hovering somewhere. Even when this pirate devil acquires a face (and endless cars), there is nothing to call him, for a long time, but McFate. Only when clues jumble near each other for a long time do they, clair-obscurely, finally spell out in patches this devil's name: Clare Quilty.

Nabokov's *Lolita* is (at last estimate) two thousand or so things—prominent among the rest, a detective story. (McFate is sometimes called Lieutenant Trapp.)

As in *Crime and Punishment*, the detective is also the criminal, but Dostoyevsky makes Raskolnikov play this double role, back and forth, through a policeman essentially outside the crime: he must stalk the man who stalks him. Humbert and Quilty, by contrast, track in on each other as mutual accuser-criminals, growing toward each other's destruction, Humbert in terror and Quilty with a leer. Not only Humbert, but Lolita herself, is possessed by Quilty, who can only be exorcised at last by murder. This detective story does not solve a crime, but *is* solved *by* one.

It is also, of course, a love story, as many have realized. All the clinical talk of girls half-nymphed into womanhood—time's mermaids, amphibious, belonging fully to neither world—is in the long run misleading. Lolita does not fulfill Humbert's obsession with nymphets, she destroys it. His concern has been for a type, co-cooned outside of time in a frozen moment of becoming. The mounted butterfly cannot decay, because it cannot (any longer) live. Humbert, with a thousand such butterfly slides to view, in his poise of remote satisfaction, meets Lolita at just her moment of chrysalis—loss and descent from nymphethood—and he follows her down. The two years of his life with her, and the two years after, are all post-nymphet years. He sees her last in a splayed and cowlike pregnancy, and never loved her more. By his own fastidious measure, cultivated half a lifeless lifetime, she represents his fall from an aesthetic state of grace. He dies into time with every sag of her flesh. Having flirted with her in his Eden of the mind, he loves her outside the fiery gates—now his and her flesh darken together back toward earth. He is redeemed by his fall, made capable of loving. And so capable of damning her.

> She was only the faint violet whiff and dead leaf echo of the nymphet I had rolled myself upon with such cries in the past; an echo on the brink of a russet ravine, with a far wood under a white sky, and brown leaves choking the brook, and one last cricket in the crisp weeds . . . but thank God it was not that echo alone that I worshipped. What I used to pamper among the tangled vines of my heart, *mon grand péché radieux*, had dwindled to its essence: sterile and selfish vice, all *that* I canceled and cursed.

Lolita is an even rarer thing than an honest love story. It is our best modern hate story. Unrequited love is, from the outset, half made up of hate. Self-hate for loving—or else, on the other side, for not loving; a shared intimacy of detesting, uncontrollable as love itself. To be the unwilling object of another's love is embarrassing, oddly debilitating. What should be a reciprocal relationship is both interrupted and uninterruptible; an intensely "personing" energy pounds at the unresponding object, thrusting an Other in on a violated Self. It gives the loved an unwanted responsibility for the lover, victimizing the loved as an unwilling victor.

It is common to say that we become, in some measure, those we love. It is a circularly weird fact that we become, will we or not, those who love us. The very lack of reciprocation forges a bond. After all, no one cares as much for anyone as does that person's lover—except each of us caring for himself. No matter what the division of barriers between a cold loved person and the lover, they agree on one crucial point—both *do* love the same person. There is a union achieved by reason of a common object, which is the one kind of union lacking in the true reciprocity of love, where the lovers have different objects—A's being B, and B's being A. In the case of the loved unlover (who is an unmoved mover), the secret tie lies in a barren uniformity under all the reversals: both A and B love A, and only A. Set apart in all things else, on this point they are undivided—and what was put apart in heaven cannot be sundered on earth. The broken circuit pours all its electro-cuting force into the point of rupture, which is a unifying focus. Bound, by division.

This is the bond Humbert and Lolita share, wedded by her unresponsiveness. She accepts that burden, and even appeals to it, later, asking for financial support as a dark marriage right. But as they both loved the same object ("Lo"), they are also linked, in a camaraderie of plague victims, by hating the same object: the Humbert mirrored back on Humbert in her own revulsion or coarsening. Eve cannot hate the serpent near as well as the serpent does. The love that freed Humbert from Eden—and now binds him—crippled and distorted her. There is nothing crueler than love. He needs her, and diminishes her by the need, and despises himself for doing so. He preys on what he admires, destroying it with admiration. He is her tempter, but also—quite sincerely, as he assures Quilty at the end—her father. Both God and Satan to her, creating and undoing her. Romantic agony over his own deterioration he could stand, and even prettify. But love breaks him out from all such excuses into a larger prison—hers, the one he forged for her in darkness. His hell is the fact that he damned her. Listening from a hill to the play of children, he muses:

> One could hear now and then, as if released, an almost articulate spurt of vivid laughter, or the crack of a bat, or the clatter of a toy wagon, but it was all really too far away for the eye to distinguish any movement in the lightly etched streets. I stood listening to that musical vibration from my lofty slope, to those flashes of separate cries with a kind of demure murmur for background, and then I knew that the hopelessly poignant thing was not Lolita's absence from my side, but the absence of her voice from that concord.

Love destroys. We all seduce and abuse one child, the one we once loved best, the one we were born as; and we mistreat all others in obscure revenge for what was done to us (mainly by us). Of course, Lolita's fall—like Margaret's—was "the blight she was born for." It is, always, Margaret we mourn for. But woe to him by whom the scandal comes into the world. Humbert, fallen, can pay that price—this constitutes his superiority to the prelapsarian dandy of the book's first pages. But he "rose" to moral responsibility by making her fall with him.

—GARRY WILLS, "The Devil and Lolita," *New York Review of Books,*
21 February 1974, pp. 4–5

JAMES TWITCHELL

It has been pointed out before that with few exceptions girls in American literature don't really grow up. Our novels are full of Huck Finns, and Nick Carraways, and

Holden Caulfields, but no one cares about their sisters. As a matter of fact if, as the Marxists have stated, literature is the litmus paper of social concern, then how girls become women has been of no big concern. But how boys become men—now, that's a different story. And it's one that has been told over and over.

To be sure, there are plenty of females in American novels, and plenty of females who change. But they change in a most peculiar way. They do not grow up the way boys do—rather, they "fall" or they "soar"; they become whores or nuns.

Historically this has always been the case "in the novel." On the one hand there are books like Richardson's *Pamela* and *Clarissa,* which are not Bildungsromans as much as they are books of etiquette, novels of manners. They do not show a girl growing into womanhood, but one frozen into ladyhood. She doesn't mature through experience; she escapes from it. And on the other extreme are novels about girls who "fall," usually through sexual experience. In such works as Defoe's *Moll Flanders* and *Roxanna,* the protagonist is initiated, yes—but into bawdyhood, not womanhood.

There has been, however, a whole genre of underground novels which present a third option for the heroine—a woman who "falls" in the eyes of society but who retains her own self-respect and personal integrity. In each case, from *Fanny Hill* to *Candy,* these are considered pornographic novels, not only because of their overt sexual content but also because of the apparent unconcern of the girl involved.

The major split in the English novel between the Defoe and Richardson heroines continued throughout the eighteenth century. By and large one had a choice between a Roxanna ("The Fortunate Mistress") and a Clarissa ("The History of a Young Lady"), a Molly Seagrim or a Sophia, a novel by Fanny Burney or one about Fanny Hill. For the Victorians the choice was still the same, except that both heroines were pressed between the covers of the same book. So Thackeray gives us both Amelia Sedley and Becky Sharp, both Rebecca and Rowena. But take your pick—either way you end up with extremes. And these extremes are carried on through the Brontës, Dickens, Meredith, Mardy, Galsworthy, up almost until our own time.

For most of the twentieth century we still find the Hobson's choice of an Edith Wharton heroine or Maggie, Girl of the Streets; Isabella Fletcher or sister Carrie; Mrs. Dalloway or Caddy Compson. The same choice Thackeray presented tin *Vanity Fair* is still with us: either a heroine ravished into sex or one ravished far above sex, either a bawd or a blue stocking, a whore or a nun. Take your choice, but you will not find many, if any, girls growing into women.

It may well be that there have been so few effective women's Bildungsromans written by men because the male realizes that for him to write "honestly" about girls growing up he will have to focus on what he considers the specific act of maturity for a woman—the rupturing of the hymen. He has been conditioned to believe this—and women have too. Men writing about boys growing up can deal with non-sexual experiences, but rarely is there a heroine who matures because of changes in the *psyche*; almost always the changes are in her *soma.* If we look back into the history of the novel, this act of deflowering is almost always tantamount to initiation. And that initiation, if not supervised by the conventions of society, usually leads to a life of sin and moral depravity.

But this attitude toward the maturing girl is not limited to male authors. Women writers in past centuries have often been equally unable to show the "all-together" female. Unconsciously the female writer may have realized that the whole genre was somehow tainted, and so she stayed away from it. The exception may be George Eliot, who took her heroines "out of the closet" but was still unwilling to let them go out of the house. And although the female Bildungsroman is finally beginning to make some headway in recent years (witness Plath's *The Bell Jar,* Chopin's *The Awakening,* Lessing's *The Golden Notebook*), progress has been slow and often awkward.

At first it seems ironic that one of the few honest attempts to create a female Bildungsroman should be a book that parodies the historical "girl growing up" novel. On second thought, perhaps the only way to write in this genre may be to write *against* the historical precedent. Vladimir Nabokov's *Lolita* is one of the few "honest" and hence pornographic treatments of a girl's maturing written by a man. It is honest not to "truth," but rather to historical truth, to the way man has been conditioned to perceive the process of growing into womanhood.

In Lolita we find a heroine who in the eyes of the "supposed" author Humbert Humbert, follows the tradition of those hundreds of virgins who are deflowered and turned into moral stinkweeds. What we must remember, however, is that it is Humbert and Humbert's view of women that is being ridiculed. For finally of course it is Humbert the man, not Lolita, who becomes the object of irony. Imprisoned by what he has been conditioned to think should happen, he is unable to see that this is not what does indeed happen.

However, Nabokov does. Where Humbert's view of Lolita's maturation is ridiculous, Nabokov's is sensible and compassionate. For Humbert, the whole "growing up" of Lolita centers around the night in The Enchanted Hunters, where Lolita is "made a woman." But what Humbert is unwilling to admit, except many years later while writing his confessional memoirs, is that it was Lolita who seduced him, not he her. This central event in the female Bildungsroman is simply turned around. Only long after the event, long after Lolita's death, just before his trial, is he able to admit:

> Frigid gentlewomen of the jury! I had thought that months, perhaps years, would elapse before I dared to reveal myself to Dolores Haze; but by six she was wide awake, and by six fifteen we were technically lovers. I am going to tell you something very strange: it was she who seduced me.

The irony is, of course, that it is Humbert who was deflowered and who turns out to be the stinkweed, not Lolita. In fact, what we learn is that sexual intercourse has virtually nothing to do with Lolita's growth into womanhood, for she "had sex" long before Humbert. Neither she nor Nabokov seems to be concerned about it at all.

Nabokov goes to considerable lengths to push against the tradition of the nineteenth-century girl's "initiation through sex" with Humbert's rendition of the seduction scene. He begins as the almost archetypal adult with his well-adjusted social conscience:

> However, I shall not bore my learned readers with a detailed account of Lolita's presumption. Suffice it to say that not a trace of modesty did I perceive in this beautiful hardly formed young girl whom modern co-education, juvenile mores, the campfire racket and so forth had utterly and hopelessly depraved. She saw the stark act merely as part of a youngster's furtive world, unknown to adults. What adults did for purposes of procreation was no business of hers.

But then the real prudish Humbert starts to seep through the facade:

> Pride alone prevented her from giving up; for, in my strange predicament, I feigned supreme stupidity and had her have her way—at least while I could still bear it. But really these are irrelevant matters, I am not concerned with so-called "sex" at all. Anybody can imagine those elements of animality. A greater endeavor lures me on: to fix once for all the perilous magic of nymphets.

This is one of the many times when the authorial voice tracks over Humbert's and we hear Nabokov speaking not far off. Like one of those Saul Steinberg drawings that Nabokov greatly admires, we see the pen hand of the artist caught for a second in the celluloid frame of art. When Humbert says, "But really these are irrelevant matters; I am not concerned with so-called 'sex' at all. Anybody can imagine those elements of animality," his words are dripping with dramatic irony. Don't let him kid you; he is concerned with sex. But Nabokov is not.

The next line is a real *tour de force*. When Humbert says, "A greater endeavor lures me on: to fix once for all the perilous magic of nymphets," we know that it is he, not Lolita, who fears her maturity. Preferring her potentiality to her actuality, he must "fix" her magic at its unrealized stage. He had imagined *years* elapsing before seducing Lolita; for her, it took a quarter of an hour. The qualities that Humbert cherishes in his "Lo"—her downiness, her "pubescence"—are negative qualities, primarily valuable to Humbert as signs of non-growth. For him, sex changes all that. According to Humbert immediately after her "sexcapades" with him, Lolita becomes a woman, a fallen woman. It is not simply his male ego, but history, that has taught him to react this way. In the lepidopteral context, she is destined to become a "butterfly" through her experience with him and is now doomed to death. He feels she can grow no more; he has taken her into maturity.

The end of the book repudiates Humbert's perception. The final reunion scene is all too often overlooked by critics, perhaps because of the rather tedious transcontinental chase. But it is an integral part of Nabokov's Bildungsroman. Humbert goes to see Lolita, already convinced that she will have gone the way of all fleshy girls in literature who have been "sexually ravished" by men. What he finds is not quite what he had expected:

> Couple of inches taller. Pink-rimmed glasses. New, heaped-up hairdo, new ears. How simple! The moment, the death I had kept conjuring up for three years was as simple as a bit of dry wood. She was frankly and hugely pregnant. Her head looked smaller (only two seconds had passed really, but let me give them as much wooden duration as life can stand), and her pale-freckled cheeks were hollowed, and her bare shins and arms had lost all their tan, so that the little hairs showed.

She is no longer a nymph; the downy pubescence is gone. But what he is coming to see is that his "girl-child" has become a woman. The pupa is now a butterfly:

> Against the splintery deadwood of the door, Dolly Schiller flattened herself as best she could (even rising on tiptoe a little) to let me pass, and was crucified for a moment, looking down, smiling down at the threshold, hollow-cheeked with round *pommettes,* her watered-milk-white arms outspread on the wood. I passed without touching her bulging babe. Dollysmell, with a faint fried addition. My teeth chattered like an idiot's.

Here she is spread out like a butterfly pinned to a collector's cork. Humbert is losing all control. Although she has matured, she is neither slut nor saint. She is, in fact—and this is what galls Humbert—happily married.

In the scene with her husband, Humbert is flabbergasted that Lolita, for all her experiences with him, could be content with another man. This was not the way it was supposed to be—sex was supposed to ruin her forever. As much as Humbert wants to believe this, he realizes that no such thing has happened. She has grown into womanhood. He watches her bending over to help her husband: "How womanish and somehow never seen that way before was the shadowy division between her pale breasts when she bent down over the man's hand!" And he is visibly shaken when Dick, Lolita's husband, tells him Lo will make a "swell mother." How can this be! Lolita a swell mother!

But gradually Humbert accepts the unacceptable. As he stares at her he realizes that she is not a sex object but a person:

> . . . and there she was with her ruined looks and her adult, ropeveined narrow hands and her goose-flesh white arms . . . and I looked and looked at her, and knew as clearly as I know I am to die, that I loved her more than anything I had ever seen or imagined on earth, or hoped for anywhere else.

Lust has become love. Humbert, who has lived a middle-aged man's masturbatory dream, awakes to find it a nightmare. Now back into a corner, he has to admit that Lolita is human and that she is a woman.

> And it struck me, as my automaton knees went up and down, that I simply did not know a thing about my darling's mind and that quite possibly, behind the

awful juvenile clichés, there was in her a garden and a twilight, and a palace gate—dim and adorable regions which happened to be lucidly and absolutely forbidden to me . . .

This is one of the rare moments when Humbert, "so tired of being cynical," lets the façade fall. Just for a second he admits that Lolita is a person with depth, with feeling, with ideas and hopes and a life of her own.

And so Lolita's growing up ends. She becomes a woman not only to herself, but also to Humbert. In realizing this, Humbert also "grows up." One need only recall the usual treatment of girls in American literature to realize that this is not the way it is supposed to be. But Nabokov, for all his fantasies and games, is finally not concerned with what is supposed to be, but rather with what actually is. He has given us one of the few girls who is initiated into life without ending up down on the sidewalk or up in the penthouse, a heroine who is neither a whore nor a lady but, finally, a woman. But to do it—and this is what is so condemning of American mores—he has to write a "pornographic novel." Ironically, however, what is obscene about the book is not what happens to Lolita with Humbert, but what happens to Humbert's psyche after he accepts the chauvinistic assumptions of what it takes for a girl to grow up.

Although *Lolita* is of course more concerned with the growing-up of Humbert Humbert, there is a valid case for the novel as one of the few successful American female-Bildungsromans of the twentieth century. In fact, decades hence *Lolita* may well be pointed to as important not as one of the best examples of Black Humor, but also as one of the first substantive changes in the literary tradition of the female Bildungsroman.

—JAMES TWITCHELL, "*Lolita* as Bildungsroman," *Genre* 8, No. 3
(September 1974): 272–77

ROBERT T. LEVINE

Lolita the Nymphet dwells on an enchanted island whose boundaries are not spatial but temporal: the age limits of nine and fourteen. Humbert Humbert aspires to live out his days on that island. He anticipates a perpetual ecstasy that will make amends for the soiled, wasted days of his youth. But he cannot live there. No adults allowed. In his desperate effort to climb onto the island, he pulls Lolita off it and into the unenchanted ocean of adulthood too soon. This essay will examine the various expressions in *Lolita* of Dolores Haze's departure from that childhood isle and the various ironies resulting from Humbert's part in her departure.

Humbert, in the first chapter of his memoir, informs us that Lolita did indeed have a precursor: the maiden Annabel Leigh. By the time we have reached the final chapter, we may realize that there was another precursor to Lolita: the prostitute Monique. Of course, she is a less prominent character than Annabel, who is echoed throughout the novel. Yet Monique is important thematically because the effect

Humbert has on her foreshadows his effect on Lolita. He has been attracted to Monique by her "curiously immature body" and her childish mannerisms. On the day after their first transaction, he observes that "she seemed to have grown less juvenile, more of a woman overnight."

On the day after the "honeymoon" night of Humbert and Lolita, as they are riding away from The Enchanted Hunters hotel, Lo says: "Let us stop at the next gas station. . . . I want to go to the washroom." A few moments later, "she started complaining of pains, said she could not sit, said I had torn something inside her." What has actually happened is that Lo has experienced her menarche. This scene has been prepared for earlier in the novel when Humbert wonders: "Has she already been initiated by mother nature to the Mystery of the Menarche?" At their next stop after the gas station, Humbert buys Lo among other items "a box of sanitary pads." So on the day following her first sexual intercourse with Humbert, Lolita—suddenly aging like her precursor Monique—biologically leaves her childhood by beginning the cycle of menstruation.

Has Humbert torn anything physical inside Lolita? Probably not. Although we have been told that "she was not quite prepared for certain discrepancies between a kid's life and mine. Pride alone prevented her from giving up." Lolita's accusation may indicate merely that she doesn't recognize the phenomenon of menstruation. Her ignorance, as well as her precocity, is stressed by Humbert: "What adults did for purposes of procreation was no business of hers." Yet, whether or not Humbert has torn anything physical inside her, we may be certain that he has torn something spiritual in her. He has destroyed her joy for living; he has induced in her a cynicism alien to the world of childhood, where magic and hope should prevail. In the course of describing Lo's tennis game, Humbert refers to his tearing of her spirit:

> She preferred acting to swimming and swimming to tennis; yet I insist that *had not something within her been broken by me*—not that I realized it then!— she would have had on the top of her perfect form the will to win, and would have become a real girl champion. (my italics)

Because of the adults cynicism induced in her by Humbert, Lolita cannot take seriously "the will to win." She senses that in the end there will always be defeat. When on one occasion Humbert promises her some childish delight (like going to a roller rink) in return for her sexual cooperation, but then reneges on the promise, her drained spirit is hauntingly expressed in her face:

> I happened to glimpse from the bathroom, through a chance combination of mirror aslant and door ajar, a look on her face . . . that look I cannot exactly describe . . . an expression of helplessness so perfect that it seemed to grade into one of rather comfortable inanity just because this was the very limit of injustice and frustration—and every limit presupposes something beyond it— hence the neutral illumination. And when you bear in mind that these were the raised eyebrows and parted lips of a child. . . .

Soon after beginning his story, Humbert exclaims: "Ah, leave me alone in my pubescent park, in my mossy garden. Let them [nymphets] play around me forever. Never grow up." But they do grow up. McFate forces them to grow up. And Humbert, entirely against his intentions, aids McFate. By the end of the novel, H.H. has fully recognized his crime, has seen that he is clearly guilty, has executed the offending part of himself—Clare Quilty. Humbert makes his crime evident to the reader when he recounts the epiphany he had on a Colorado mountain slope while listening to the voices of children welling up from the mining town in the valley:

> I stood listening to that musical vibration from my lofty slope, to those flashes of separate cries with a kind of demure murmur for background, and then I knew that the hopelessly poignant thing was not Lolita's absence from my side, but the absence of her voice from that concord.

This passage, cited by Nabokov as one of the novel's "subliminal coordinates" and frequently commented on by critics, asserts that Lolita still belongs in the world of childhood, where both sex and tennis can be dealt with simply. In that concord, Lolita can experiment behind the bushes with Charlie Holmes and see "the stark act merely as part of a youngster's furtive world, unknown to adults." She can enjoy herself playing tennis even if the game is "formless pat ball" and even if she and her girl opponent "rush out after every ball, and retrieve none." The reader may, retrospectively, appreciate the irony in Lo's frivolous account of the activities at Camp Q (she is mimicking the Camp Q advertising brochure): "We loved the sings around the fire in the big stone fireplace or under the darned stars, where every girl *merged her own spirit of happiness with the voice of the group*" (my italics). For all its phoniness, Camp Q did provide a setting for the concord of children and Lo's voice was part of the concord.

It would seem that Nabokov has chosen the word "concord" to produce an important pun. As the final word of a long sentence and a long paragraph, "concord" receives great emphasis. The word may echo the French phrase *"hors concours,"* used by Humbert many pages earlier to characterize the experience of fondling a nymphet. This phrase, meaning "out of the competition, with no rivals," is applied to an exhibition entry which "is so superior to the rest of the exhibition that it is barred from receiving the awards or prizes." The French *"hors"* means "out of" and *"concours"* means "a running together, gathering, crowd, or competition." Thus the word "concord," in echoing *"hors concours,"* may remind the reader (or the re-reader) of the novel's central irony: Humbert and his nymphet cannot exist together on that "intangible island of entranced time." Humbert's dream of joy with an nymphet is impossible because any nymphet he lives with will thereupon lose her nymphet-ness. By fondling Lolita, by seeking the experience that is *"hors concours,"* he forces her *hors concours* and *hors concorde,* out of the concourse and concord of children into the dolorous world of adults. Significantly, the term that H.H. has used to describe his association with the motherless Lolita is "concourse": "From the very beginning of our concourse, I was clever enough to realize that I must secure her complete co-operation in keeping our relations secret . . ."

This concourse of Humbert and Lolita supersedes her concourse with other children: she is taken out of wonderland and into "umber and black Humberland."

But some readers have felt that Humbert is not to blame for Lolita's leaving the enchanted land of childhood. They argue that Lolita lost her childhood and innocence when she lost her virginity with Charlie Holmes at Camp Q. They argue that it is Lolita who seduces Humbert at The Enchanted Hunters hotel. Lionel Trilling, for example, writes about Humbert: "Perhaps his depravity is the easier to accept when we learn that he deals with a Lolita who is not innocent, and who seems to have very few emotions to be violated." Such arguments are, in my opinion, misguided. They confuse virginity with innocence. As Paul Lauter has discerned, "the moral point of *Lolita* lies . . . in what the *recherché* European discovers behind the billboards of America: purity of landscape beside depravity in motels and beneath the 'philistine vulgarity' a kind of fruitless innocence which his own creative debauchery can only kill." Before cohabiting with H.H. at The Enchanted Hunters, Lolita—however precocious, however cynical in her teenybopper way—is still just a kid, dwelling in a youngster's furtive world." Her state immediately after leaving Camp Q, as she rides with Humbert toward The Enchanted Hunters, is neatly depicted in the following exchange:

> "It's a sketch, you know. When did you fall for my mummy?"
> "Some day, Lo, you will understand many emotions and situations, such as for example the harmony, the beauty of spiritual relationship."
> "Bah!" said the cynical nymphet.

She is not yet a nymph, still a nymphet. Copulation in the forest with Charlie Holmes will not destroy the perilous magic of nymphets, but that magic will surely be destroyed by congress with a pentapod monster.

Another expression of Lolita's lost childhood—an expression rivaling *"hors concours"* in its artistry—occurs in the town of Wace, where Lo and Hum attend a play by Clare Quilty and Vivian Darkbloom. The only feature of the play that pleases Hum is "a garland of seven little graces . . . seven bemused pubescent girls in colored gauze." In the play, each girl represents one of the seven visible colors of the rainbow. Taken together, these visible colors may be seen as representing childhood. A few lines later, H.H. refers to Lo as "my own ultraviolet darling. Why "ultraviolet"? Well, she is of course deeply tanned from the sun's ultraviolet rays. And she does go beyond the ordinary children-colors in her beauty and charm. But also—as in *"hors concours"*—there is the sense that she has left childhood. As her voice is no longer present in the musical scale of children's shouts, so has she lost her proper place in the visible spectrum of children. How appropriate that Nabokov, a confessed synesthete, should mark in both auditory and visual terms Lolita's passage from childhood.

In removing Lolita from that concord and spectrum, Humbert is caught up in the Sophoclean irony of being an agent against his happiness and of being ignorant when he thinks he is wise. He seems to know his world:

I knew I had fallen in love with Lolita forever; but I also knew she would not be forever Lolita. She would be thirteen on January 1. In two years or so she would cease being a nymphet and would turn into a "young girl," and then, into a "college girl"—that horror of horrors.

And then (if we may continue the series by adding H.H's words from elsewhere) into "that sorry and dull thing: a handsome woman." He knows, but he does not know. Does not know what he will do to her life. *"Lolita, qu'ai-je fait de ta vie?"* He may be "a great big handsome hunk of movieland manhood," but his adulthood is not a disguise. He is no faunlet. Woolly-chested Professor Humbert will deprive his favorite North American girl-child of her childhood.

A further irony in Humbert's behavior stems from his presenting himself to the reader as a champion of individual freedom. In his disquisition on nymphets, he complains about society's restrictions: "I found myself maturing amid a civilization which allows a man of twenty-five to court a girl of sixteen but not a girl of twelve." He frequently laments the intellectual imprisonment imposed upon Americans by the clichés of Madison Avenue and Hollywood. Yet the major act of life has been to take away the freedom of Dolly Haze, the freedom necessary to nymphetage.

Humbert views Charlotte Haze as a prime threat to his freedom. Nevertheless, he intrudes into Lolita's life in the same way that Charlotte has intruded into his. He has despised Charlotte for wanting to pry into his present and past so that she can own him, so that she can render him entirely Our Hum, to stand on the shelf with her other possessions—Our Great Little Town, Our Christian God, Our Glass Lake, Our Beach, Our Doctor. Charlotte insists on learning all about Hum's prior lovers. She makes big plans concerning Monsieur Humbert without consulting him: "In the fall we two are going to England." She burgles his desk to invade his diary, whose "microscopic script" can be deciphered only by a prying and loving wife. (Lolita, who does not love Humbert, cannot decipher the diary's "nightmare curlicues.")

Now consider Humbert's behavior toward Lolita. Hum is to Lo as Charlotte has been to Hum. Humbert tries to imprison Lo in every way. He must know all about her sexual history: "Was it Grace Angel?" He tries each day to map out her life. In the tradition of Charlotte, he burgles her room. He opens her mail. For all his European breeding and sensitivity, he wants to make of her an *objet d'art* for his own shelf. Is his goal of My Lolita any less selfish, any less smothering, than Charlotte's goal of Our Hum? He is shocked at Lolita's indifference to his love: "Never did she vibrate under my touch." He can scarcely accept that he "had never counted," that "in her washed-out gray eyes, strangely spectacled, our poor romance was . . . dismissed like a dull party, like a rainy picnic to which only the dullest bores had come, like a humdrum exercise, like a bit of dry mud caking her childhood."

He urges the reader to recognize kinship with the despicable Humbert: "Reader! *Bruder!*" Yet Humbert, too, must recognize kinship with people whose tendencies he has despised: Quilty and Charlotte. To understand Lolita's feelings about him, he need only recall that, rather than "sit for a while on the piazza" with Charlotte, he preferred to "nurse that tooth." Humbert must disperse the fog of solipsism and lust so that he can get a clear view of himself. The many mirrors of Pavor Manor seem to provide that view at last. From the final enlightened perspective of his narration, when he can look back on events and see clear guilt, he acknowledges his cursed intrusion into Lolita's life: "children under 12 free, Lo a young captive."

The captivity of Dolores Haze was taken so seriously by certain unimaginative segments of the reading public, when *Lolita* first appeared, that the novel was branded as immoral, degenerate. Humbert's sensitivity and moral growth were not fairly weighed. But the critical counter-reaction to this early Philistine assessment of the novel may have led to a complementary distortion. It seems to me, judging from recent criticism, that now Lolita's plight is not taken seriously enough. And one can understand how, even without the provocation of Philistines, Lolita's side may be slighted. After all, the novel narrated by so fascinating a figure as witty, sensitive, artistic, unpredictable Humbert Humbert centers—despite its worship of Lolita—on H.H. Our narrator, toward the end of his memoir, admits:

> It struck me . . . that I simply did not know a thing about my darling's mind and that quite possibly, behind the awful juvenile clichés, there was in her a garden and a twilight, and a palace gate—dim and adorable regions which happened to be lucidly and absolutely forbidden to me, in my polluted rags and miserable convulsions.

If the reader is to get closer to those "dim and adorable regions" of Lolita's mind, he must at times sift the information H.H. gives from the misleading interpretation which H.H., befogged by lust, imposes on that information. Previously, this essay has discussed the reluctance of some readers to appreciate Lolita's innocence. Such readers are too much influenced by H.H.'s notion of a nymphean evil." As Paul Lauter has aptly remarked, "Humbert at the moment of seduction . . . [finds] solace for his own perversion in what he wishes to see as Lolita's depravity." And Julian Moynahan has perceived that Humbert eventually abandons "his corrupt rationalizations concerning the natural depravity and sexual precocity of American little girls." Similarly, Humbert and a number of his readers are slow to recognize Lolita's intelligence; for some time, H.H. believes that her I.Q. of 121 is too high. Her sensitivity, also, is not always appreciated. One critic, for instance, has recently written that "the poignancy of this loss [Lolita's loss of her childhood] afflicts only Humbert" and that Lolita "is quite as indifferent to the injury he supposes he has done her as she is indifferent to his love of her." But how can the reader ever forget "her sobs in the night—every night, every night—the moment I feigned sleep"?

Humbert yearns for the timeless world. He wants to dwell with his Lolita in places of fantasy like the Hotel Mirana and Our Glass Lake. He wants to keep a hermetic seal around room 342 of The Enchanted Hunters. He, however, is the one who breaks the seal of Lolita's childhood, making the grains of sand fall even faster in the hourglass. His plan to live with Lolita in the magic world of nymphets is as "out of reach" as the anonymous nymphet seemingly seen undressing at "a lighted window across the street" whose "tender pattern of nudity" is abruptly "transformed into the disgusting lamp-lit bare arm of a man in his underclothes reading his paper by the open window in the hot, damp, hopeless summer night." Only in art can Humbert have his way. In the world of the imagination. Lolita can stay on the enchanted island. She can be spoken of eternally in the present tense: "that intangible island of entranced time where Lolita plays with her likes."

Yet art is not life for Humbert. Art is not a cure, just a "very local palliative." He is driven to seek that "incomparably more poignant bliss" of nymphet love not in the world of imagination but in the real world of "lovely, trustful" America, where his cumbersome presence fatally dissolves the magical mist of Dolly Haze.

—ROBERT T. LEVINE, " 'My Ultraviolet Darling': The Loss of Lolita's Childhood," *Modern Fiction Studies* 25, No. 3 (Autumn 1979): 471–79

SUSAN ELIZABETH SWEENEY

In Ovid's *Metamorphoses*, the myth of Io and Argus (1.583–779) immediately follows the tale of Daphne's pursuit by Apollo and her transformation into a laurel tree. It includes, as a story within a story, the tale of Syrinx's pursuit by Pan, and her subsequent change into the reeds from which his pan-pipes were fashioned (1.689–712). Io's story, like theirs, is one of sexual pursuit and metamorphosis; however, her change yields no respite.

According to Ovid, the nymph Io, daughter of a river god, is pursued and finally raped by Jupiter, who promptly changes her into a heifer to avoid Juno's jealousy. Unfortunately, Juno admires the animal and demands it as a gift. Still more unfortunate is that she remains suspicious—even though Jupiter reluctantly bestows the altered Io upon her—and assigns hundred-eyed Argus to guard the heifer.

Io's father does not recognize her until she traces her name in the dust with one hoof; and even then he can't help his daughter, because Argus herds her away to distant pastures. Jupiter feels responsible for Io's plight, and asks the god of theft and trickery, Mercury, to rescue her. Mercury disguises himself as another herdsman, and upon meeting Argus begins playing on his reed pipes and telling him stories, one of which—the myth of Pan and Syrinx—lulls the monster to sleep, after which Mercury beheads him. Outraged by this murder, Juno adorns the tail of her peacock with Argus' hundred eyes. She also sends a Fury to torment Io and drive her over the earth—until Jupiter finally confesses, begs Juno's forgiveness, and forswears Io's charms, upon which the nymph returns to her former state. Subsequently, according to Ovid, she is worshipped as a minor goddess.

There are several striking similarities between this myth and *Lolita*, especially in plot, character, and theme. In each a beautiful young-girl—a "nymphet," in Nabokov's classically-inspired neologism—is raped by a powerful older man; is led from family and home, and forced to go on what Ovid calls "interminable wanderings"; and undergoes a metamorphosis directly linked to male sexuality and female objectification.

The various male characters in the myth parallel Humbert's multiple roles as Lolita's surrogate stepfather (Io's father); as her powerful lover (Jupiter); and, finally and most importantly, as the self-described monster who imprisons her (Argus). Mercury, the god of thieves, trickery, ingenious devices, and roads, whose name has become a synonym for "quicksilver," is a suggestive parallel for Quilty, the "veritable Proteus of the highway," and Humbert's double. Just as Mercury lulls Argus to sleep with a story, and then attempts to steal Io, so Quilty begins his liaison with Lolita during the performance of *The Enchanted Hunters* (his play within the play of Nabokov's novel), and ultimately steals her during Humbert's delirium. It is Humbert who murders Quilty, of course, and not the other way around; yet the confusion of roles is appropriate, because their doubling is stressed throughout the novel.

In addition to these similarities in plot and character, *Lolita* elaborates upon important themes from Ovid's myth: love and metamorphosis; vision, recognition, and abnormal perception; enchantment, hypnotism, and sleep; and self-conscious art. The organization of these themes is even more significant, however, because the transformations of Io and Argus, as chronicled in the myth, correspond to the most important aspects of Nabokov's novel: the interrelated metamorphoses undergone by Lolita and Humbert Humbert.

The major attribute shared by Io and Lo, beyond the initial similarity in their names, is their designation as nymphs (or "little nymphs"). Although, according to Charlotte, Lolita is "a sturdy, healthy, but decidedly homely kid," Humbert is able "to discern at once, by ineffable signs—the slightly feline outline of a cheekbone, the slenderness of a downy limb, and other indices which despair and shame and tears of tenderness forbid me to tabulate—the little deadly demon among the wholesome children." Thus he pronounces her a nymphet. Nabokov's use of this word and its sibling, "faunlet," derives, of course, from the minor deities of classical mythology, neither human nor divine, who haunt specific natural locales. Nymphs seduce men yet flee their embrace, sometimes even changing from anthropomorphic to natural shape (trees, water, and so on) in order to escape human sexuality; thus it's especially appropriate that in Quilty's play *The Enchanted Hunters*, Lolita plays "a woodland witch, or Diana, or something," who enchants stray men in Dolly's Dell.

The nymphet's most distinguishing characteristic is her prepubescence, which implies an undefined, incomplete state of metamorphosis. Like the lepidopteral nymph or pupa (a usage with which Nabokov was familiar, and which he certainly intended), who is neither caterpillar nor butterfly; or the classical nymph, who is neither human nor divine—Lolita is no longer a child and yet not quite an adult. In such fairy tales as *Snow White* or *Sleeping Beauty*, to which Nabokov also alludes, this same state of arrested development is manifested as an enchanted trance from which the sleeper awakes into womanhood. In the *Metamorphoses*, it is indicated by the changed shapes—a laurel tree, or a handful of reeds—which nymphs adopt

to protect themselves from sexuality and sexual experience. That Nabokov referred deliberately to such magical changes is evident when Humbert describes his
shopping trip for Lolita: "There is a touch of the mythological and the enchanted in
those large stores where according to ads a career girl can get a complete desk-
to-date wardrobe, and where little sister can dream of the day when her wool
jersey will make the boys in the back row of the classroom drool." It is this "quiet
poetical afternoon," in fact, that prompts their stay at The Enchanted Hunters.

It is not surprising, given this emphasis on arrested development, that Io and
Lolita are defined by their specific metamorphoses and by a general tendency
towards transformation. Io changes from a nymph to a heifer, and back again,
before becoming a goddess. Not only does Lolita undergo similar transformations
from ordinarily little girl, to nymphet, to teenager, to ordinary wife and expectant
mother, but Humbert also worships her in various other avatars—as Aphrodite,
the Madonna, and other deities; as famous mistresses of history and legend; and as
the Hollywood starlet she aspires to be. Ultimately she, too, achieves immortality,
through the medium of Humbert's art.

Yet why are Io and Lolita victimized by these changes, instead of protected by
them? Rather than having organic cause—as in other myths from the *Metamorphoses* (for instance, those of Daphne and Syrinx) or traditional fairy tales—their
respective transformations signify a rape brought about by male sexuality, male
perceptions, and female objectification. Consider the mistaken recognitions and
false male perceptions which recur throughout Ovid's myth: Jupiter disguises Io as
a heifer; her father fails to recognize her; Argus, her captor, is characterized by his
deviant vision; and in order to kill Argus, Mercury disguises himself as a herdsman.
Consider such themes as voyeurism, disguise, and mistaken identity, in Nabokov's
novel, as well as its frequent allusions to visual media from billboards to movies.
More significantly, Lolita's involuntary metamorphosis into a "nymphet" is caused
solely by Humbert's self-absorbed perception of her: "What I had madly possessed
was not she, but my own creation, another, fanciful Lolita—perhaps, more real than
Lolita; overlapping, encasing her; floating between me and her, and having no will,
no consciousness—indeed, no life of her own. The child knew nothing. I had done
nothing to her. And nothing prevented me from repeating a performance that
affected her as little as if she were a photographic image rippling upon a screen and
I a humble hunchback abusing myself in the dark." Humbert's vision of Lolita at The
Enchanted Hunters, when he experiences "a confusion of perception metamor-
phosing her into eyespots of moonlight or a fluffy flowering bush," goes even
further to exemplify such solipsism on his part in terms of an apparent change in
Lolita herself.

Io's and Lolita's respective metamorphoses not only reflect their objectification by male voyeurs, as we have seen, but also their corruption by male sexuality—
for both are corrupted, despite the innate sexuality of nymphs, the supposed
sexuality of nymphets, and the fact that Lolita is not a virgin (she is traumatized
more by premature exposure to adult sexuality than by sex itself). Thus Io's
metamorphosis symbolizes her changed social and sexual status as a result of the

rape. Becoming a heifer, in particular, emphasizes her gender and sex role, and connotes bestiality—especially in contrast to the asexual changes undergone by Daphne and Syrinx. Lolita's transformation is also specifically sexual, because nymphets are characterized by both their implied sexuality and the eroticism they afford the discerning male. In addition, the polarities represented by Io's two lives (humanity and bestiality, innocence and depravity) neatly parallel what Humbert identifies as the perverse "twofold nature of this nymphet . . . this mixture in my Lolita of tender dreamy childishness and a kind of eerie vulgarity." "The beastly and beautiful merged at one point," Humbert muses, attempting to describe their first fateful night in The Enchanted Hunters, "and it is that borderline I would like to fix."

Humbert's descriptions of Lolita as an animal not only fix that borderline, but also delineate such "eerie vulgarity." At The Enchanted Hunters he gazes at her "glimmer of nymphet flesh, where half a haunch and half a shoulder dimly showed." "Now and then it seemed to me that the enchanted prey was about to meet halfway the enchanted hunter, that her haunch was working its way toward me under the soft of a remote and fabulous beach." Later Humbert characterizes their relationship in terms of "the quiet murmured order one gives a sweatstained distracted cringing trained animal even in the worst of plights (what mad hope or hate makes the young beast's flanks pulsate, what black stars pierce the heart of the tamer!)." The implied connotations of bestiality in such imagery stress the perversion of Humbert's relationship with Lolita, "our singular and bestial cohabitation."

Despite such references to Lolita as an animal, or as "enchanted prey," Nabokov's novel never directly refers to Io or her changed shape. Yet the following dialogue, preceding Humbert's and Lolita's arrival at The Enchanted Hunters, and unexplained by the text, is so significant that it represents Lolita in the "Hegelian synthesis linking up two dead women" at the novel's end: " 'Look, Lo, at all those cows on that hillside.' 'I think I'll vomit if I look at a cow again.' " And immediately before retiring to their bedroom that night, Humbert spies in the hotel lobby "a delightful child of Lolita's age, in Lolita's type of frock, but pure white, and there was a white ribbon in her black hair. She was not pretty, but she was a nymphet, and her ivory pale legs and lily neck formed for one memorable moment a most pleasurable antiphony (in terms of spinal music) to my desire for Lolita." (After Io was changed back into a nymph, according to Ovid, "de bove nil superest formae nisi cando in illa," 1.743.) Abashed at Humbert's gaze, the little girl turns away "in specious chat with her cow-like mother." Two other passages from the narratives seem oddly similar. Ovid says of Io: "si modo verba sequantur,/oret opem nomenque suum casusque loquatur;/littera pro verbis, quam pes in pulvere duxit/corporis indicium mutati triste peregit" (1.647–650). In Nabokov's novel, Lolita reads advice to victimized children aloud from a newspaper: " 'If,' she repeated, 'you don't have a pencil, but are old enough to read and write—this is what the guy means, isn't it, you dope—scratch the number somehow on the roadside.' 'With your little claws, Lolita.' "

Such possible allusions to Io's role in the myth are more suggestive than conclusive, however; Io and Lolita resemble each other not in specific detail but in

general circumstances, in their shared status as victims of rape, sexual objectification, mistaken recognition, and captivity, and in the metamorphoses they undergo.
Similarities between Argus and Humbert, on the other hand, are not only more
convincing, but are supported by unmistakable references to the myth. Yet the
apparent incongruity isn't contradictory, because the roles of captor and captive are
always interdependent; and, although Argus may not be a narrator and hero in
Ovid's myth, Humbert is the major character of *Lolita*.

> —SUSAN ELIZABETH SWEENEY, "Io's Metamorphosis: A Classical Subtext
> for *Lolita*," *Classical and Modern Literature* 6, No. 2
> (Winter 1986): 80–84

KATHERINE TIERNAN O'CONNOR

In a written interview with Herbert Gold, Nabokov was queried about the "sense
of immorality" said to be conveyed in Humbert's relationship with Lolita. He readily
acknowledged that it was there but, characteristically, denied that it emanated from
him: "No, it is not *my* sense of immorality of the Humbert-Lolita relationship that
is strong; it is Humbert's sense. *He* cares, I do not. *I* do not give a damn for public
morals. In America or elsewhere . . ." The rest of his comments, however, suggest
that despite his assertions of authorial distance regarding matters of morality and
immorality, he took umbrage at the way in which his interlocutor, Herbert Gold,
had phrased his remarks. Gold had written "Your sense of the immorality of the
relationship between Humbert Humbert and Lolita is very strong. In Hollywood
and New York, however, relationships are frequent between men of forty and girls
very little older than Lolita. They marry—to no particular public outrage; rather
public cooing. After denying that the "sense of immorality" is his, Nabokov goes on
to say: "And anyway, cases of men in their forties marrying girls in their teens or
early twenties have no bearing on Lolita whatever. Humbert was fond of 'little
girls'—not simply 'young girls.' Nymphets are girl-children, not starlets and 'sex
kittens." Lolita was twelve, not eighteen, when Humbert met her. You may remember that by the time she is fourteen, he refers to her as his 'aging mistress.' "
The message is clear it seems: Nabokov regards Gold's reference to banal Hollywood couplings as grossly inapplicable to the Humbert-Lolita relationship. Humbert's violation of a girl-child is, by implication, incomparable in its magnitude.

When considered within a present-day context, Nabokov's Lolita is a much
more realistic victim of child abuse than Dostoevskij's sentimentally drawn near
caricatures. Likewise, Humbert Humbert is an all too plausible child abuser. Like
Svidrigajlov, he is "a man of taste and culture," and, in addition, as a sophisticated
European he inspires a kind of automatic deference in culturally insecure Americans. But most important of all, he enjoys the protective cover of fatherhood. Lolita,
moreover, is an orphaned only child when she finally falls into his clutches, and in
Humbert's own words: "you see, she had absolutely nowhere else to go." Humbert
may have been a "pentapod monster," but he is ultimately redeemed by his voice,
for it is through the narration of his story that he actually comes to see the truth

of its content. The reality of his violation and enslavement of Lolita is revealed through the truth of his art, and a "sense of immorality" is intrinsic to that art. In view of the fact that all of Nabokov's own comments on Lolita herself, Lolita the girl-child, Lolita the nymphet, are unfailingly kind and compassionate, it seems unlikely that he could have felt that Humbert's "sense of immorality" was misplaced.

In his lecture on Dostoevskij Nabokov says that he "subscribes to Kropotkin's statement that 'men like the examining magistrate and Svidrigajlov, the embodiment of evil, are purely romantic invention.' " We may not, in fact, agree with Kropotkin's statement, but it is clear why Nabokov says that he subscribes to it. He sets the stage, as it were, for the entrance of his own counter-creation, Humbert Humbert, and as if in acknowledgement of his not being "the embodiment of evil," Nabokov himself has said "there is a green lane in Paradise where Humbert is permitted to wander at dusk once a year" (foreword to *Despair*). Unlike Svidrigajlov, who self-destructs on stage, Humbert is granted a natural death off-stage, as is Lolita who outlives him by little more than a month. Unlike the Dostoevskij model, neither Lolita nor Humbert, neither child-victim nor victimizer, die by their own hand. On the contrary, both die giving birth, the ultimate act of self-regeneration. Lolita dies giving birth to a stillborn baby girl, whereas Humbert is delivered of the narrative itself, his textual atonement for the sins committed against a girl-child who had perished long ago. By having Humbert die *before* Lolita, the stillborn baby girl she gives birth to "in life" is miraculously replaced by the girl-child who comes to life again in art. The "sense of immorality" said to pervade the Humbert/Lolita relationship may be Humbert's own, as his author insists, but the perfectly timed death of the two protagonists of Humbert's narrative is a gift of Nabokov himself.

When asked about the "genesis" of Lolita, Nabokov· made reference to a newspaper story he *claimed* to have read in *Paris Soir* in 1939: "[It told of] an ape in the Paris Zoo, who after months of coaxing by scientists produced finally the first drawing ever charcoaled by an animal, and this sketch, reproduced in the paper, showed the bars of the poor creature's cage." The association between the "poor creature" and Lolita herself is, of course, obvious—too obvious perhaps—but it is also more interesting, I think, than its obviousness may initially suggest. First of all, by the author's own account the inspiration for Lolita was pity. Pity for the captive and pity for the hyperconsciousness of captivity which blinds the captive to the world beyond its bars. Not surprisingly, therefore, the narrator of the story is not the captive, Lolita herself—her voice is silent—but rather the captor, Humbert Humbert. Ultimately, of course, Humbert is a victim as well, but it is his metaphoric imprisonment behind the bars of his own obsession that is responsible for his quite literal imprisonment of a child. Also, although both Humbert and Lolita are themselves the captives of their author, the voice which he has lent to Humbert, Humbert has silenced in Lolita.

Perhaps the most poignant feature of Nabokov's alleged zoo story is the charcoal sketch which the ape produced after it had been coaxed and prodded by "scientists." Its forced drawings is both the result of coercion and the reflection of it. Perhaps something other than pity was also aroused by this story, namely, anger and resentment directed at the "scientists" who may, incredibly, have been surprised at the drawing the ape produced. Maybe they had forgotten about the ape's imprisonment until the bars of the cage made an appearance in its sketch. Not encaged themselves, and interested primarily in making the ape perform, perhaps they were theretofore oblivious or insensitive to its captivity. In the beginning of Humbert's narrative he, too, seems insensitive to his captive's captivity, and it appears, moreover, that he is trying to seduce the reader into complicity. Humbert, however, *is* an artist, and ultimately the beauty of his art is true to the reality it portrays, and that reality includes the bars, the captive's incapacity to see beyond them, and the captor's realization that he and he alone is responsible.

In Nabokov's lecture on Kafka's "The Metamorphosis" he offers the following definition of art: "*Beauty plus pity*—that is the closest we can get to a definition of art. Where there is beauty there is pity for the simple reason that beauty must die: beauty always dies, the manner dies with the matter, the world dies with the individual." Lolita dies, Dolly dies, Humbert dies . . . but *Lolita* the book lives on. *Lolita* is *my* Lolita as Nabokov was wont to say, but it is also the broken and violated prior text which can only be truly savored when it has been made whole again in art. The beauty of Humbert's narrative stands in marked contrast to the aesthetic impoverishment of Stavrogin's and Svidrigajlov's first-person narratives of their transgressions. Their voices convey neither beauty nor pity. For *that* you have to look to the novels that contain their voice but do not speak through it. Dostoevskij the author is needed to lend the "sense of immorality" that is often absent from the voice of his characters. Humbert Humbert, on the other hand, can stand alone. He has to, in fact. His author takes responsibility for the "shudder of inspiration" that made both him and Lolita possible, but once it is his voice that is heard, his author remains ostentatiously offstage. Humbert is empowered to say all that is necessary and needs no prompting, but when he has finished, there is a hint of applause coming from the wings.

—KATHERINE TIERNAN O'CONNOR, "Rereading *Lolita*, Reconsidering Nabokov's Relationship with Dostoevskij," *Slavic and East European Journal* 33, No. 1 (Spring 1989): 74–77

CRITICAL ESSAYS

Gabriel Josipovici

LOLITA: PARODY AND THE PURSUIT OF BEAUTY

To comment in print on the work of Vladimir Nabokov one must be either very foolish or very daring. For Nabokov has never made a secret of his contempt for critics; in preface and postscript, in interviews with the papers, on radio and on television, he has poured scorn on all those who would try to 'place' him in relation to his contemporaries, who would examine his 'themes' or decipher the 'messages' his novels contain. In the preface to his son's translation of *Invitation to a Beheading* he tells us that critics have found in his work the influence of Cervantes, Kafka, Tolstoyevsky and many others. He himself denies it. The only influence he will admit is that of the French writer Pierre Delalande, whom he has invented. And in his essay 'On a Book Entitled *Lolita*' he asserts that critics who have not read his earlier novels—the best of which, he claims,[1] have not been translated from their original Russian—are in no position to pass judgement upon him. He has, more-over, no message, nothing to communicate, and writes 'with no other purpose than to get rid' of a book—to get it out of his system.

In the face of this onslaught there seems little for the sympathetic critic to do except praise the author's mastery of invective and self-protective irony and turn to more amenable writers. And such an attitude would seem to find justification in the novels themselves, and in Nabokov's way there of destroying the pretensions of all the shallow and pretentious bores who throng his pages, talking of Freud or Marx, Ball Zac or Doll's Toy. Yet it is just such passages as these which should make the critic pause in his understandable desire to escape as quickly and silently as possible. For is there not more in Nabokov's personal attitude than a simple dislike of the critical profession as such? The theme of the critic as buffoon, of the academic mind run mad, of the moral perversion involved in explaining human beings in terms of heredity or environmental and books in terms of mechanism or organism—these themes are so central to Nabokov's work that it is impossible not to see his attitude towards his own critics as an extension into real life of the

From *The World and the Book: A Critical Study of Modern Fiction* (Stanford: Stanford University Press, 1971), pp. 201–20. First published in *Critical Quarterly* 6 (1964): 35–48.

preoccupations of his novels. Indeed by an irony which cannot have failed to appeal to him, the patterns of misinterpretation established in his novels have been faithfully reproduced in the critical reception accorded to these novels. Perhaps if we look at Lolita as, among other things, a model of the relationship between the writer and his book and the reader and the writer, we may come closer to grasping its real nature. As Nabokov knows—it is one of the reasons for his profound melancholy—it is the critic's prerogative always to have the last word.

All the tragic events recorded in the 'Memoir of Humbert Humbert' spring from his desire for certain kinds of girl-children. It is therefore necessary, if we are to understand the meaning of these events, to make sure that we understand the nature of the desires. In his foreword to the Memoir, John Ray Jr., Ph.D., gives one interpretation, when he explains that 'had our demented diarist gone, in the fatal summer of 1947, to a competent psychopathologist, there would have been no disaster'. Ray, that is to say, sees Humbert's craving for nymphets as an abnormal condition, but one susceptible to psychiatric treatment. The events narrated in the Memoir he regards as 'a general lesson . . . "Lolita" should make all of us—parents, social workers, educators—apply ourselves with still greater vigilance and vision to the task of bringing up a better generation in a safer world'.

These are noble sentiments, and such an interpretation of the tragic tale of Humbert Humbert is clearly in keeping with the character of a man who has just been awarded the Poling Prize for 'a modest work ("Do the Senses Make Sense?") wherein certain morbid states and perversions have been discussed'. But it is not Humbert's interpretation, and even the most cursory reading of the Memoir should be enough to convince us that it is grossly inadequate. Humbert, it is true, does for a while believe that his love for nymphets may be the result of his unconsummated passion for little Annabel in the Kingdom by the Sea; but what he recognises all along, and what is made clear beyond all possible doubt by his ironic attempt to relive that youthful experience with Lolita and the Pacific as substitutes for Annabel and the Mediterranean, is that an explanation in psychological terms can never account for the nature of his case. For even if that unconsummated youthful passion did change him from a child like other children into a man different from other men, who is to say that it is not he who is normal and the others abnormal? What Humbert challenges is not the method but the assumptions of the psychiatrist:

> I am ready to believe that the sensations I derived from natural fornication were much the same as those known to normal big males consorting with their normal big mates in that routine rhythm which shakes the world. The trouble was that those gentlemen had not, and I had, caught glimpses of an incomparably more poignant bliss.   (20)[2]

What that bliss was he explains later:

> Indeed, it may well be that the very attraction immaturity has for me lies not so much in the limpidity of pure young forbidden fairy-child beauty as in the

security of a situation where infinite perfections fill the gap between the little given and the great promised—the great rose-grey never-to-be-had. (257)

It is not that Humbert does not have the same desires as other men. He has those, but he has additional ones too. And these are not of the body but of the spirit: he longs for unattainable beauty—for that which is beautiful *just because* it is unattainable. In an earlier novel of Nabokov's, *Laughter in the Dark,* we find the hero, Albinus, in a somewhat similar situation. Although he is quite handsome he has never been able to satisfy his very strong sexual desires. He has had a few affairs, but they have not given him what he really craves for:

> Alongside of these romances there had been hundreds of girls of whom he had dreamed but whom he had never got to know; they had just slid past him, leaving for a day or two that hopeless sense of loss which makes beauty what it is: a distant lone tree against golden heavens; ripples of light on the inner curve of a bridge; a thing quite impossible to capture.[3]

Humbert's desires, like those of Albinus, are much closer to those of the poet than of the sexual maniac. And it is in fact as a poet that he sees himself. 'We poets never kill', he says at one point, and 'we poets' is one of his favourite expressions in the early sections of the Memoir. In one passage he explicitly makes the distinction between poet and maniac, for of his night in The Enchanted Hunters with the not-so-drugged Lolita he says:

> If I dwell at some length on the tremors and gropings of that distant night, it is because I insist upon proving that I am not, and never was, and never could have been, a brutal scoundrel. The gentle and dreamy regions through which I crept were the patrimonies of poets—*not* crime's prowling-ground. Had I reached my goal, my ecstasy would have been all softness, a case of internal combustion of which she would hardly have felt the heat, even if she were wide awake.   (130)

But what gives *Lolita* a depth lacking in the earlier novels is the fact that Humbert *does* reach his goal, and that his ecstasy proves to be far more than a case of internal combustion. As soon as he has made love to Lolita for the first time he recognises his terrible error: by possessing Lolita, who was desirable precisely because she appeared to be unpossessable, Humbert seems to have destroyed everything in himself which had hitherto set him above the 'normal big males'. He is quite clear, as he recounts the story, where the watershed of his fortune lies. Having locked the drugged Lolita into the hotel bedroom he goes downstairs to give her time to go soundly to sleep:

> In a few minutes . . . I would let myself into that '342' and find my nymphet, my beauty and bride, imprisoned in her crystal sleep. Jurors! If my happiness could have talked, it would have filled that genteel hotel with a deafening roar. And my only regret today is that I did not quietly deposit key '342' at the office, and

leave the town, the country, the continent, the hemisphere—indeed, the
globe—that very same night.   (122)

From the moment they make love, despite all Humbert's attempts to rationalise
away the feeling by telling himself that he was not even her first lover, he is caught
in a web of guilt and remorse. He cannot understand the reason for this since he
has only followed his desires, the desires of a poet: 'I have but followed nature. I
am nature's faithful hound. Why then this horror that I cannot shake off?' He feels
that by making love to Lolita he has destroyed not only something *in* her, but that
somehow he has destroyed *her:* 'More and more uncomfortable did Humbert feel.
It was something quite special, that feeling: an oppressive, hideous constraint, as if
I were sitting with the small ghost of somebody I had just killed.' From that moment
too any love Lolita may still have had for the handsome lodger disappears and they
remain bound together only by fear on her side and lust on his. In this way they set
out on their aimless journey through the circles of hell-America, a parody of that
parody of the love of parents and children which is incest, each of them forced into
a role that is not his, he into deliberately superficial witticisms, she into her magazines and her tough talk. Now that he has at last attained the goal for which his
mind and body had striven for so long he finds himself in a realm where values have
ceased to exist, and where the mind turns against the body and the body against
the mind.
    And when eventually, inevitably, Lolita escapes, his artificial world collapses
and he arrives at the heart of his spiral of hell. But—and this is the miracle—out of
this descent there emerges a quality which the earlier Humbert, with all his talk of
poets and beauty, had most conspicuously lacked: the quality of love:

> Somewhere beyond Bill's shack an afterwork radio had begun singing of folly
> and fate, and there she was with her ruined looks and her adult, rope-veined
> narrow hands and her goose-flesh white arms, and her shallow ears, and her
> unkempt armpits, there she was (my Lolita!), hopelessly worn at seventeen,
> with that baby, dreaming already in her of becoming a big shot and retiring
> around 2020 A.D.—and I looked and looked at her, and knew as clearly as I
> know I am to die, that I loved her more than anything I had ever seen or
> imagined on earth, or hoped for anywhere else.... What I used to pamper
> among the tangled vines of my heart, *mon grand péché radieux,* had dwindled
> to its essence: sterile and selfish vice, and *that* I cancelled and cursed. You may
> jeer at me, and threaten to clear the court, but until I am gagged and half-
> throttled, I will shout my poor truth. I insist the world know how much I loved
> my Lolita, *this* Lolita, pale and polluted, and big with another's child, but still
> grey-eyed, still sooty-lashed, still auburn and almond, still Carmencita, still
> mine....   (270–1)

It is this new love which makes it possible for the Memoir to be written. The early
Humbert, for all his talk of 'we poets', had not written one line of literature. It is

only with the replacing of lust by love that he becomes a poet in deed as well as in name.

But what is this change if not the recognition that he cannot possess Lolita, that she is a human being with a destiny of her own and not merely the object of his desires? At the very end, when he has lost her for ever, Humbert goes to a Catholic priest to try what he calls 'an old-fashioned Popish cure' for the remorse that is tormenting him. But naturally the cure fails; he has deprived another human being of her childhood, of the possibility of freedom, and he finds it impossible to believe that this sin can ever be wiped out. So, having failed, he sees 'nothing for the treatment of my misery but the melancholy and very local palliative of articulate art'. The descent into hell to which he was led by his attempt to possess the unpossessable is only made bearable, in the end, by the transformation of that hell into art and the partial redemption of the girl he had destroyed in his pursuit of beauty by the conferring upon her of the immortality of art:

> And do not pity C[lare] Q[uilty]. One had to choose between him and HH, and one wanted HH to exist at least a couple of months longer, so as to have him make you live in the minds of later generations. I am thinking of aurochs and angels, the secret of durable pigments, prophetic sonnets, the refuge of art. And this is the only immortality you and I may share, my Lolita. (300)

In the course of his exposition of the theory of nymphets Humbert makes the following curious statement: 'Humbert was perfectly capable of intercourse with Eve, but it was Lilith he longed for.' Now Lilith was the first wife of Adam who was dispossessed by Eve, according to Rabbinic mythology, and she is linked, in folklore and legend, with the snake and the vampire. In case it may be thought that Humbert is here indulging in a scholarly antithesis without realising the implications of what he is saying, he refers a short while later to Lolita as 'the body of some immortal demon disguised as a female child'—it is only the villains in Nabokov who use language without realising its full implications. Humbert knows exactly what he is saying about the nature of nymphets in general and Lolita in particular: she is none other than that amoral, ever-desirable female who leads those who pursue her to destruction. It should occasion no surprise that Humbert, who regards himself as a poet and his pursuit of nymphets as essentially a poetic endeavour, who is fond of literary allusions and who, it will be recalled, is the author of a learned paper on Keats, should link Lolita in his mind with the Belle Dame Sans Merci, and Lamia, who figures so prominently in Romantic mythology as a symbol for that which lies beyond reason and language and which the poet seeks to capture, even at the risk of his life, and always in vain.[4]

Margot, the vulgar little cinema usherette in *Laughter in the Dark,* who leads Albinus to his destruction, is similarly presented in terms which link her to this conception. We have already seen the close resemblance between the desires of Albinus and of Humbert, and the two books have many other parallels. What lends *Lolita* a depth quite foreign to the flat grotesquerie of the earlier work is that Lolita herself is not only a Lamia but also a little American girl whose mother is dead and

who now has nowhere else to go except into a home for orphans or into the arms
of her monstrous stepfather. Margot is herself without any feeling, a young woman
out to get what she can and not unversed in the ways of doing so. How different
it is with Lolita! It is her helplessness that makes Humbert's lust so terrible for both
of them. Neither her nymphet charms nor his violent desires really belong to them.
It is as though their bodies had been taken over by powerful alien forces, leaving
their true selves helpless onlookers in a ghastly tragedy being played out with those
bodies. It is because Lolita is more than a Lamia that the story is tragic rather than
grotesque. It is because she is a human being who can be pathetic as well as vicious
that Humbert's lust can ultimately turn to love. When this happens her story can be
written, her nymphet charms immortalised.

Beside Humbert's sudden surges of tenderness, his constant ability to put
himself in her place, Lolita's total lack of imagination is horrifying. She is quite unable
to imagine his state of mind, and thinks of him only as a dirty old man. But she is
not wholly to blame. The weight of Humbert's hatred and sarcasm falls not on her
but on the country which has nurtured her, and especially on its system of education.

America enters the novel in the person of Mrs Haze, with her *ne montrez pas
vos zhambes*, her interminable questionnaires, and her pathetic attempts to behave
as she imagines a lady should behave. Towards her Humbert feels only a slight awe
and a good deal of pity. Not so the camp where Lolita is sent to live the healthy
outdoor life and where she loses her flower to hideous red-haired Charlie-boy.
Lolita explains how 'we loved the sings round the fire . . . where every girl merged
her own spirit of happiness with the voice of the group', and we recall Paduk, the
dictator in *Bend Sinister*, with his injunctions to his subjects to merge their individual
egos in the virile oneness of the state. Such a merging can only lead to the
destruction of a man's freedom and imagination. Imagination is what enables a man
to put himself in the place of others and lack of it can only lead to cruelty and
brutality, when people are no longer treated as human beings but as objects. After
their first love-making Humbert comments:

> Suffice it to say that not a trace of modesty did I perceive in this beautiful
> hardly-formed young girl whom modern coeducation, juvenile mores, the
> campfire racket and so forth had utterly and hopelessly depraved. She saw the
> stark act merely as part of a youngster's furtive world, unknown to adults . . .
> My life was handled by little Lo in an energetic, matter-of-fact manner as if it
> were an insensate gadget unconnected with me.   (132)

Although the tone here and throughout the novel is gentler than in *Bend Sinister*,
the offence is the same: through a total lack of imagination man has been reduced
to a gadget, love to a form of gymnastics, and beauty to a saleable commodity.

But for Nabokov, as for Swift or Chaucer, give a fool enough rope and he is
sure to hang himself. Nabokov's satire is at its most biting in the long set speeches
he gives to the materialist perverters of the imagination. The pompous bonhomie
of the foolish and the corrupt arouse his especial hatred, beneath the common-

sense façade, the folly and bestiality of their unvoiced assumptions. *Bend Sinister* is full of people who try to fool themselves and others into substituting the beast for the man under cover of professed reasonableness and high motives. But language, which for Nabokov, as for the writers of the Renaissance, is the clearest evidence of man's unique place in the universe, always takes its revenge on such hypocrisy. In *Lolita* the best example of this is perhaps to be found in the wonderful speech delivered by the Principal of Beardsley College to poor Humbert:

> We are not so much concerned, Mr Humbird, with having our students become bookworms or be able to reel off all the capitals of Europe which nobody knows anyway. . . . What we are concerned with is the adjustment of the child to group life. . . . To put it briefly, while adopting certain teaching techniques, we are more interested in communication than in composition. That is, with due respect to Shakespeare and others, we want our girls to *communicate* freely with the live world around them rather than plunge into musty old books. We are still groping perhaps, but we grope intelligently, like a gynecologist feeling a tumor. We think, Dr Humburg, in organismal and organisational terms. . . . What do we mean by education? In the old days it was in the main a verbal phenomenon. . . . [But] we live not only in a world of thoughts, but also in a world of things. Words without experience are meaningless. (173–4)

The utter moral and intellectual confusion of a person who believes communication to be the most important thing and yet would do without words reminds one of Swift's Grub Street Hack and of Swift's indictment, in *A Tale of a Tub*, of both the scientist who would make one word equal one thing and the religious enthusiast who would raise words to the status of objects. As we have seen, what both try to do is to by-pass the free and conscious mind which translates language into meaning, and they thus reduce man to either a simple mechanism or a simple organism. There is no need to analyse the Principal's speech to discover the kind of education her pupils are really going to get.

In each of Nabokov's novels there is one person who stands out as even more grotesque and terrifying than the brutal subhuman and unimaginative creatures who oppose the hero. The horror induced by this character stems from the fact that he has so many of the characteristics of the hero and yet these are so perverted as to present us with a hideous parody of everything for which the hero stands. The clearest portrait of the type is once again to be found in *Laughter in the Dark*. Axel Rex, once a brilliant faker of Old Masters, now a successful caricaturist, has all the characteristics of the artist except one: he lacks the capacity to love. Love is essentially disinterested but Axel Rex sees all art as reducible to a trick played by the artist upon the world for the furthering of his own ends:

> It amused him immensely to see life made to look silly, as it slid helplessly into caricature. . . . The art of caricature, as Rex understood it, was . . . based . . . on the contrast between cruelty on one side and credulity on the other. And if,

in real life, Rex looked on without stirring a finger while a blind beggar, his stick tapping happily, was about to sit down on a freshly painted bench, he was only deriving inspiration for his next little picture.[5]

Art has here been diverted from its true function, which is to give pleasure by making available to the realm of consciousness more of the world than we can normally grasp, and has been used for a purely selfish purpose, to humiliate and hurt. The disinterestedness which is the basis of art has been replaced by a deliberate meaning of art and life to provide amusement for the artist at the expense of another human being. There is an imagination at work here but it is a parody of the natural function of the imagination and springs not from love but from envy and hatred. In *Bend Sinister* the different forms that this perversion can take are almost clinically examined and contrasted to the attitude of the hero; in *Invitation to a Beheading* it is the executioner, M. Pierre, who embodies the type; and it is probable that if *Pale Fire* leaves one vaguely dissatisfied, despite its brilliance, this is because the equivalent figure there is of course Kinbote, the editor of the poem, who has now moved from a position as the foil of the hero into the very centre of the picture. An experiment with such a scheme was obviously to be expected of Nabokov sooner or later (in some of the early books it is not so much that the villain is the protagonist as that all the characters are infinitely dislikeable), but it is difficult not to feel that he was making things too hard for himself by denying himself any outlet for the sympathy and understanding that are as much a part of his vision as the bitterness and satire.

Clare Quilty is the anti-hero of *Lolita,* the parody of Humbert. With his collection of erotica and his arty plays, his hobbies (as *Who's Who in the Limelight* informs us) of fast cars and pets, he is a worthy member of that grotesque company. Humbert himself, at the height of his despair, when he has lost Lolita and is driving back over a thousand miles of American highway to find a clue to her kidnapper, half-grasps the part played by Quilty in the tragedy, though he remains ignorant of his identity:

> The clues he left did not establish his identity but they reflected his personality, or at least a certain homogeneous and striking personality; his genre, his type of humour . . . the tone of his brain, had affinities with my own. He mimed and mocked me. . . . His main trait was his passion for tantalization. . . . With infinite skill, he swayed and staggered, and regained an impossible balance, always leaving me with the sportive hope—if I may use such a term in speaking of betrayal, fury, desolation, horror and hated that he might give himself away next time. He never did. (243–4)

Quilty, it will be recalled, had abducted Lolita from the hospital where Humbert had been forced to leave her, by posing as her uncle. It is doubtful whether the nurse realises the horrible irony of her statement when, after refusing for a long time to reveal to Humbert the identity of the kidnapper, she finally whispers, her eyes on the hundred-dollar note he has put into her hand: 'He is your brother.'

Lacking the power to love, Quilty can escape unhurt from the relationship that destroys Humbert. For him Lolita, like all human beings, is an object to be used for his own amusement and thrown away if she won't play the games he devises for her. But, despite this, and by a final irony, he remains the one man Lolita ever really loves. Neither her education nor her imagination allow her to distinguish between the truly perverted and nature's faithful hounds. Or rather, she does distinguish, but wrongly, seeing in Humbert only a dirty old man and in Quilty a genius whose superior qualities render necessary a slightly eccentric way of life.

Humbert's story ends in prison. Here, alone, consumed by guilt and remorse, he is forced to sit idly and await his trial for the murder of Clare Quilty. In such a situation the only thing that can keep him from going mad is to write down the story of his passion. After the frenzied activity of the last few months he finds himself shut up in a tiny room with nothing to do but play with words. 'Oh my Lolita,' he cries, 'I have only words to play with!' No wonder then that he plays with them which such controlled frenzy, such fiendish concentration. Words are now all he has left and only by playing with words can he keep the spectre of madness at bay. So that behind the dazzling barrage of wit lies the sad and disillusioned Humbert, the man who had once seen himself as infinitely superior to other men, a poet of poets. Occasionally the mask drops and he allows us to catch a glimpse of his: 'Oh let me be mawkish for the nonce! I am so tired of being cynical.' But before the reader can extend his sympathy, the mask is on again and the hectic play with language once more under way.

The story of Humbert Humbert and Lolita comes to us refracted through Humbert's baroque prose. Never does Humbert allow the reader to forget the fact that what he has in front of him are words and that these words are being manipulated by one man: himself. In order to keep this fact constantly before the reader he continually interrupts his narrative to address him: 'Your Honour', 'Winged Gentlemen of the Jury', 'touché, reader'. He slips in an aside: 'You can count on a murderer for a fancy prose style'; he writes down a sentence and then takes it back: 'Then I pulled out my automatic—I mean that is the kind of fool thing the reader might suppose I did'; he warns an imaginary secretary not to correct a mistake he has made transcribing something into the Memoir and orders the printer to 'repeat till the page is full'. Everywhere he burlesques the conventional novelist who, with the connivance of the reader, blurs the distinction between art and reality, words and events: 'But now I am convinced that prude and prurient Miss East—; or, to explode her incognito, Miss Finton Lebone. . . .' He may be a murderer, and he may be in prison, but he knows the power even mere words can exert and he uses it to the full.

The most notable instance of this kind of play with the reader occurs not in any single episode but in the way he keeps Quilty's identity hidden until the very end of the book. Even when Lolita divulges it to him he carefully withholds it from the reader:

She said really it was useless, she would never tell, but on the other hand, after all—'Do you really want to know who it was? Well, it was—'

And softly, confidently, arching her thin eyebrows and puckering her parched lips, she emitted, a little mockingly, somewhat fastidiously, not untenderly, in a kind of muted whistle, the name that the astute reader has guessed long ago.

Waterproof. Why did a flash from Hourglass Lake cross my consciousness? I, too, had known it, without knowing it, all along. There was no shock, no surprise. Quietly the fusion took place, and everything fell into order, into the pattern of branches that I have woven throughout this memoir with the express purpose of having the ripe fruit fall at the right moment; yet with the express and perverse purpose of rendering—she was talking but I sat melting in my golden peace—of rendering that golden and monstrous peace through the satisfaction of logical recognition, which my most inimical reader should experience now.   (265)

Humbert appears to be playing with the reader exactly as Clare Quilty had played with Humbert himself, leading him on, tantalising him with the knowledge that the answer lies just round the corner, and taking a perverse delight in his power to withhold this answer for as long as he pleases. But there is an important difference between them. Clare Quilty was dealing with Humbert's life, his game was played out only with the reader's imagination. So long as he persists in confusing the two the reader will indeed feel cheated and frustrated, but if he recognises the difference he will see that such devices not only help but are the necessary condition for the fulfilling of Humbert's task. For Humbert does have a task: 'I am not concerned with so-called "sex" at all,' he says, as he cuts short the narrative of his seduction by Lolita. 'A great endeavour lures me on: to fix once and for all the perilous magic of nymphets.' Unlike Axel Rex and Clare Quilty, his motives are not selfish, he does not use art for his own ends or his own private pleasures, he uses it to try to render once and for all that magic and ineffable beauty which he had once dreamt of possessing but now only wishes to articulate.

For if Humbert's story can be said to end in prison, from another point of view we can see that it is only in prison that it begins. It is only there that he writes down the Memoir that is to be the sole testimony to his strange and tragic passion. Nor is it the simple retelling of something that is over and done with, the artistic imitation of a reality that has ended. Rather, it is itself the culmination of Humbert's lifelong quest, a quest of which his life with Lolita was only the penultimate episode. Humbert's desire for nymphets, we saw, was never that of the sex maniac. It was the manifestation of a longing for unpossessable beauty, for that which is beautiful just because it cannot be possessed. As such it was closer to the desire of a poet. Yet this simple faith in himself as somehow above ordinary mortals, because more imaginative, more sensitive than they, was shattered when he did in fact finally possess Lolita and found, instead of the fulfillment of his desire, the despair of mingled guilt, lust and futility. With Lolita's escape and subsequent marriage, Humbert's lust is replaced by love, which means that though he still longs for her more than for anything in the world, he recognises her right to choose her own life. It is as if, no longer having any hold on her, Humbert himself had been released from an atrocious burden. And it is this new love which Humbert carries with him into prison, and which allows him, once there, to set about the task of capturing Lolita's mysterious beauty not through carnal possession but through language. Thus, if from one point of view, Humbert is forced into writing the Memoir by the fear of impending madness and the impossibility of ever possessing Lolita in the flesh, if, that is, the Memoir is simply a poor substitute for the living girl, from another point of view the shift from life to art is the logical outcome of his discovery that he had somehow gone wrong in his previous attempts at capturing the elusive beauty of nymphets. It is not a poor substitute, but the true and only way of capturing Lolita and fulfilling his poetic longings. Thus the Memoir, like Proust's novel, spirals in upon itself, being at once the history of how it came to be written and the climax of that history, at once the quest and the goal. For the goal is the quest transmuted into language.

Let us look again at what Humbert himself recognised as the decisive moment in his life, a moment where, if things had gone differently, there would have been no tragedy for Humbert and no Memoir for us to read:

> In a few minutes . . . I would let myself into that '342' and find my nymphet, my beauty and bride, imprisoned in her crystal sleep. Jurors! If my happiness could have talked, it would have filled that genteel hotel with a deafening roar. And my only regret today is that I did not quietly deposit key '342' at the office, and leave the town, the country, the continent, the hemisphere—indeed, the globe—that very same night. (122)

Because he doesn't, because he decides to stay, Humbert destroys Lolita *and* eventually writes the Memoir that captures her charms for ever. What is the explanation of this paradox? Why does Humbert need to leave 'the gentle and dreamy regions' which are the patrimonies of poets, and enter 'crime's prowling-ground' before he can indeed become a poet? We can see that before that decisive event Humbert's life was all potentiality; that every girl he longed for held out the promise of indescribable bliss precisely because she was out of reach, because the only boundaries of that bliss were those of the imagination and the imagination knows no boundaries. But once he has made love to Lolita he has crossed a threshold, made a choice, and he is constrained by an external reality in the form of Lolita herself. Thus we could say that before that event he was like the poet whose boundless imagination creates a thousand masterpieces, but who, because he will not submit to the discipline of language, because he will not accept the fact that language and subject-matter restrict and falsify, never writes anything at all. On the other hand we see that people like Clare Quilty, or Axel Rex in *Laughter in the Dark*, will make use of reality for their own subjective ends, arbitrarily using life for the purposes of their private whims. In a sense they are like the novelist, whose irresponsibility lies in the fact that he manipulates people and events in a completely arbitrary way in order to create his fictions. Nabokov brilliantly conveys this at the end of *Laughter in the Dark* when the blind Albinus is made to rely wholly on Rex and Margot for information about the house in which he is living, just as the reader is made to depend on the whims of the novelist.

Quilty and Rex remain unaffected by people and events because they are completely lacking in feeling, which means feeling what another person is suffering. And it is because Humbert feels so strongly the pain he is causing Lolita that his entanglement with her is so tragic. Once that night at The Enchanted Hunters has been gone through he realises that there is no turning back; it all becomes a dark necessity, as Hawthorne would have said. But again *Laughter in the Dark* provides an instructive contrast. Margot, the vulgar little cinema attendant with whom Albinus falls in love, and Lolita are both, as we saw, identified with the Lamia/Belle Dame Sans Merci figure. Both Albinus and Humbert, once their decisive choice has been made, are like the Romantic poet, longing for the chaos which will engulf him but which will give meaning to a life which before had seemed purely arbitrary and meaninglessly free. *Laughter in the Dark* follows the Romantic pattern closely: Albinus is wrenched out of his comfortable bourgeois existence by his passion; Margot, quite without scruple, drains Albinus of his money and slowly reduces him to utter dependence on herself and her lover Axel Rex, helped by the accident in which Albinus loses his sight. Inevitably, the novel ends with his death. The first paragraph, in six succinct phrases, presents us with the Romantic pattern, which the rest of the novel simply fills out. But in *Lolita* things are not so simple. Because Lolita is seen by Humbert to be a little girl as well as Lilith, a human being forced to suffer his lust as well as a creature of myth, there is, in the later work, the possibility of tragedy and the possibility of love. Or perhaps we could say that Humbert is able to respond to Lolita as a human being other than the creature of his desires because he is a richer, more imaginative being than Albinus. Since the story comes to us through Humbert's own words the two cannot be disentangled.

The imaginative equivalent of the physical destruction of Lycius in Keat's *Lamia* is the surrender of the mind to unconscious impulses. But this, as we saw in the last chapter, leads not to art but to silence or to a loss of control which expresses itself in cliché. Both Humbert and Albinus take the Romantic plunge, but where this leads quickly and inevitably to Albinus's death, Humbert changes profoundly on the way. If, as we said, the decisive event is the one that takes place in room '342' of The Enchanted Hunters, there is another crucial change, less easy to chart, which transforms Humbert's lust into love, his desire to possess Lolita carnally into the desire to immortalise her in art. His recognition of his error in this respect, like Marcel's similar error with regard to Albertine, is what allows him to write the Memoir that he does; for it is recognition of the fact that the world is not amenable to my desires, that the longings of my imagination will always be at odds with the will of other people. When he realises this, Humbert steps forever outside the world of Clare Quilty and Axel Rex, and is able at last to achieve his lifelong aim of capturing the elusive beauty of nymphets. And because he realises this Lolita comes to us as more than a Romantic myth, but more too than one more fictional heroine. One could say that the traditional novel tries to make us forget that what we are reading is only a book: transparent words give the illusion of reality; while the Romantic poem tries to deny reality and turn the world into pure imagination. Humbert's Memoir moves and mediates between the two, and the point at which the two meet is in Lolita herself. For her and for the book which conveys her to us there can be only one language: the language of parody.

In the place of Romantic daydream or the novelist's commonsense, Humbert accepts the language that is given him and proceeds to undermine it from within. What he does is to use his *situation* as a means of creating the language he needs. His situation—that of a grown man, the legal father of Lolita, and yet her lover against her own wishes—is a parody of the conventional notions of love between the sexes and of the love of parents and children. These conventional notions are embedded in our language and cultural traditions. Humbert thus takes this language and this culture as his field for a monumental exercise in parody and burlesque. Just as he is caught by a dark necessity as soon as he makes love to Lolita for the first time, so the writer is caught by the logic of language once he has set pen to paper. He can either ignore this, as does the traditional novelist, or chafe against it, as does the Romantic poet. Humbert does neither. He accepts it and then parodies his situation. He establishes himself not outside language and culture, as the Romantic hero would try to do, but, so to speak, in their interstices, and from there proceeds to reveal to us the conventional and contingent quality of what we unthinkingly take to be both natural and necessary. And at every turn the language and culture play into his hands: the Mann Act is deplored as 'lending itself to a dreadful pun, the revenge of the God of semantics against tight-zippered philistines'; the harmless title of a popular book, *Know Your Own Daughter,* becomes a cynical comment on society when confronted by Humbert and his Lolita; the shops are found to sell pumps of crushed kid—for crushed kids, notes Humbert—and pyjamas in popular butcher-boy style—for Humbert the popular butcher. And the well-known, quasi-mythical love of Dante for Beatrice, and of Petrarch for Laura, takes on equivocal colouring when ironically brought up in defence of Humbert's vice.

The movement, however, is two-way. Just as Humbert makes of America a magic land by frequently taking literally the exalted claims of the advertisements he meets *en route,* so the evocations of Poe and Ronsard, Horace and Catullus, place the work within an elegiac frame which perfectly sets off the theme of a lost Eden. Yet the reader is never allowed to bask in these elegiac echoes. Ovid's *noctis equi* become nightmares and the sentences twist and turn in mid-air, straighten out abruptly and finish where we least expect them to:

> Ah, gentle drivers gliding through summer's black nights, what frolics, what twists of lust, you might see from your impeccable highways if Kumfy Kabins were suddenly drained of their pigments and became transparent as boxes of glass!
>
> (116)

The constant two-way movement between the tone of culture, of the entire Western heritage, and the present horror of Humbert's situation forces us to experience the past as actuality and the present itself as part of that Western tradition. The clichés of habit by which we view what is past and what is in books as one thing and what we experience daily as another are constantly being shattered by Humbert's extraordinary style. Parody reveals the gap between world and book, past and present, tradition and experience, the private and the public, the desires of men and the nature of the world. To be subjected to this style is less like reading a story than like having a prism pressed to one's eyes and suddenly seeing everything glow with a new life.

Just as Humbert had come to love Lolita only when he accepted the fact that she was not his to do what he liked with, so it is only when he accepts the fact that words are all he has to play with and that we cannot each of us forge a new language but must take words as they are, with all their unwanted and irrelevant associations—it is only then that he can succeed in his poetic attempt. For the true poet has power over words only in so far as he realises that it is only over words that he has power, that this power is only that of bringing them together in new ways, never of creating new meanings. To accept this is the first step to the moulding of a language which can bring into the consciousness, articulate and communicate, the mysterious beauty of that which lies perpetually out of reach. It is the way of creative parody, which Valéry understood so well when he wrote that 'a literary *langue mandarine* is derived from popular speech, from which it takes the words, figures, and "turns" most suitable for the effects the artist seeks' and invents contrasts, juxtapositions, contractions or substitutions 'which excite the mind to produce more vivid imitations than those sufficient for understanding ordinary language'.

Humbert's story, then, can only be seen through Humbert's words, the baroque language capturing Lolita as could no other medium. But Humbert himself is of course only made up out of the words of Nabokov. Humbert's burlesque of the traditional novelist in the 'Miss East' episode is mirrored in Nabokov's insistence that the whole Memoir is a fiction, through the device of the parody preface, with its information about the destinies of the 'real' people beyond the 'true' story, 'for the benefit of old-fashioned readers'. Humbert's situation mirrors that of his creator, Nabokov, who also has only words to play with and the violent urges of a poet to articulate. When Nabokov said that his novel was about his love affair with the English language he spoke more literally than his critics realised. The novel is about his love affair with language, but since there are many languages it is necessary to make a choice. A language not his native one was forced on Nabokov by tragic circumstances; but since no language is ever 'our own' perhaps the circumstances were in one way fortunate.

For the reader to ask what the novel is 'about', for him to try and extract its 'theme' or 'message' is for him to be guilty of Humbert's initial error: to try and possess carnally what can only be apprehended imaginatively. The novel does not reveal its secret once and for all; the imaginative effort must be renewed each time it is reread. Ultimately the theme is the imaginative effort itself, that progress towards inevitable failure and loss which is the pattern of success. In the end Humbert does fail. The beauty is not there for us to behold. Lolita has once again slipped through his hands. In the actuality of the fiction he is about to die and all that is left of his story is a pile of paper: art is only a *local* palliative, it will not save anybody's life. He has had his vision, made his effort, and now it is the turn of life, of the ordinary, of that which is silent and without meaning. Despite Humbert's disclaimer, he was *not* one of nature's faithful hounds, his initial act was not natural, no matter how much he desired it. Just as Nabokov's first act, his choice of subject-matter and of how and when to start, was not natural. And for this un-natural act life will have its revenge. As Kafka wrote in another context: 'I perhaps am the stronger and more skillful of the two; he, however, has more endurance.' When the novel comes to an end there is nothing *there* for us to hold. The palliative of art works only while Humbert is actually writing, or the reader actually reading. But the miracle of art lies in the fact that we can reread this novel as often as we like.

NOTES

[1] That essay was written in 1956. Since then a good deal of the early work has been translated, but there are still one or two novels behind which the author can hide from non-Russian-reading critics.

[2] All references are to the English edition published by Weidenfeld & Nicolson, London, 1959.

[3] *Laughter in the Dark* (London, 1961) 11.

[4] John Jones in *John Keats's Dream of Truth*, has some pertinent things to say about Keats's use of the Lamia figure. Keats's failure to make of her both a credible being *and* a symbol finds its parallel in the work of the other Romantics. In this sense *Lolita*, like *Herzog*, is a critique of Romanticism: it shows what happens when the Romantic imagination is placed in the real world.

[5] Op cit. 102–3.

Steven Swann Jones

FOLK CHARACTERIZATION IN *LOLITA*

Vladimir Nabokov has been quoted as saying, "Great novels are above all great fairy tales"; this assertion is especially appropriate for his novel *Lolita*.[1] As Alfred Appel, Jr. points out, "The simplicity of *Lolita*'s 'story' ... and the themes of deception, enchantment, and metamorphosis are akin to the fairy tale; while the recurrence of places and motifs and the presence of three principal characters recall the formalistic design and symmetry of those archetypal tales" (p. 346). I believe, however, that there are more explicit parallels between Nabokov's *Lolita* and the European fairy tales or *Märchen* than the general resemblances and numerous allusions that Appel has discovered.[2] Not only has Nabokov created similarities in plot and theme between *Lolita* and certain European fairy tales (most notably "Snow White"), he has also consciously borrowed the stock characters of the European fairy tale, lock, stock, and barrel. These include the jealous mother, the fairy princess, the prince charming, the ogre father, and the hunter. In this paper, I shall examine in some detail Nabokov's depiction of these traditional characters in *Lolita* and shall propose an interpretation to account for his use of these folkloristic figures.[3] The conclusion I shall reach is that Nabokov uses these characters in *Lolita* for three reasons. First, he simply wishes to give his story some of the magical appeal of fairy tales. He recognizes the success with which these enchanting figures appeal to the imagination, and he wants to emulate their fanciful perspective. Second, he simultaneously uses these traditional characters to expose the unrealistic way that fairy tales and their stock figures portray life and its actual participants. He forces us to recognize that actual events and persons do not always fit these folkloristic fabrications. And third, in a kind of Blakean or Hegelian synthesis of these contradictory perceptions of the value and usefulness of fairy tales (as magical and yet unrealistic), Nabokov ultimately employs the folk characterizations in *Lolita* to make a statement about the paradoxical relationship of art (mirage) and reality (fact). Nabokov seems to suggest through his treatment of the folkloristic material in *Lolita* that man lives between two worlds, the imagined one and the

From *Western Folklore* 39, No. 4 (October 1980): 269–83.

"true" one (the ideal and the real) and that art—folk and literary—is a conscious exploitation of this situation. Ultimately, Nabokov uses folk characters to suggest that human epistemology, philosophy, and morality must proceed from this paradoxical premise that the life we lead is part fantasy, part fact.

One logical way to consider the occurrence of folk characterization in *Lolita* is to examine that novel's major characters and ascertain what folkloristic roles they play. We can identify four main characters: Charlotte, Lolita, Richard Schiller, and Humbert (whom we see sometimes in the guise of his double, Quilty). In the novel, we find that Nabokov continually casts them in folkloristic roles.

Charlotte Haze, for example, is cast as the jealous mother (or stepmother) who is so frequently the villain in folktales such as "Cinderella" (Type 510A), "Cap o'Rushes" (Type 510B), "One Eyes, Two Eyes, Three Eyes" (Type 511), and "Snow White" (Type 709).[4] Repeatedly, Charlotte is presented as an unwanted obstacle, an old, undesirable impediment to our protagonist's desires. Humbert refers to her as "The Haze woman" (p. 47), "the old cat" (p. 49), the "detested mamma" (p. 51), and "busybody Haze" (p. 63), and he describes her as having "rubber-red lips writhing in angry, inaudible speech" (p. 68) and "a possessive streak" that makes her "crazily jealous" (p. 81). Furthermore, like other evil fairy mothers and stepmothers "she simply hated her daughter!" (p. 82). Humbert admits himself that "Mrs. Haze was to me but an obstacle" (p. 73), and he longs "for some terrific disaster" in which the "mother is messily but instantly and permanently eliminated" (p. 55).

An interesting parallel in actions can be seen between Charlotte and the Queen or stepmother in "Snow White." Both women compete with their daughters (stepdaughters) for the attentions of the father figure. For instance, in *Lolita* Humbert overhears Charlotte and Lolita fighting over him: "I heard a great banging of door and other sounds coming from quaking caverns where the two rivals were having a ripping row" (p. 50). And in "Snow White," the Queen repeatedly asks her magic mirror who is fairer, herself or her daughter. In one German version, she throws a temper tantrum, breaking plates and glasses, and asks the father to choose between Snow White and herself. (Coincidentally, in this version, the father consents to send the child away, as does Humbert, and then, again, like Humbert, he falls victim to Snow White's charms and helps her to escape.) Furthermore, in response to their parallel jealously, both women send their daughters out to the wilderness—Camp Q. in *Lolita* and the dwarfs' house in the woods in "Snow White"—in an attempt to rid themselves of their rivals. While there, both daughters are initiated into certain mysteries and rites. This initiation is partly motivated by the mothers' examples. In *Lolita*, Charlotte's marriage to Humbert can be seen as a sexual model that prepares Lolita for her experiences with Charlie. And, in a sense, Lolita is imitating her mother when she eventually seduces (if that is the right word) Humbert. Meanwhile in "Snow White," the Queen gets Snow White to eat the poisoned apple (symbolically partake of sexuality) by eating half herself. Finally, both Charlotte and the Queen in "Snow White" conveniently die as a result of their emotional response to the realization of the sexual attractiveness of their daughters. In one version of "Snow White," the Queen drops dead out of rage upon hearing of Snow White's marriage. In *Lolita,* Charlotte runs crying out of her house and straight into a car when she reads Humbert's diary and realizes that he loves Lolita.

Nabokov's characterization of Charlotte as the jealous mother serves two purposes. Initially, it makes the characters and actions appear as if they are part of some traditional fairy tale, with Charlotte in the role of the wicked and repressive witch, who is the main obstacle to our protagonist's desires. The removal of that obstacle, as in "Snow White" and most folktales, should lead to a satisfactory conclusion of the drama. However, the ironic turn of events in *Lolita* that follows the disposing of the jealous mother reveals the second reason why Nabokov employs this folk characterization. He subverts the traditional folkloristic formula by having Charlotte's death lead, not to a happy ending as is the case in most fairy tales after the death of the witch or evil stepmother, but instead to a sordid and unhappy relationship between Humbert and a less-than-willing Lolita.

Lolita herself is cast in the role of a traditional folk character. For example, she is described as a "little princess (lost, kidnapped, discovered in gypsy rags through which her nakedness smiled at the king and his hounds)" (p. 41) and as "a fairy princess between her two maids of honor" (p. 54). In addition to being called a fairy princess, Lolita is described as a "nymphet" living in an "enchanted island of time" who possesses the fey grace, the elusive charm, and the fantastic and demonic power to bewitch others; she is also the incarnation of Humbert's "initial fateful elf" (Annabel) who cast a spell over him (see pp. 18–20). All of these folkloristic allusions demonstrate Nabokov's conscious exploitation of a traditional folk character in his depiction of Lolita, that of the nymphic or elphin fairy princess, whose essential quality is her supernatural power to enchant by her beauty all who behold her (as, for example, Snow White does). This figure possesses all the ideal beauty and charm that the human mind can imagine. As Humbert says, "She was the loveliest nymphet ... Priap himself could think up" (p. 44). This idealistic representation of the magic and beauty of life in the folk character of the fairy princess is what Nabokov borrows for Lolita, character and novel. The character Lolita borrows the magical power of the fairy princess to enchant our imaginations by her desirability. And the novel *Lolita* borrows the philosophical perspective of the fairy tale that allows us to see and enjoy the romantic fantasy in our own lives. By his depiction in *Lolita* of the enchanting power of folkloristic characters such as Lo, Nabokov is both appropriating some of that magical appeal for his novel and celebrating the special "wonderful" way in which fairy tales are able to view life.

However, Nabokov qualifies his folkloristic fantasy of Lolita by presenting her also as a crass American teenager, undercutting, or cutting against, her role as a delicate and desirable fairy princess. Nabokov exposes Lolita's crudeness through her conversation, "Oh, yah?" (p. 207); her vulgar vocabulary," 'revolting,' 'super,' 'luscious,' 'goon,' 'drip' " (p. 67); and through her appearance, "her complexion was now that of any vulgar untidy highschool girl who applies shared cosmetics with grubby fingers to an unwashed face" (p. 206). Lolita is thus both a crude adolescent and a beautiful fairy princess with "lips as red as licked candy" (p. 46). Nabokov even has Humbert explicitly note "this mixture in my Lolita of tender dreamy childishness and a kind of eerie vulgarity" (p. 46).

Returning to Lolita's depiction as a folkloristic character, we find that in her actions she emulates the heroines' roles in numerous *Märchen*. For example, Lolita's attempts to avoid her stepfather's advances and final escape from her stepfather parallel the dilemma and actions of the heroine of "The Maiden without Hands" (Type 706), who must flee from her lecherous father. The dramatization of the heroine's attempts to avoid the unwanted advances of the father has been interpreted as a projection of the subconscious incestuous desires of the daughter for the father.[5] The *ironic* use of folk characterization by Nabokov can be seen here, however, for it is not a fantasized and unfulfilled incestuous union that is eventually successfully avoided (as the scenario is usually presented in folklore), but instead it is a too real, fatherly passion that has its way with the young heroine. In this case, the young girl's fears are not harmless fantasies or projections as the folktales suggest but instead are brutal facts as evidenced by Humbert's manifest desires and explicit lust.

Another resemblance between Lolita's actions and those of *Märchen* heroines occurs during Lolita's entrapment by Humbert when she enters a kind of static, dormant state which parallels the enchanted sleep of the heroines in "Snow White" and "Sleeping Beauty" (Type 410). The image of a dormant Lolita is suggested by Humbert, for example, when he recalls certain moments after having his fill of her when she was "for all the world a little patient still in the confusion of a drug," "her grave gray eyes more vacant than ever" (p. 287). In the folktales of "Snow White" and "Sleeping Beauty," the heroine lies comatose until she is rescued by her prince charming. This period of dormancy in the folktales is interpreted as a metaphor for the internal psychological maturation that is necessary for the heroine eventually to participate successfully in a sexual relationship with her future mate.[6] The latency period, then, is seen as a benign and necessary part of the process of growing up. (Nabokov satirically comments on this psychological interpretation of children and fairy tales in *Lolita* when he has "the child therapist in [Humbert] regurgitate neo-Freudian hash and conjure up a dreaming and exaggerating Dolly in the 'latency' period of girlhood" [p. 126]). In *Lolita*, however, this psychological metaphor is presented in a rather ironic and macabre way. Lolita's cocoon is made up of the web of Humbert's cruel threats about her fate in a reformatory school or another state institution should they ever be discovered and Humbert jailed (p. 151). And her sleep is not the untroubled sleep of Snow White and Sleeping Beauty but is continually harassed by Humbert's attentions, to which she responds in incredulity and exasperation, "Oh no, not again" (p. 194). Furthermore, Lolita does not emerge from her adolescent sleep into the waiting arms of a prince charming, but sneaks away instead to Humbert's double, Clare Quilty, who tries to get her to take part in "weird, filthy, fancy things" (p. 278), i.e., various sexual perversions. All the positive possibilities suggested by the folkloristic motif are inverted by Nabokov, so that the silver cloud of the fairy tale has a darkened lining.

In addition to this general parallel between Lolita's life with Humbert and the dormant state of certain *Märchen* heroines, an explicit parallel to the poisoned sleep in the folktale of "Snow White" occurs in *Lolita* when Humbert attempts to drug Lo at The Enchanted Hunters. He tricks Lo into taking one of his sleeping pills by pretending to take one himself, much as the Queen tricks Snow White into biting the drugged apple by taking a bite herself. Ironically, however, the resulting sleep is not the deep one that Humbert wishes for. Instead, once more life does not fulfill the folkloristic formula, and Lolita is awakened by the slightest movement by Humbert.

Finally, the idea of Lolita experiencing a kind of dormant state akin to those of Snow White and Sleeping Beauty is also suggested and underscored in *Lolita* by the numerous entomological allusions. As Appel points out, "A 'nymph' is also defined 'a pupa,' or the young of an insect undergoing incomplete metamorphosis."[7] So, Nabokov's description of Lolita as a nymph suggests she is both a fairy tale figure undergoing psychological metamorphosis and a chrysalis undergoing physical metamorphosis. However, the metamorphosis is not the ideal and complete transformation of the immature girl or pupa into a radiantly beautiful princess or butterfly as we conceive of it in folklore and nature. The process in Nabokov's more darkly naturalistic world is incomplete. Lolita does not emerge as the beautifully complete and physically whole individual that we picture the heroines of our fairy tales to be. Instead she undergoes a second period of gestation, during which we lose track of her, until she reappears as the married and pregnant wife of Richard F. Schiller. When we finally see her, she is "frankly and hugely pregnant," her "head looks smaller," and she is wearing "pink-rimmed glasses"; all in all, "her looks have faded" (pp. 271–272). The fairy tale princess has not ended up as the beautiful wife and mistress of the castle. Instead she is the frowzy housewife with "watered-milk-white arms" and "sloppy felt slippers" (pp. 271–272)—not the glass slippers of "Cinderella." In sum, Nabokov has toyed with our folkloristic expectations by depicting Lolita as a fairy princess or *Märchen* heroine and then has invalidated those expectations by revealing the more vulgar and quotidian reality or fate that underlies the romantic fantasies.

Nabokov ironically undercuts his use of folk characterization in the case of Richard F. Schiller as well. From the folkloristic perspective, Schiller's obvious role is that of the prince charming who rescues Lolita from her terrible predicament. He is the male of her own age who marries her and carries her away, much as the fairy tale heroes do in "Snow White," "Cinderella," and "Sleeping Beauty." His description fits that of a prince charming: "Arctic blue eyes, black hair, ruddy cheeks . . . nice sad eyes with beautiful lashes, and very white teeth" (pp. 275–276). However, on closer inspection we find he has "little blackheads on the wings of his perspiring nose" (p. 276). The romantic perspective gives way to the critical as we become aware that our prince charming is hard of hearing and consequently appears clownish when Humbert shouts, "And so, you are going to Canada? Not Canada—I mean Alaska, of course," and Dick, "nodding sagely" replies: "Well, he cut it on a jagger, I guess. Lost his right arm in Italy" (p. 277). Our fairy tale prince is a buffoon in real life; he cannot even converse coherently. Finally, Nabokov reveals how he is subverting the entire fantasy of the prince charming motif by naming his prince Dick *Schiller*—a hero who is a shill or impostor, a stand-in or decoy. He is not the perfect prince of fairyland, just as Lolita is not the perfect princess. We live in an imperfect world, try as we might to imagine otherwise.

The prince and princess do not live happily ever after once they escape from the clutches of the ogre. "Mrs. 'Richard T. Schiller' dies in childbed, giving birth to a stillborn girl, on Christmas Day 1952, in Gray Star, a settlement in the remotest Northwest" (p. 6). This is a final undercutting of the expected roles of the fairy tale characters of Lolita and Richard Schiller. It is also an ironic reversal of the Christian myth of the Nativity. The bright and guiding star of Bethlehem has become the cold, gray half-light of the modern world, and the symbolic day of rebirth and regeneration has instead produced two deaths. It is a bleak contrast indeed to the optimistic tone of the Christian myth and to the "they lived happily ever after" endings of fairy tales.

When we turn to Humbert Humbert, we find that Nabokov depicts him not as one particular folk character but as a composite of many. He is alternately described as the prince, the ogre, and the hunter—sometimes the protagonist and sometimes the antagonist. Nabokov has Humbert call himself "a comic, clumsy wavering Prince Charming" (p. 111), implies that he is "an old ogre" (p. 188), and refers to him as "the enchanted hunter" (p. 13). In addition to these characters, Humbert also plays the part of the wicked Queen drugging Lolita, and he even assumes briefly the role of "the fairy-tale nurse" (p. 41).

When we compare Humbert's actions to his fairy tale models, we find that he behaves like some of these traditional folk characters. For instance, Humbert tries to emulate the typical prince charming when he asks Lolita the last time he sees her to go away with him: "Come just as you are. And we shall live happily ever after" (p. 280). And he resembles the fathers in "The Maiden without Hands" and in "Cap o'Rushes" in the way both these lecherous, ogre-like fathers incestuously desire to marry their daughters who are forced to flee from them. Furthermore, Humbert acts like the dwarf-ogre in "Rumpelstiltskin" (Type 500). As Appel notes (p. 396), Nabokov probably exploits this similarity consciously in the scene where Humbert quizzes Lolita about her abductor's name. It is Quilty, Humbert's double, who makes this scene mimic the incident in "Rumpelstiltskin" where the heroine must identify her captor's name or lose the child she bears (appropriately enough, Lolita is pregnant at the time). Finally, Humbert acts like the wicked Queen in the folktale of "Snow White" when he attempts to drug Lolita at The Enchanted Hunters. As previously noted, he tricks Lolita into taking one of his sleeping pills by pretending to take one himself, just as in some versions the Queen tricks Snow White into biting the drugged apple. Thus, like a chameleon, Humbert assumes the role of a variety of folk characters, revealing in his ambiguity and inconsistency his lack of heroic stature. He is a mock hero, just as Schiller is a mock prince charming, because these kinds of simplistic characterizations are only masks that we can put on or take off.

Humbert's major impersonation of a traditional hero can be seen in his role as an enchanted hunter. The folkloristic figure of the enchanted hunter is perhaps not as well defined or commonly employed as the folk characters of the fairy princess, prince charming, jealous mother, and lecherous or ogre-like father. Nonetheless, the hunter or huntsman is a traditional figure in folklore. We find him in fairy tales such as "Snow White," "Little Red Riding Hood" (Type 333), and "The Hunter" (Type 304). One quality generally associated with these hunters is their skill with guns or bows and arrows. The phallic connotations of these articles suggest that hunters possess the knowledge and ability to achieve sexual congress, and that, in a sense, what they are hunting for (their prey) is a sexual partner. As Humbert puts it when he is in bed with Lolita, "it seemed to me that the enchanted prey was about to meet halfway the enchanted hunter" (p. 133).

Nabokov mimics this phallic symbolism and sexual significance of the hunter in his depiction of Humbert. Humbert first sleeps with Lo at the inn with "the seductive name of The Enchanted Hunters" (p. 110). After Humbert has arranged his ravishment of Lo and is contemplating his box of sleeping capsules, he asks himself, "Was he not a very Enchanted Hunter as he deliberated with himself over his boxful of magic ammunition?" (p. 111). However, as we have seen before, Nabokov continually parodies his use of folkloristic motifs. Humbert's magic bullets are impotent; Lolita wakes at the slightest sound. And in the final scene where Humbert attempts to kill Quilty by shooting him, "the weapon feels limp and clumsy in his hand" (p. 299). Humbert's marksmanship is poor and his bullets seem to have little effect when they do hit their mark: "he shivered every time a bullet hit him as if I were tickling him" (p. 305). According to Nabokov, in real life we do not have the sexual (and social) mastery or efficacy that we see idealistically portrayed in fairy tales.

One explicit instance of the hunter in folklore that Nabokov overtly borrows for both the play *The Enchanted Hunters,* in which Lolita performs and thereby meets Quilty, and for the seduction scene at the inn called The Enchanted Hunters, in which Humbert finally consummates his lust, is the Circe episode of the *Odyssey* (an allusion that Appel seems to overlook). The folkloristic narrative that Nabokov borrows and parodies for both scenes describes how Odysseus's men fall under the spell of the enchantress Circe and are turned into pigs. Odysseus, who had originally spied Circe's woodland hall while hunting with a bow and arrow, arrives and breaks her spell by seducing her. Thus, in the folk version, the narrative suggests that by controlling and directing his sexual impulses, the hero can free himself of his bestial nature and take charge of his life.

In the play *The Enchanted Hunters,* which Nabokov calls "just another, practically anonymous, version of some banal legend," "Dolores Haze was assigned the part of a farmer's daughter who imagines herself to be a woodland witch, or Diana, or something [Nabokov may as well come right out and say Circe], and who, having got hold of a book on hypnotism, plunges a number of lost hunters into various entertaining trances before falling in her turn under the spell of a vagabond poet" (p. 202). Nabokov's heavy-handed hints and the borrowed plot confirm his conscious use of the legend of Circe for *The Enchanted Hunters.* However, once again

Nabokov chooses to invert the meaning, and in his version the enchantress ends up instead seducing the adventurer-hunter. Thus, he has Dolores lead the poet "to the paternal farm behind the Perilous Forest to prove that she was not a poet's fancy, but a rustic, down-to-brown-earth lass" (p. 203).

Nabokov also parodies the Circe narrative in his account of Humbert's seduction of Lolita at the inn. To begin with, Humbert, in his lusting after Lolita, is presented as an enchanted hunter; like Odysseus's men he is bewitched by his desire for the beautiful enchantress. The folkloristic version of the legend of Circe suggests that if the hunter (presented collectively as Odysseus's men) does not know how to control his carnal appetite, he may behave like a beast. This problem of exaggerated, rampant sexual appetite plagues Humbert; he describes his sexuality as "the hidden tumor of an unspeakable passion" and as "my gagged, bursting beast" (p. 61). What the hunter requires is the maturity and discipline to control his desires, and he acquires this (as Odysseus does) by exercising his sexual potency and consummating his desires with an appropriate partner. This sexual ritual is what Humbert strives to emulate in his attempt to seduce the bewitching Lolita at the inn, aptly named The Enchanted Hunters. When Humbert and Lolita arrive at the inn, they are confronted by "a row of cars like pigs at a trough" (p. 119), suggesting the pre-coital bestiality (like Odysseus's men). One of the desk clerks is named Mr. Swine, and when he and his co-worker put Humbert and Lolita in the same room, Humbert declares those "two pink pigs were among my best friends" (p. 120). And, according to the folkloristic formula, after the coitus, when Humbert checks out Mr. Swine has been transformed into Mr. Swoon (p. 141). However, this use of the folk characterization of Humbert as the sexually potent adventurer-hunter is ironically reversed in the end, because, as it turns out, "it was she who seduced me" (p. 134), just as the heroine of the play *The Enchanted Hunters* seduces the poet. Nabokov's parodying of the Circe legend reveals that, in his view, man cannot assume control over his physical or intellectual longings. He is controlled as much by them as they are by him. The point is, ordinary people do not have heroic prowess—Humbert suffers from heartburn while he ponders how to approach Lolita—and we are more likely to be the victim of sexual and emotional urges (and of the human condition in general) than their masters, despite the optimistic and rosy pictures found in traditional folk narratives.[8]

Quilty, Humbert's double, reinforces the role of the hunter figure. He is the author of the pay *The Enchanted Hunters,* and we meet him at the inn named The Enchanted Hunters. Furthermore, he serves as an instrument in Lolita's escape, much as the huntsman frees Little Red Riding Hood from the belly of the wolf (Humbert). Additionally, as Appel points out, Quilty signs himself with the anagram "Ted Hunter, Cane, N.H." (p. 253), when he makes off with his captured prey, Lolita. However, he too is a victim of Lolita's charm, chasing her half way across the country and ultimately, albeit indirectly, losing his life as a result of his attraction to his prey. He is an unconscious victim of his own lust, his own humanity, but he is a victim just the same. In the end, in his foppishness, cowardice, and simple humanness in the face of his impending death, he is a brutal parody of the superhuman prowess and courage we associate with the virile, heroic hunters of folklore and a convincing portrait of the human frailty more commonly associated with the average man.

In the final analysis, Nabokov's treatment of folk characterization in general and the folkloristic motif of the enchanted hunter in particular does leave open the possibility for a transcendent perspective that synthesizes the dialectically opposed fanciful and factual points of view so often contrasted in *Lolita*. This transcendent perspective is hinted at in the novel when Humbert describes his romance with Annabel: "The spiritual and the physical had been blended in us with a perfection that must remain incomprehensible to the matter-of-fact, crude, standard-brained youngsters of today.... Oh, Lolita, had *you* loved me thus!" (p.16). Love, the power to be enchanted by someone or something, is the key to transcending the two initial stages of viewing the world simply as fantasy or simply as fact.

This transcendent enchantment, however, is not just a return to what Nabokov has presented as the naive, fanciful perspective of fairy tales. *Lolita* does not conform to the folktale formula. In fact, Lo refuses Humbert's love, and he ends up a prisoner describing the events, the human condition or fate, that have made him a prisoner. If the fairy tale, in general, is a comic affirmation of the victory of the fructifying forces of nature over the dissolutive powers of death, of the eternal or inevitable triumph of the individual psyche over the Scylla of existential despair and the Charybdis of sexual anxiety, in short, of the happy possibilities of existence, then *Lolita* is no simple fairy tale. Despite the obvious parallels, allusions, and overt borrowings in Nabokov's *Lolita,* the novel does not, as do many fairy tales, validate the will-to-live by invalidating the fact of death. The grim face of death and destruction is not itself destroyed or locked away as is so often the case in fairy tales, such as "Snow White," for example, where the stepmother who represents the inevitable onslaught of old age and maturation that threatens the child heroine, is, in the conclusion, locked up in a tower or room or nailed up in a barrel. Instead, Nabokov uses the folkloristic references to assert essentially the opposite message—that life is inevitably qualified by death and plagued by dissatisfaction. In the end, it is the hero and heroine of *Lolita* who, like the god Baal in Canaanite mythology, are killed and entombed. Humbert faces a life alone in "tombal seclusion" and Lolita dies in childbirth in Gray Star. According to Nabokov, the only resurrection possible in this life of ours is in the paradoxical and imaginary refuge of art; as Humbert puts it, in the concluding sentence of the novel, "this [the refuge of art] is the only immortality that you and I may share, my Lolita" (p. 311). Nabokov's *Lolita* is, from this perspective, as sombre, sober, and tragic a depiction of the human condition as any existential novel (e.g., *Man's Fate, The Stranger, The End of the Road*).

On the other hand, this blunt acceptance of the grim facts of life does not mean that Nabokov opts for a purely rational skeptical outlook on life either. In his comment about today's youngsters above and in his cold, factual account of Lolita dying in Gray Star, Nabokov satirizes a modern world overly given to rationality, cynicism, and doubt. Although Nabokov rejects naive belief in fairy tales and other romantic depictions of life, such as Christian mythology, in his description of Lolita's death he also criticizes a modern world that fails to appreciate the romance underlying and motivating the myths. So, according to Nabokov, in our post-existential society the bright, guiding star of Bethlehem, which symbolizes religious faith, romantic inspiration, and the magical essence of fairy tales, has deteriorated to the dim and uninspired illumination of Gray Star. To some extent, the creation of *Lolita*, especially the use of folk characterization, is an attempt to rekindle the fires of imagination in a vulgar world. Nabokov's *Lolita*, especially its pilfering and parodying of folk characterizations, is a comic affirmation of the *joie de vivre* underlying fairy tales, a celebration of the romantic and humorous elements in life simply because they are there. As the "comic, clumsy, wavering Prince Charming" (Humbert) says, "I am so tired of being cynical" (p. 111).

Ultimately, then, *Lolita*, the novel, is trying to enchant us as much as Lolita, the character, enchants Humbert. But it is an enchantment that does not cloud the vision. The transcendent perspective the novel is ultimately attempting to communicate suggests that we should acknowledge reality—the frank picture of Lolita at the end—and still be enchanted by it—still be in love with Lolita, as Humbert finds he is. Fascination with life should not proceed from ignorance or avoidance of the brute facts of life and death, but in full knowledge of those facts.

In the end, perhaps there is some truth in Humbert's tongue-in-cheek statement concerning the "profound message" of *The Enchanted Hunters* that "mirage and reality merge in love" (p. 203). This conclusion argues that Nabokov is using folk characterization in *Lolita* not only to reveal dialectically opposed ways of viewing the world as fantasy or fact, but also to suggest that through love—which represents the ability to be enchanted by life despite its inherent limits and which is synonymous with artistic and esthetic appreciation of life—we might transcend the initial perspectives of fantasy or fact and become enlightened, as well as enchanted, hunters ourselves.

NOTES

[1] Vladimir Nabokov, *The Annotated Lolita*, edited by Alfred Appel, Jr. (New York, 1970), 347. All page references in the body of this paper are to this text. The influences and sources for Nabokov's work have been discussed previously by Appel and other students of Nabokov. This study is not intended to be a biographical examination of sources but rather an analytical consideration of Nabokov's consistent use of certain folkloristic materials and stereotypes in his development of the characters in *Lolita*. For considerations of the general backgrounds and sources of *Lolita*, biographical and textual, one should consult: Alfred Appel, Jr., "Backgrounds of *Lolita*," *TriQuarterly* 17 (1965): 17–40; Alfred Appel, Jr., "*Lolita*: The Springboard of Parody," *Wisconsin Studies in Contemporary Literature* 8 (1967): 204–241; Alfred Appel, Jr., "Tristram in Movieland: *Lolita* at the Movies," *Russian Literature TriQuarterly* 7 (1973): 343–388; Felicia F. Campbell, "A Princedom by the Sea," *Lock Haven Review* 10 (1968): 39–46; Andrew Field, *Nabokov: His Life in Art* (Boston, 1967); James Joyce, "*Lolita* in Humberland," *Studies in the Novel* 6 (1969): 339–348; Charles Mitchell, "Mythic Seriousness in *Lolita*," *Texas Studies in Literature and Language* 5 (1963): 329–343; and Carl Proffer, *Keys to* Lolita (Bloomington, 1968).

[2] Nabokov continually alludes to fairy tales, princesses, prince charmings, ogres, castles, magic potions, and a host of other figures and objects from the world of folklore in general and European fairy tales in particular. This study is by no means a comprehensive attempt to identify all those references; rather it is an attempt to show the method and purpose behind Nabokov's use of certain of these allusions in

his development of character and to suggest that there exists a meaningful connection between the traditional fairy tale, which is the common property of authors such as Nabokov and readers such as ourselves, and *Lolita*, which is the special creation of one mind. For general surveys of allusions (folkloristic and others) which appear in *Lolita*, see the studies cited above, especially Carl Proffer, *Keys*, and Alfred Appel, "Notes," in *The Annotated Lolita* (especially pp.346–347). Some of the allusions that Appel points out are to "a fairy tale vampire" (p. 141), "Grimm Road" (p. 293), a door that swings "open as in a medieval fairy tale" (p.296), and a number of well known fairy tales such as "Hansel and Gretel," "Sleeping Beauty," "The Emperor's New Clothes" (p. 203) and "Bluebeard" (p. 245).

[3] I have examined previously the question of the literary use of folklore, (S. Jones,"The Legend of Perseus and John Barth's *Chimera*," *Folklore Forum* 11 [1978]: 140–151), and I noted in that article that the study of the relations of folklore and literature has received consideration by a number of prominent folklore scholars: Archer Taylor raises the subject in his "Folklore and the Student of Literature," in *The Study of Folklore*, ed. Alan Dundes (Englewood Cliffs, N.J., Written Literature," *Acta Ethnographia* 19 (1970): 389–99; Stith Thompson examines it in his "Folklore and Literature," *PMLA* 55 (1940): 866–74. Furthermore, the folklore/literature connection was extensively discussed in the "Folklore and Literature" symposium in the *Journal of American Folklore* 70 (1957): 1–24, which included contributions by Richard Dorson, John Aston, Carvel Collins, and Daniel Hoffman. Hoffman additionally gives the question of the literary use of folklore more detailed consideration in his *Form and Fable in American Fiction* (New York, 1961). And Hennig Cohen and Tristram Coffin discuss the issue in *Our Living Traditions: An Introduction to American Folklore* (New York, 1968). Ultimately, though, the three most useful investigations, in my opinion, are Alan Dundes, "The Study of Folklore in Literature and Culture: Identification and Interpretation," *Journal of American Folklore* 78 (1965): 136–41; Daniel Barnes, "The Bosom Serpent: A Legend in American Literature and Culture," *Journal of American Folklore* 85 (1972): 111–22, and Wolfgang Meider, "The Proverb and Anglo-American Literature," *Southern Folklore Quarterly* 38 (1974): 49–62. As Dundes, Barnes, and Meider suggest, the point of investigating the appearance of folklore in literature is not simply to identify the proper tale type or motif numbers, but to explicate the purpose and significance of the folkloristic allusion in a literary text. It does us little good to know that an author employs a particular item of folklore unless we can begin to understand what it is doing there. In this paper, I attempt to demonstrate this dual purpose of the study of the role of folklore in literature (to identify and to interpret) by examining Nabokov's use of folklore in his character depictions in *Lolita*.

[4] Antti Aarne and Stith Thompson, *The Types of the Folktale*, FF Communications no. 184 (Helsinki, 1973). Quotation marks are employed in this paper to identify the titles of folktales, rather than the italics employed in Aarne-Thompson.

[5] Alan Dundes, " 'To Love My Father All': A Psychoanalytic Study of the Folktale Source of *King Lear*," *Southern Folklore Quarterly* 40 (1976): 353–366.

[6] Bruno Bettelheim, *The Uses of Enchantment* (New York, 1976), 194–215.

[7] Alfred Appel, Jr., ed., *The Annotated Lolita*, 340.

[8] Another intriguing interpretation of Nabokov's use of the Circe legend involves the possibility that Nabokov is using this narrative as a metaphor for the creative process and the artist's relation to his subject or world. The artist attempts to master his subject by recreating it, but ultimately it seduces him, by forcing his involvement and participation in it on a pragmatic, quotidian, and carnal level. Man's humanistic limitations are always apparent to Nabokov, no matter whether he be writer or lover.

Lucy B. Maddox
NECROPHILIA IN *LOLITA*

I

Nabokov's *Lolita* is a novel about love and death in two of their most pathological forms: child rape and murder. The narrator, Humbert Humbert, admits
without blinking that he is guilty of both offenses, but insists on believing that his
motives, whatever they were, were radically innocent. In the process of trying to
sort out and explain his compulsions, he writes an allusive, confessional memoir in
which he refers the reader to certain literary precursors that he sees as like-
minded. These allusions are part of Humbert's appeal for sympathetic understanding from the hypothetical jury that will pass judgment on him. In making his appeal,
however, Humbert overlooks an obvious and crucial distinction, since there are
actually two potential juries involved: the courtroom jury that will judge the crim-
inality of his actions, and the jury of readers that will be more interested in the
psychology of his motivation than in the legality of his actions. Failing to make this
important distinction between his two audiences leads Humbert into another,
equally crucial, failure of discrimination. He assumes that for all those who judge
him—whether they be members of a panel of his peers, literate and skeptical
readers, or noble-winged seraphs—the final criterion will be stylistic. That is, if the
juryman who reads or listens to his confession can be persuaded, through the
language of the confession, to give assent to Humbert's explanation of the essential
innocence of his desires, then that juryman must also see his criminal acts as a kind
of aesthetic requirement, a necessary and even satisfying denouement.

By alluding to writers like Poe, the source of his most frequent allusions,
Humbert suggests that our judgment of some writers is likely to be most admiring
precisely when that writer's subjects are most morbidly pathological and when his
style is accordingly most eccentric and most seductive. Either of his juries would, of
course, easily recognize in this defense another, overriding irony that Humbert

From *Centennial Review* 26, No. 4 (Fall 1982): 361–74.

misses; that is, Poe wrote about morbid obsessions, but Humbert persisted in trying to live them out. While the Poe allusions are therefore useless as a courtroom defense, they succeed in introducing the reader to some essential errors of dissociation in Humbert's perception of himself and his audience; consequently, they point to the sources of Humbert's psychological and emotional conflicts and help determine the reader's final judgment of him.

Nabokov's working title for *Lolita, A Kingdom by the Sea,* is an obvious allusion to Poe's "Annabel Lee," a poem that figures prominently in Humbert's apologia for the seemingly unpoetical sordidness of his life. Humbert makes an implicit comparison between himself and the grieving speaker of Poe's poem as a way of partially accounting for his own distraction: he too has suffered a loss so disturbing that he can describe it only as a personal apocalypse, the result of an unfair contest between his most profound desires and the whims of the phantom powers that determine human fate. But because Humbert's purpose is to explain and perhaps justify his own criminal acts, he does not have the same imaginative and stylistic freedom that Poe does. That is, he cannot translate his situation into imagined disorder caused by imagined grief and thus represented in the evocative but evasive language of a poetic fantasy. He is a confessed murderer, limited to "a fancy prose style" to explain to himself and others a bewildering complex of remorse, grief, self-loathing, and self-justification: "Ladies and gentlemen of the jury, exhibit number one is what the seraphs, the misinformed, simple, noble-winged seraphs, envied. Look at this tangle of thorns." [1] If Poe's poem is psychologically, emotionally, and tonally uncomplicated, Humbert's prose narrative is a tangle of conflicting emotions and attitudes that moves back and forth between cynicism and sentimentality, as he tries to retrace his progress—which he sees as fated—from the paradisiacal "princedom by the sea" (p. 11) of his childhood through the madness and self-loathing of his adult life to, finally, remorse, guilt, and prison.

Humbert's strategy is to follow his progress chronologically, on the supposition that sequence, rightly understood, must eventually lead to significance. He begins, therefore, at the beginning: "I was born in 1910, in Paris" (p. 11). The narrative proceeds rather lazily through a brief summary of his "happy, healthy" childhood, until it reaches the crucial period of his frustrated boyhood love for his "initial girl-child," Annabel Leigh (p. 11). Here the narrative takes a curious and important turn, for in describing his experiences with Annabel, Humbert violates the chronological order he has been keeping to; he describes his last encounter with Annabel first, and concludes the Annabel passage with a description of their first sexual encounter. The disrupted order of the passage, and the striking tonal differences between the two descriptions, indicate that the first episode (the second one described) is the one Humbert most wants to remember and write about. For reasons the reader comes to understand much more clearly than he does, Humbert is compelled to verify and dispense with endings before he can speak freely about beginnings. Recalling that distant period, he now detects in his sexual frustration first evidence of the deliberate cruelty of fate, which he sees as determining the entire course of his subsequent life. But what Humbert identifies as the working of fate the reader can recognize as a compulsion to seek finality, because of the emotional and imaginative freedom it gives him. For Humbert, beginnings—whether of texts or of lives—can be seen as significant only when the endings are known, so that both are parts of a pattern that is fixed, complete, and knowable.

The image of Annabel Leigh that Humbert retains comes from a blurred photograph, now lost, that was taken "on the last day of our fatal summer and just a few minutes before we made our second and final attempt to thwart fate" (p. 15). In this case, to thwart fate means to have sexual intercourse; given the hyperbolic weight of "fatal" and "fate," it seems curiously inconsistent that Humbert's description of the episode is accomplished in two cynically brisk sentences:

> Under the flimsiest of pretexts (this was our very last chance, and nothing really mattered) we escaped from the cafe to the beach, and found a desolate stretch of sand, and there, in the violet shadow of some red rocks forming a kind of cave, had a brief session of avid caresses, with somebody's lost pair of sunglasses for only witness. I was on my knees and on the point of possessing my darling, when two bearded bathers, the old man of the sea and his brother, came out of the sea with exclamations of ribald encouragement, and four months later she died of typhus in Corfu.   (p. 15)

Only after dispensing with this second "desperate" sexual encounter and Annabel's sudden death, in a tone that attempts detachment, does Humbert get around to the part of his Annabel story that he clearly finds most tantalizing—the account of their first attempt at love-making.

In this account the prose style of the murderer is unapologetically fancy. The matter-of-fact brusqueness of the first episode gives way to sustained, lyrical, sensuous, and erotically detailed description:

> One night, she managed to deceive the vicious vigilance of her family. In a nervous and slender-leaved mimosa grove at the back of their villa we found a perch on the ruins of a low stone wall. Through the darkness and the tender trees we could see the arabesques of lighted windows which, touched up by the colored inks of sensitive memory, appear to me now like playing cards, presumably because a bridge game was keeping the enemy busy . . . A cluster of stars palely glowed above us, between the silhouettes of long thin leaves; that vibrant sky seemed as naked as she was under her light frock. I saw her face in the sky, strangely distinct, as if it emitted a faint radiance of its own. . . . Her quivering mouth, distorted by the acridity of some mysterious potion, with a sibilant intake of breath came near to my face. . . . My darling would draw away with a nervous toss of her hair, and then again come darkly near and let me feed on her open mouth, while with a generosity that was ready to offer her everything, my heart, my throat, my entrails, I gave her to hold in her awkward fist the scepter of my passion.
>
> I recall the scent of some kind of toilet powder . . . a sweetish, lowly, musky perfume. It mingled with her own biscuity odor, and my senses were

suddenly filled to the brim; a sudden commotion in a nearby bush prevented them from overflowing. . . . But that mimosa grove—the haze of stars, the tingle, the flame, the honey-dew, and the ache remained with me, and that little girl with her seaside limbs and ardent tongue haunted me ever since— until at last, twenty-four years later, I broke her spell by incarnating her in another.   (pp. 16–17)

Here the sentiments are self-indulgent and the language emotionally charged; the description of this recollected experience is self-consciously pushed in the direction of a vision of ecstatic sensual transfiguration. Clearly, for Humbert this frustrated encounter with Annabel is a more compelling and affecting memory than the second, last-ditch effort, and decidely more affecting than the memory of her death.

Humbert offers no explanation for the puzzling emphasis and order of these recollections, except to announce that he has "reserved for the conclusion of my 'Annabel' phase the account of our unsuccessful first tryst" (p. 16). In fact, the lack of restraint in the style and emotional content of the second passage accounts for the violation of chronological order: Humbert is unable to express strong, un-guarded emotion for Annabel until he first establishes, for himself and his audience, that she is dead. Recognizing this psychological stipulation, which Humbert reveals in the opening pages of his narrative, gives new meaning to the legal stipulation he makes at the end: "The following decision I make with all the legal impact and support of a signed testament: I wish this memoir to be published only when Lolita is no longer alive" (pp. 310–11). In both instances the living child inhibits and frustrates him; the dead child liberates and exhilarates him.

Seen in this context, the Poe allusions in the narrative seem exactly appro-priate. "Annabel Lee," a love poem about a dead girl, is spoken by a distraught lover who is now free to lie beside his child bride, nightly, in her tomb. While the speaker's lament is very obviously prompted by the loss of the living girl, its actual subject is the lover's *present* love for the child in the tomb. In Humbert's second Annabel passage, the long one, he mixes the "Annabel Lee" references with allu-sions to Poe's story "Ligeia," another appropriate analogue of Humbert's psycho-logical and emotional conflicts. The narrator of Poe's story describes his passion for the beautiful Ligeia, especially his obsession with the mysterious expression of her eyes. Ligeia dies, and the grieving narrator, still haunted by thoughts of her, sub-sequently marries a woman he does not love. This wife, Rowena, soon falls ill. Her death-chamber is lined with tapestries whose "arabesque" figures are kept con-stantly in motion by currents of air. As the narrator ministers to his wife he sees, or thinks he sees, drops of a ruby-colored liquid falling from the air into her goblet of wine. The fair-haired Rowena dies, but as the narrator keeps watch by her corpse it stirs into life, then once again subsides into death. The process is repeated several times, the corpse appearing to "struggle with some invisible foe," until finally it arises from the bed and the fallen shroud reveals the dark hair and eyes of the reincarnated Ligeia.[2] In Humbert's long descriptive passage, the "arabesques" of the windows, the "mysterious potion," the conflict with the "enemy" family, Annabel's movement of drawing away and then coming "darkly near," and the metaphoric reincarnation of the dead lover in a living substitute all suggest that Humbert has deliberately drawn on Poe for the language of his own description.

The narrators of "Annabel Lee" and "Ligeia" provide Humbert a literary context, a genealogy, for his own kind of madness: the psychological distortion resulting from love for a female who is immune to change and who therefore cannot be lost. In Poe, the suggestions of necrophilia—that is, of morbid sexual desire—are there primarily to deepen certain intentionally fuzzy emotional effects. In *Lolita*, on the other hand, Nabokov exploits the psychological implications of necrophilia, but without taking any of them literally. Humbert's version of necrophilia—that is, his need to verify a lover's death before he can speak without irony of his erotic desire for that lover—becomes a metaphor for a complex set of responses to the living, in which desire, guilt, and aesthetic sensibility become inextricably tangled. (The presence of necrophilia in the background of Humbert's confession is further suggested by the appearance of the name "Rosato, Emil" in the list of Lolita's classmates that Humbert peruses lovingly—an allusion to Faulkner's "A Rose for Emily," the story of a woman who sleeps with the corpse of her murdered lover.)

II

In his actual dealings with the living, Humbert is repeatedly a failure—as lover, husband, rival, father, and friend. His two marriages are both disasters: his sexual affair with Lolita is a nightmare, his role as her parent a charade; he suffers minor setbacks in his rivalries with Lolita's various boyfriends, a devastating defeat in his contest with Clare Quilty, and a final, irreversible loss to Richard Schiller, whom Lolita marries; his acquaintances never become friends because he values them only for their usefulness in his schemes to get and keep his nymphet. Because these social failures result in constant self-reproach, his response is sometimes to contemplate murdering the person before whom he feels guilty, especially if she is a woman. In each case, however he is morally incapable of using murder as an escape. The worst he can do to his first wife, Valeria, is slap her and wish she were dead. With his second wife, Charlotte Haze, he goes so far as to plan her death by drowning, but the reality of her physical presence paralyzes him:

> She swam beside me, a trustful and clumsy seal, and all the logic of passion screamed in my ear: Now is the time! And, folks, I just couldn't! In silence I turned shoreward and gravely, dutifully, she also turned, and still hell screamed its counsel, and still I could not make myself drown the poor, slippery, big-bodied creature.... Were I to catch her by her strong kicking foot; were I to see her amazed look, hear her awful voice; were I still to go through with the ordeal, her ghost would haunt me all my life.   (p. 89)

In ways that Humbert himself doesn't understand, because he is afraid to, this murder of Charlotte haunts him anyway, imaginary or not. Near the end of his narrative, he confesses that in rereading it he finds "bits of marrow sticking to it, and blood, and beautiful bright-green flies. At this or that twist of it I feel my slippery self eluding me, gliding into deeper and darker waters than I care to probe" (p. 310). "Slippery" Charlotte, now dead, is present in the passage, as is Clare Quilty, the one person Humbert does murder, and whom he last sees as a grotesquely disfigured and bloody corpse, "a quarter of his face gone, and two flies beside themselves with a dawning sense of unbelievable luck" (p. 306). Humbert was strongly tempted to kill both Charlotte and Quilty, but succeeded only with Quilty. Yet he seems to equate the two events in the metaphors of this passage, as if the imaginary murder were as psychologically burdensome as the actual one; Charlotte and Quilty are equally potent ghosts. Here again a crucial failure of discrimination leads Humbert to equate motives with acts, to assume that a desire for finality is the same as murder.

In fact, the successful murder of Quilty is in two important ways the psychological reverse of the failed murder of Charlotte. In the first place, Humbert's hatred for Quilty is not the expression of a guilty desire to escape, but of a more aggressive moral outrage at Quilty's gloating and brutish amorality. Second, even though he has no trouble justifying his motives this time, he is able to go through with the killing only by seeing the whole procedure as a surreal nightmare, part of an "ingenious play" (p. 307). When the feel of blood and the sight of the flies destroy the sense of unreality, Humbert feels unexpected disgust: "Far from feeling any relief, a burden even weightier than the one I had hoped to get rid of was with me, upon me, over me. I could not bring myself to touch him in order to make sure he was really dead" (p. 306). Hidden in those deeper psychological waters that he fears to explore is an apparently irreconcilable conflict: Humbert the poet manqué is drawn toward death as an abstraction, while Humbert the ordinary mortal is terrified by its actuality. Rather than comfort the conflict, Humbert surreptitiously puts the abstraction to work as a psychological palliative, allowing it to provide a more acceptable version of a part of reality that, undisguised and untransfigured, he finds intolerable.

Humbert's dilemma thus has two fundamental sources, both unacknowledged: his fear of death, and his literal belief in the ability of the transforming imagination to confer immortality. The nympholepsy which is the bane and blessing of his life is symptomatic of a more general, essentially aesthetic impulse to possess and preserve the beautiful, while his abhorrence of the mature woman, the "coffin of coarse female flesh within which my nymphets are buried alive" (p. 177), is a specific instance of a general horror of physical decay. He is attracted to the *idea* of death, therefore, as a saving stasis, a way of preventing the loss of the beautiful. His desire becomes focused on certain young girls, first because they are an available source of uncorrupted physical beauty, and second because they are very erotic creatures, and therefore invite, or at least allow, possession. For Humbert, ordinary sexual intercourse, "that routine rhythm which shakes the world" (p. 20), is a frustratingly dull business. The mere contemplation of nymphets, on the other hand, offers "glimpses of an incomparably more poignant bliss" (p. 20), in part because nympholepsy promises a very dramatic violation of the routine rhythms of normal life. Humbert's desires converge, then, in the need for the extraordinary combination of stasis and apocalypse—a union possible only in death, or in the figures of art.

III

The same moral paralysis that prevents Humbert from murdering Charlotte Haze also makes it impossible for him to possess her daughter sexually without the kind of psychological dislocation that allowed him to enjoy the prospect of drowning the mother. That is, he must first mentally translate the actual Dolores into the fantasized Lolita. His first attempt works well, in part because it amounts only to masturbatory teasing and thus Lolita is not physically violated, and in part because he successfully accomplishes the necessary mental transactions: "What I had madly possessed was not she, but my own creation, another, fanciful Lolita—perhaps, more real than Lolita; overlapping, encasing her; floating between me and her, and having no will, no consciousness—indeed, no life of her own" (p. 64). As long as the child he possesses is lifeless, she cannot be harmed physically or morally, nor can she reproach him, nor can she ever be buried in the coffin of mature female flesh—a slow and, for Humbert, particularly disgusting death. The success of this first attempt at sexual contact with Lolita makes him frantic for more, while at the same time making it clear that he has to sustain the illusion of lifelessness in Lolita if his own feelings are to remain uncomplicated. He therefore devises the strategy of drugging Lolita in order to "kill" her temporarily. (The setting for this second safe encounter is to be the Enchanted Hunters hotel; as it turns out, the hotel provides an appropriately funereal atmosphere for a mock death, since it is hosting one convention of clergymen and one of horticulturists.) In prospect, with Humbert looking forward to the moment when "she would be dead in his arms" (p. 118), the ploy works well: "Naked, except for one sock and her charm bracelet, spread-eagled on the bed where my philter had felled her—so I foreglimpsed her" (p. 127). In practice, the plan fails; Lolita sleeps too fitfully for his peace of mind, then awakens to propose to an astonished Humbert that they make love.

Humbert's reaction to having sexual intercourse with the wide-awake, chattering child is exactly the reaction he will have later when he contemplates the mutilated body of Quilty lying in a bloody bed; sitting beside Lolita in the car later that day Humbert feels "More and more uncomfortable. . . . It was something quite special, that feeling: an oppressive, hideous constraint as if I were sitting with the small ghost of somebody I had just killed" (p. 142). From this point on Humbert's anxiety becomes more and more pathological and his language increasingly morbid. The pattern of the language helps to locate the source of his psychological distress in his deepening guilt for what now seems to him the unpardonable crime of having killed something vital in the child in the process of trying to isolate and "fix" the nymphet. The ecstatic vision of nymphet-love cannot survive the actuality of physical possession, and so degenerates into a nightmare of remorse and conflicting desires.

When Lolita leaves him for Quilty, Humbert becomes haunted by erotic dreams of her in which she appears as "a complex ghost," "in strange or ludicrous disguises as Valeria or Charlotte, or a cross between them" (p. 256). That ghost is a composite of three women Humbert has made love to and desired to kill. With Valeria and Charlotte, both of whom he despised, his moral fastidiousness kept him from succeeding at murder; with Lolita, whom he loved, the same moral qualms led him to succeed, as he now sees it, in destroying her life as a child. On a return visit to the Enchanted Hunters, Humbert has a sudden urge to look up a photograph of the conventioneers which was taken during the first visit, and which he thinks may help him to recall that evening more clearly. The imagery he uses in describing his search for the photograph in a back issue of the local newspaper is particularly morbid: the librarian helps him "disinter" a bound, "coffin-black volume almost as big as Lolita"; he speculates that his reason for the search is of the same order as the curiosity that "impels one to examine with a magnifying glass bleak little figures— still life practically, and everybody about to throw up—at an early morning execution" (p. 264). Clearly, Humbert was more successful than he meant to be in his desire to render Lolita lifeless; the real child dies for him—with an unapocalyptic whimper—at his own hands, and the daemonic nymphet becomes a Fury.

It remains for Humbert to unravel, as far as he can, the tangled desires and fears that have produced his Lolita nightmare. Much of the unravelling occurs in his description of a scene that is recorded near the end of the narrative, although the episode actually took place long before Lolita's disappearance. In the passage, Humbert recalls his reaction to Lolita's sarcastic question about where her "murdered mummy" is buried:

> I named the cemetery.... "Moreover," I added, "the tragedy of such an accident is somewhat cheapened by the epithet you saw fit to apply to it. If you really wish to triumph in your mind over the idea of death—" "Ray," said Lo, for hurray, and languidly left the room, and for a while I stared with smarting eyes into the fire. Then I picked up her book. It was some trash for young people. There was a gloomy girl Marion, and there was her stepmother who turned out to be, against all expectations, a young, gay, understanding redhead who explained to Marion that Marion's dead mother had really been a heroic woman since she had deliberately dissimulated her great love for Marion because she was dying, and did not want her child to miss her.... Now, squirming and pleading with my own memory, I recall that on this and similar occasions, it was always my habit and method to ignore Lolita's states of mind while comforting my own base self. When my mother, in a livid wet dress, under the tumbling mist (so I vividly imagined her), had run panting ecstatically up that ridge above Moulinet to be felled there by a thunderbolt,

I was but an infant, and in retrospect no yearnings of the accepted kind could I ever graft upon any moment of my youth, no matter how savagely psychotherapists heckled me in my later periods of depression. But I admit that a man of my power of imagination cannot plead total ignorance of universal emotions. I may also have relied too much on the abnormally chill relations between Charlotte and her daughter. But the awful point of the whole argument is this. It had become gradually clear to my conventional Lolita during our singular and bestial cohabitation that even the most miserable of family lives was better than the parody of incest, which, in the long run, was the best I could offer the waif.   (pp. 288–89)

Encoded in this important passage are Nabokov's justification for the exotic subject matter of his novel and a qualified defense of the moral monster who is its main character.

IV

When Lolita interrupts Humbert's incipient lecture on fear of death, her abbreviated "Ray" takes the reader back to the foreword to *Lolita*, written by the fictitious John Ray, Jr., moralist and specialist on "certain morbid states and perversions" (p. 5). Ray's advice to the reader is to read the book for its ethical lessons; he points out that had Humbert gone to "a competent psychopathologist, there would have been no disaster," but concedes, significantly, that "then, neither would there have been this book" (p. 7). In his pedantic way, Ray is exactly right. He recognizes just the distinction—between the literal perversity that is morally and psychologically destructive and the metaphoric perversity that is aesthetically liberating—that Humbert has so far failed to make. Humbert tries to triumph over his own fear of death by uniting himself with a nymphet, a creature immune to change and decay, and so makes a sordid parody of his own life as husband, lover, and father. Ordinary familial love, self-denying and unobsessive, may make for lifeless art, as Lolita's novel seems to demonstrate, but is absolutely necessary for sane living. The reason for Humbert's brilliance as a novelistic narrator is also the reason for his abysmal failure as a social being: the extraordinary power of his imagination. The effect of that power on Humbert's relationship to his nymphet-daughter also ultimately results in the awkward reversal of the usual expectations in this artificial family; here the child longs to be average and unexceptionable, while the parent finds normalcy frustrating and insulting. At this stage, Lolita is a thwarted realist on the way to becoming a cynic, Humbert a thwarted idealist and already a confirmed sentimentalist.

Humbert's description of his mother's death, which he admits is pure invention, contains all those conflicting elements which he has tried to transfer to his actual experience; the vision catches a sexually-charged moment of simultaneous apocalypse and stasis, a moment of ecstatic death, frozen in time and preserved in a compelling visual image. The arrangement is Laocoön-like, except that the horror has been translated into ecstasy: an artist's conception of the kind of death that a man who is terrified of its physical reality might find consoling. The *caveat* about "yearnings of the accepted kind" is an undisguised effort to obviate Freudian inter- pretations of the vision, while the name "Moulinet," with its suggestions of Don Quixote's windmill, directs the reader to an alternate source of explanations for Humbert's obsessive behavior, in the literary tradition of the radically idealistic character. The narrative has introduced other potential models of this kind through Humbert's penchant for allusion—among them the Poe narrators and, frequently, Emma Bovary, Flaubert's female Quixote.

When Humbert's vision clears he sees his relationship to Lolita as tragically parodic: each cast the other in an unwelcome role, one as a surrogate for a dead father and the other a surrogate for a dead lover, each failed in the role, and each punished the other mercilessly for the failure. The reader, on the other hand, because he is sensitive to novelistic structures and methods of characterization, sees the whole of *Lolita* as comically parodic, with Humbert as the caricatured romantic idealist and Lolita as a grotesquely misconceived incarnation of the ideal. The distinction between tragedy and caricature—between Lolita and *Lolita*—goes to the heart of the novel, and, of course, it requires the sacrifice of Humbert to Nabokov's ironic design. Humbert cannot make the kind of distinction between psychological metaphor and moral perversion that the reader of the novel makes almost reflexively. The reader understands, as Humbert doesn't, that the anatomy of a morbid obsession such as necrophilia can be a useful, flexible metaphor for complex psychological patterns of desire which are not necessarily pathological, or even perverse. Nabokov clearly understands the difference, as does John Ray, Jr., who reminds the reader that " 'offensive' is frequently but a synonym for 'unusual' " (p. 7). Consequently, Nabokov, Ray, and the reader are all much more willing than Humbert is to qualify their final judgments of his moral culpability, if not to pardon him.

If Humbert never succeeds in sorting out the muddle of his motives, he does manage, before he finishes, to disentangle his two very different responses to the two Lolitas—the impervious nymphet and the vulnerable girl. This new and psy- chologically healthy adjustment is prompted by the memory of rediscovering Lolita after having lost her for several years. What he finds in recalling their last meeting is that in the course of the missing years the nymphet died into the mature woman, who is not only living but healthy, cheerful, pregnant, and—to Humbert's surprise— evidently unscarred by her "bestial cohabitation" with him. In the final sentences of his narrative, Humbert, who once abhorred the coffin of adult female flesh that suffocated his nymphets, bids an appropriately paternal farewell to the living woman, now Mrs. Dolly Schiller, and wishes her a long and happy life with her new, very normal family. His ultimate farewell is reserved for Lolita the nymphet, who never lived except as an imagined projection of his desires, and whom he can now place where she belongs. By writing his book, Humbert explains, he may be able to "make you live in the minds of future generations. I am thinking of aurochs and angels, the secret of durable pigments, prophetic sonnets, the refuge of art. And this is the only immortality you and I may share, my Lolita" (p. 311). The essential irony of Humbert's story is that he was clearly thinking of aurochs and angels all along, right from the beginning, while living with imperfect, ordinary mortals who stubbornly resisted transfiguration. Without knowing it, Humbert ends by accomplishing what he set out to do, through his decision to treat his past life as a literary text and thus not only allow himself the luxury of an ecstatic vision, but also allow his compulsions and desires to be read, appropriately, as metaphoric. In the process, he preserves his ecstatic vision of Lolita in the frozen images of his book, and so gives them both at least a fair shot at a metaphoric immortality.

NOTES

[1] Vladimir Nabokov, Lolita (New York: Putnam, 1972), p. 11. All subsequent references to Lolita are to this edition.
[2] The Complete Tales and Poems of Edgar Allan Poe (New York: Modern Library, 1938), pp. 661, 665.

Richard H. Bullock

HUMBERT THE CHARACTER, HUMBERT THE WRITER

The black and umber world of Humberland begins with the words, "Lolita. Light of my life, fire of my loins. My sin, my soul," [1] and a first reading of the novel suggests that the terms "fire of my loins. My sin" summarize the book. This view, though, which makes of the narrator and protagonist Humbert Humbert a faithful recorder of his own evil acts with an overly complicit adolescent, fails because it ignores the text's rococo entanglements of fact and fiction, reality and fantasy, artist and art. Humbert is the narrator and he narrates his own story, but serious problems exist in verifying the facts of his narrative, due to his solipsistic nature and to the closed, circular nature of the story he tells. Moreover, these problems suggest a view of Humbert as an artist who fails in his attempt to "safely solipsize" Lolita, the object of his desires. That Humbert fails in this attempt is obvious. But the Humbert who fails as an artist of the flesh and imagination must not be confused with the Humbert who narrates the novel; the two Humberts must carefully be distinguished if the problems involving their natures, their roles, and their success or failure are to be solved.

Yet, Humbert himself complicates and confuses the search for answers. As the narrator, Humbert is seemingly only superficially believable, a narrator whose word cannot be trusted, his memory being in his words "sensational but incomplete and unorthodox" (p. 219). As long as the novel is seen as a confession, as Humbert recounting his life as it happened, Humbert's reality as protagonist and the truthfulness of all his statements as narrator of the events of Humbert the character's life must not be regarded as confessor. Rather, he is an artist engaged in the creation of a work of art centered in his own being but existing outside the realm of fact by its nature as art. In other words, the Humbert who performs the actions of the novel, along with Claire Quilty and Lolita herself, must be read as fictions created by a second Humbert, the narrator and novelist.

* * *

From *Philological Quarterly* 63, No. 2 (Spring 1984): 187–204.

Humbert the character lives divided in a divided world. A half-English, half-Swiss European living in America, his heritage and location bespeak a divided self, and this cultural split creates conflicts within him, as when on arriving at the Haze house he must repress his desire to leave because of his "old world politeness" (p. 40). In addition, his emotions are capable of expression in two opposing directions simultaneously. When Valeria departs with her Russian, Humbert feels anger, an intense emotion, and boredom, an extreme affectlessness, at once (p. 38). Humbert's mind thinks in terms of divisions, as the consuming passion of his life, "to fix once for all the perilous magic of nymphets" (p. 136), is a search for that point at which "the beastly and beautiful merged" (p. 137). In a sense, Humbert is man's representative in the great chain of being, caught between spirituality and animality and trying to merge them in his own self. But his obsession with divisions and bifurcations goes far beyond that, leading to a radical division between the world of physical objects and that of mental events.

In childhood the enamored Humbert talked with his Annabel of solipsism (p. 14), showing an early interest in exclusively mental events, and much of his preferred world is solely mental, especially his world with Lolita. After masturbating against her leg and rendering her "safely solipsized" (p. 61), Hum speaks constantly of "the hermetic vision of her which I had locked in" (p. 125) and replaces Dolores Haze with another, fantastic, imaginative Lolita (p. 64). Humbert's hermetically sealed mind affects his life in other ways, too. For one thing, his isolation affects his speech, as Lo points out saying, "You talk like a book, *Dad*" (p. 116). In other words, Humbert talks as he would write, replacing in his mind his actual audience with a created, semifictional and somewhat indeterminate audience—his oral language is directed at a fiction, not a genuine other.[2] He wonders if his fantasies will affect the girls he uses as subjects, later in their lives, despite their never knowing it. So he posits a mental world of cause and effect in which by thinking one might influence the thoughts or destinies of others, a power available only to the solipsist for whom everyone else is imaginary. In effect, his disease of depravity might be contagious (p. 23). This contagion does seemingly happen; Valeria, Charlotte, and Lo all die prematurely after being caught up in his "voluptas," Val and Lo dying in childbirth, as if his influence renders them incapable of surviving fruitful union or of producing possible future nymphets—his prey. In the physical world, the references to mirrors, to Our Glass Lake, and to that room at The Enchanted Hunters, among others,[3] all point to a closed, sealed, inwardly-turned universe, and Hum's efforts while in Beardsley, as well as on the road, to keep Lo from seeing anyone are attempts to "safely solipsize" his relationship with her, to make physical reality a function of his own mind. Even more important to the novel are the treatments of mental isolation as a prison of one sort or another, as Andrew Field correctly points out.[4] In a very real way, Humbert is even imprisoned in the words of his text and exists only in their context while demanding another mind's assistance to make his life: "I shall not exist if you do not imagine me" (p. 131).

Time as Humbert conceives it also contributes to his closed universe. After Lo deserts him, he writes a scholarly article in which he postulates "a theory of time based on the circulation of the blood and conceptually depending . . . on the mind's being conscious not only of matter but also of its own self, thus creating a continuous spanning of two points (the storable future and the stored past)" (p. 262). Blood circulates in a closed system, and what activates and drives it is the heart. If Humbert's model is valid for him, the physical and emotional disease of his heart (which we know to be fatal) must affect his perceptions, memories, and the interplay of his past and future. In fact, they are affected; he states,

> When I try to analyze my own cravings, motives, actions, and so forth, I surrender to a sort of retrospective imagination which feeds the analytic faculty with boundless alternatives and which causes each visualized route to fork and re-fork without end in the maddeningly complex prospect of my past.   (p. 15)

In short, in looking at his past he cannot separate fact from fantasy, and he cannot obtain verification of past events, as when he searches for the news photograph of himself in The Enchanted Hunters to find that it shows only a blurred, unidentifiable shoulder. The blood circulating in its closed system will apparently retain fantasies, while facts lose their veracity; when he declares that he has "fallen in love with Lolita forever," he acknowledges that "she would not be forever Lolita . . . The word 'forever' referred only to my own passion, to eternal Lolita as reflected in my blood" (p. 67). Time goes by, people age, circumstances change, but Humbert's mental construct remains, a mythically circular world in which time is abolished and Lolita is ever as she was, "golden and brown, kneeling, looking up, on that shoddy veranda" (p. 169).

This position, as we shall see, is not the novel's final statement, for Humbert at the close of the novel, just before its rebeginning, affirms a nobler sense of love for Lolita and no longer relies on his constructed world of nymphets. Nevertheless, the novel as Humbert the narrator crafts it follows a circular pattern by relating events leading up to the relating of the events and so participates in a larger sense in a closed, circulatory, and ultimately artistic world. In fact, many aspects of the world of Humbert the narrator have cyclical patterns which reflect their narrator's mind. Annabel, Valeria, Charlotte, and Lolita all die prematurely following relationships of one sort or another with Humbert. In a related pattern, Val and Lo die in childbirth after abandoning Hum for other men, reflecting the pattern of gain and loss Humbert follows with women throughout his life, Rita being the only exception. Moreover, after his long journey across the United States with Lolita, a journey that forms a great circle, Humbert repeats the trip a second time with Lo and then a third with Rita. These cycles, however, are only echoes of the larger, complex cycle that forms the structure of the book itself, centers on the changing relation of Humbert the character's fantasy world to reality, and so demonstrates Humbert's growth as he changes from actor to storyteller.

In the third paragraph of the first chapter, Humbert explains that "there might have been no Lolita at all had I not loved, one summer, a certain initial girl-child"

(p. 11). Had there been no Annabel Leigh to bewitch him and take him out of normal time and normal relationships, neither Lolita the nymphet nor *Lolita* the novel would have been possible. However, Annabel did exist, at least for him, and Humbert did fall in love with her and her kind, leading him to Lolita. Until he meets Lolita, though, his sexual activities are twofold: to relieve his body he frequents prostitutes, and to relieve his mind he frequents park benches, where he can watch nymphets playing while "pretending to be immersed in a trembling book" (p. 22). In these parks filled with nymphets playing in pulsating and melting shadows, Hum watches and fantasizes, never considering interfering with a child's innocence. He repeatedly disavows any criminal intent, insisting that "the gentle and dreamy regions through which I crept were the patrimonies of poets—*not* crime's prowling ground" (p. 133). His physically sexual life and his life of sexual fantasy are at this time completely split, and he is "aware of not one but two sexes, neither of which was mine" (p. 20). When this division of sexual satisfaction into physical and fantastic becomes intolerable to him, he marries Valeria, at first childlike (or -ish) and cute, in an attempt to merge his body's needs and his fantasies, but soon Valeria violates his dream with a vengeance. From "fluffy and frolicsome" she becomes a "large, puffy, short-legged, big-breasted and practically brainless *baba*" (pp. 27–28) and Hum again begins to think of children (p. 29).

His fantasy world intact and possibly strengthened in its isolation from reality by his experience with fat Valeria, Humbert arrives in the U.S. and eventually meets Lolita. Immediately his fantasies take on a new aspect: no longer does he look at nymphets indiscriminately, glad for a peek at lacy underthings, but now he directs all the power of fantasy toward his image of Dolores Haze. Dolly becomes for Hum Annabel's exact image down to a mole, and time ceases to exist: "The twenty-five years I had lived since then, tapered to a palpitating point, and vanished" (p. 41). Lolita becomes the object of all of Humbert's fantasies, and she in turn cooperates with them to a remarkable degree, first passively, allowing Hum to take liberties while removing an object from her eye and while sitting with Hum and Mrs. Haze in the dark (pp. 45–58), and later initiating small intimacies herself. Then, one Sunday while her mother is in church Humbert nabs "the honey of a spasm" by masturbating against Lo's thigh as she sits passively on his lap (pp. 60–64). At this point Humbert's fantastic vision of Lolita is most intense, and she is "safely solipsized"; his sexual activities, he believes, are completely divorced from their object ("Blessed be the Lord, she had noticed nothing!" [p. 63]) and "still Lolita was safe—I was safe. What I had madly possessed was not she, but my own creation, another, fanciful Lolita having no will, no consciousness—indeed, no life of her own (p. 64).

Once Lo's mother is killed and Hum picks up Lo from camp, this internalization is threatened by their proximity and lack of external constraints, and with their first act of intercourse, Hum's mentally-oriented fantasy must change. According to Humbert, Lolita seduces him after a night of agony and failed narcotics, but this momentary merger of fantasy and reality is only the capstone of a night in which the borders between the two realms blur. At one point Lolita frees herself "from the shadow of [Hum's] embrace" and at others Hum "would dream I regained consciousness, dream I lay in wait" (pp. 132–34). Maintaining this blend of reality and unreality could only result in schizophrenia, so beginning with the pair's first coupling, the two realms exist in a contiguous state, rather than an identical, blended one. Upon leaving The Enchanted Hunters that morning, Humbert realizes that "whether or not the realization of a life-long dream had surpassed all expectation, it had, in a sense, overshot its mark—and plunged into a nightmare." More specifically, he begins to feel "an oppressive, hideous constraint as if I were sitting with the small ghost of somebody I had just killed" (p. 142). In the sense of the archaic pun or the Freudian identification of intercourse and dying, he indeed sits with such a ghost, but he analyzes his state correctly in a more important sense: his pure fantasy, killed by its realization, must be replaced by something less pure, less ideal, less exclusively fantastic because it has been made flesh. Instead of owning a shadow to play with in his fantasies, he possesses the object throwing the shadow, too, forcing a deeply ironic twist to his use of the term "ghost"—the ghost of a shadow, it must, in terms of a dualistic universe of mentality and physicality, be corporeal.

Humbert's control over Lolita as another person and not merely as a figment of his imagination must be less than absolute, so he cements his hold on her by revealing her mother's death. This simple fact—that "she had absolutely nowhere else to go" (p. 144)—colors Humbert's intertwined fantasy and reality from now on, as he may now command her to perform sexually with him; her complicity now involves obedience.

At the beginning of Part Two, when the two are on the road, Humbert describes a rented cabin as "a prison cell of paradise, with yellow window shades pulled down to create a morning illusion of Venice and sunshine when actually it was Pennsylvania and rain" (p. 147). The prison cell echoes the various themes of prisons and sealed minds running through the book, but it also alludes to Humbert's severely limited options at this point. His fantasy become reality is a young girl, technically an orphan, and far below the age of consent. He must keep her compliant, if not willing, to do his bidding in bed and at the same time he must avoid possible legal ramifications. In an even more direct way, the cabin is a prison for Lolita, who is constrained to be there, and her incarceration is dramatized by "her sobs in the night—every night, every night—the moment I feigned sleep" (p. 178). At the same time, Hum's use of the window shades to illustrate the illusion, rather than reliance on his powers of imagination, suggests a twofold change in Humbert's imaginative powers: he cannot imagine as well as he could before since objectively he finds Lolita "a disgustingly conventional little girl" (p. 150), but neither does he have to—his dream has come true. Still, she is his nymphet Lolita, his to do with as he pleases *if he can convince her to,* a qualification bespeaking the altered nature of their relationship. At first he relies on threats of isolated farmhouses and reformatories to make her compliant, along with the device of the trip itself, "whose sole *raison d'être* . . . was to keep my companion in a passable humor from kiss to kiss" (p. 156). These strategems, however, lose efficacy and must be replaced by a system of bribes as her reluctance to be part of Humbert's world grows and he perceives her to be ready "to turn away from it with something akin to plain repulsion" (p. 168).

With the play *The Enchanted Hunters* the figure of Claire Quilty enters overtly, exerting his influence directly as if in answer to Lo's growing distaste for Humbert. At this point, Humbert and Lolita have been drifting apart for many pages, and Humbert's control over her is ebbing fast. As if through a chink in the armor of Hum's solipsistic fantasy world, Quilty steals in and Lolita falls in love with him, her new emotions demonstrated by her sudden change in demeanor: "with a yelp of amorous vernal laughter, she . . . rode back, feet at rest on stopped pedals, posture relaxed, one hand dreaming in her print-flowered lap" (p. 204). Clearly, this behavior is not a reaction to Humbert, who for crawling to Lo on his hands and knees receives for his pains only an " 'Oh no, not again' " (p. 194).

In this new situation, Humbert's fantasy cannot survive intact. On discovering Lo's absence from her piano lessons, he finds her in the living room, and "with a sickening qualm" his nymphet-forming "focal adjustment" disappears and he sees, not Lolita, light of his life, etc., but Dolores Haze:

> Her complexion was now that of any vulgar untidy highschool girl. . . . A coarse flush had now replaced that innocent fluorescence. . . . Everything about her was of the same exasperating impenetrable order—the strength of her shapely legs, . . . her wenchy smell, and especially the dead end of her face with its strange flush and freshly made-up lips.

No longer a nymphet, she reminds him instead of a prostitute (p. 206), and after a fight and her escape from the house, she becomes aware of her ability to control the situation and does so immediately: " '*this* time we'll go wherever *I* want, won't we?' " (p. 209).

As a symbol of her new-found control over Humbert, Lolita demands intercourse while Humbert, having "adjusted" and seeing her again as a nymphet, is now her prisoner. He sheds "torrents of tears," and then they begin a new round of travels, but travels very differently from the first, as Quilty now becomes an ever-present force hanging in the background and obviously influencing Lo. Early in the trip she slips away to make a phone call (p. 213) and shortly after that rids herself of Hum for a few hours, apparently to see and possibly to have intercourse with Quilty. When Hum returns, he suspects her infidelity and pursues its "shadow" only to declare that "the scent I travelled upon was so slight as to be practically undistinguishable from a madman's fancy" (p. 217). From creating fantasies almost palpable with reality, Humbert moves to searching futilely for evanescent shadows created by someone else, thereby confessing to a complete breakdown of his ability to control the reality he has created and implying that another figure, Quilty, is at this point a stronger controller of Lolita's reality than he.

With this display of Humbert's impotence, Quilty becomes visible, hanging behind the doomed pair's aging automobile in a car Humbert knows is stronger than his by "many times" (p. 221). Quilty's car seems to be attached to Humbert's by a silken rope reminiscent of the threads Humbert sent through the Haze house in search of Lolita in an earlier, happier time when he was the spider, not the fly. After seeing another of Quilty's plays, Hum and Lo move on to Waco, where Lo gives him the slip as if rehearsing for her big escape to come. Humbert, powerless to stop her, responds not imaginatively, but physically; he slaps her across the face and then dissolves in remorse, for "it was of no avail. Both doomed were we" (p. 229).

Hum's knowledge of his coming fate does not cure him of his delusions, though, and neither does his loss of control. Even after Quilty has entered the scene, after Hum has realized that he must lose Lolita, after he sees his imminent defeat and his powerlessness to defend himself against it, he is still capable of declaring that "despite her advanced age, she was more of a nymphet than ever" (p. 232). He dwells at this time for nearly five pages on her tennis game and finds her yet a true nymphet because her movements, her style, reveal a childlike innocence grounded in her lack of a will to win and a "cheerful indifference" to competition (pp. 234–35). This lack, though, is not a trait inherent in her, but rather results from Humbert's having broken something in her, making her continued nymphetcy a result of traits imposed on her by Humbert in the realization of his fantasy, to her great expense, and ironically, her adoption of traits formerly only aspects of his fantasy removes these traits from his control. Clearly, too, Quilty is the controller now, daring to appear and play tennis with Lo and then impudent enough to stand in the distance and watch Lo play with a dog in full sight of Humbert. Observing this scene, Humbert internalizes it ("The turquoise blue swimming pool some distance behind the lawn was no longer behind that lawn, but within my thorax" [p. 239]), but he cannot retain such a distasteful scene, in which Quilty controls Lolita's actions merely by watching her, and he vomits "a torrent of browns and greens that I had never remembered eating" (p. 204).

When, finally, Humbert's two-year romp with Lolita is discontinued by Lolita's escape from the hospital in a town called Elphinstone after a bout with a virus, he begins his painstaking trip, alone and searching for Lolita and her abductor, whose character, if not his name, begins to solidify for Humbert. Essentially, he is a literary tantalizer, a sower of false clues and blind allusions designed to keep Humbert looking but to prevent him from finding. He has, Humbert discovers, strong affinities with Humbert, and the people of Elphinstone insist he is Humbert's brother. Even if his identity is unclear, his power remains indisputable: "He succeeded in thoroughly enmeshing me and my thrashing anguish in his demoniacal game" (p. 251). This game may be another aspect of Humbert's perverted imagination, however; Quilty's affinities with Humbert may result from Humbert's diseased mind. His reality for Humbert and Lolita is evident. But it may be for Humbert the character the reality of "safely solipsized" imaginative constructs run amok, reminiscent of his earlier musing on the contagiousness of his depravity.

In despair, Humbert eventually gives up the search, destroys or gives away Lolita's things, and commits himself to an institution, bereft not only of Lolita in the flesh, but also of his fantasies of Lo as a nymphet:

My accursed nature could not change, no matter how my love for her did. . . . But one essential vision in me had withered: never did I dwell now on possibilities of bliss with a little maiden, specific or synthetic, in some out-of-the-way place; never did my fancy sink its fangs into Lolita's sisters, far far away in the coves of evoked islands. *That* was all over, for the time being at least.

(p. 259)

The borderline between beautiful and beastly, fantastic and physical, has become a vast, impenetrable no-man's land, this separation and renunciation completing the rebound from the total merger Humbert and Lolita experienced so long ago. Hum no longer has an object for his fantasies, and he has no fantasies either. In a gray reality untinted and untainted by his mind, he finds solitude "corrupting" (p. 206) because his depraved sexual tastes remain; but then he finds Rita.

Rita occupies a very special place in Humbert's world and in his book: she is the only woman with whom Hum carries on a genuinely mutual, illusion-free relationship. Hum admits that he needs "company and care," and Rita, "the most soothing, the most comprehending companion that I ever had" (p. 261), gives him that care freely. In return, Humbert devotes two pages of the warmest prose of the novel to her, words honestly and openly affectionate and a little nostalgic: "hi, Rita—wherever you are, drunk or hangoverish, Rita, hi!" (p. 261). While with her, Hum abandons his vengeful search and lives, like the mysterious Jack Humbertson whom the pair find in their hotel room one morning, in the gray present for two years, as a fairly normal, productive scholar. As Field implies, the prison of his past no longer controls him during this period,[5] and it is during this time that Humbert realizes that his fantasies and realities do not mix: "There was in the fiery phantasm a perfection which made my wild delight also perfect, just because the vision was out of reach, with no possibility of attainment to spoil it by the awareness of an appended taboo" (p. 266). As he learns too late, his fantasies were wonderful precisely because of their impossibility and his being granted his desire has led, as in tales of genies and fairies too numerous to count, to woes he never expected. His all-too-rich imaginative life has brought him to a complete loss of fantasies and to a new maturity of outlook and behavior, but not before dragging him through a nightmarish underworld, from which he has emerged a wiser, if sadder, man.

But this is not the end of his story. He receives a letter from Lolita, now the pregnant seventeen-year-old wife of a Mr. Robert Schiller. Leaving Rita and his life with her, he packs "Chum," his revolver, and begins yet another vengeful journey to her and Dick Schiller, who Humbert thinks is his tormenter. After consulting with a modern Oracle of Delphi (two voices emanating from manholes or abysses in the floor), Hum goes off in a parodic search for the monster he must slay in order to rescue his mistress.

All is gray and sunless when he arrives at the Schiller house, and on talking with the very pregnant Lo he realizes that she sets their "poor romance" at no value whatever, "like a bit of dry mud caking her childhood" (p. 274), and that despite it all, despite her having demonstrably outgrown nymphetcy, he

knew as clearly as I know I am to die, that I loved her more than anything I had
ever seen or imagined on earth, or hoped for anywhere else . . . What I used
to pamper among the tangled vines of my heart . . . had dwindled to its essence: sterile and selfish vice, all *that* I cancelled and cursed. . . . I loved my
Lolita, *this* Lolita. . . .   (p. 280)

He abandons his vice as he later abandons his legacy from dead Charlotte
Haze and recognizes in himself mature love for Lolita as she is, as a human being.
While Field asserts that Hum's love for Lo cannot be realized except "in the pain
and purity of memory and art,"[6] in actuality the influence of fantasy-free (and
consequently artless) life with Rita matures Humbert and makes him capable of
loving more than a fantastic image. Hum sees Lo as she is, worn out and hugely
pregnant, and loves her. He also notes traces of her former nymphetcy, but
"thank[s] God it was not that echo alone that I worshipped" (pp. 279–80). In this
new state of consciousness and love, he must ask Lo to come with him or at least
to say she someday might, but of course she declines, her refusal a reproof to him
of his wretched treatment of her. Her refusal makes "all the difference" because it
proves that his perverted past still exerts control and influence on the events of his
life. His perversion does matter; hence the death of Quilty, who has assumed the
pervert's role after wrenching it away from Humbert during his and Lo's second
trip West, is a necessity for Humbert—to exorcise his demons, he must kill this
projection of his Frankensteinian fantasies.

   This projecting does not require that Quilty be a fiction of Humbert's, a
possibility Page Stegner vehemently denies[7]—it requires only that Humbert see
Quilty in that way.[8] Humbert realizes now that his perversion has always controlled
him, while his control has always been minimal at best. During "icebergs in paradise," moments akin to those in which he saw Lo as a person instead of a nymphet,
he would feel the despair and shame of his acts and be ready to ask forgiveness and
repent—but "all at once, ironically, horribly, lust would swell again," and his depravity would take control of him again (p. 287). This recognition, Douglas Fowler
argues, forms the book's "final vision," Humbert's acknowledgement of his culpability in stealing Lolita's childhood as a real child away for her.[9]

   His duty now clear to him, Humbert becomes a new person. His "old world
politeness" disappears in his visit to Ramsdale, and he prepares for the death of
Quilty by first casing Quilty's house in the darkness of a black, landscapeless night
and then returning the next morning dressed in black, the sun "burning like a man"
(pp. 294–95). He acknowledges his presence in the monster's lair and his slavery
to the perversions that Quilty represents by referring to Quilty as "master," but
now Humbert is the "enchanted hunter," the master, and Quilty the prey. Quilty
does retain power, for his presence makes Humbert's weapon with its mock-
Freudian associations feel "limp and clumsy" in his hand, and Hum feels that his first
shot might "trickle out" of the rug after penetrating it. Forcing Quilty to read Hum's
poem/death sentence/invocation gives Humbert new strength, though, and he
objectifies his adversary as "the person" (p. 303). The distancing renders Quilty

powerless—words bounce off, offers of new depravities go unheeded, and after an absurd and mythic number of wounds, Quilty, the repository and personification of Humbert's evil, finally, melodramatically, dies.

Although Hum asserts that "this . . . was the end of the ingenious play staged for me by Quilty" (p. 307), it is not the ending written or planned by Quilty, as Brent Harold implies.[10] Instead it is Humbert's ending, his final purgation of his old, evil self[11]—in his victory he becomes the playwright. However, Humbert cannot rest easy, for, as he says, "I see nothing for the treatment of my misery but the melancholy and very local palliative of articulate art" (p. 285). Quilty's death on a physical level is not enough; after Humbert's incarceration, he writes *Lolita,* for his solace and to give himself and Lolita "the only immortality [she and he] may share." Thus, in its spiralling circuit, the novel moves into and through the realm of art as it moves from ending to rebeginning, and Quilty, along with all the other characters, gains in symbolic significance as the question of his reality as a distinct character is nullified. Whatever he may have been, he is now Humbert's exorcised demon, and the narrative no longer poses as a chronicle of real events, but reveals itself as a fictional construct in which the "reality" of events and characters is no longer troublesome: all is symbol, all is fiction, all is art.

Much of the available criticism on *Lolita* condemns Humbert as a failed artist, either because of his actions throughout the novel or because of his somehow faulty narrative ability. In effect, for the critics Humbert's art fails because Lolita leaves him and never loves him or fails because he is an inept narrator of a story—two very different sorts of failure reflecting equally different types of art. In the first kind of art Humbert attempts to fashion a living work of art in Lolita, and he interacts with his creation in his physical experience, while in the second kind, imprisoned and removed from society, he writes but does not live in his art. Each of these artistic poses has been explored by Maurice Beebe, who calls the first the "Sacred Fount" concept of the artist and the second, the "Ivory Tower."[12]

According to Beebe, the tradition of Sacred Fount literature "equates art with experience" and sees the genuine artist as one who lives more intensely and more fully than others; art, in its best form, recreates experience. Moreover, this view usually posits a single source of creative or procreative energy, so that the artist, in order to create, must sacrifice some other, usually sexual, part of his being. "Life can be converted directly to art, but to do so is to destroy life."[13] The Humbert who participates in the action of the novel is, as Carol T. Williams suggests, clearly a Sacred Fount artist who forms an imaginative construct, a nymphet, from the raw material of his interactions with Dolores Haze.[14] Humbert attempts to circumvent the energy problem by creating a work of art which also fulfills sexual needs, so that his physical energy will not be drained through intercourse with his creation. His escape, it turns out, is only illusory. Instead of depleting himself physically, his imaginative juices dry up, leaving him as empty as any other artist working in this tradition.[15]

On the other hand, the Ivory Tower tradition raises art above life and assumes that art is only possible when the artist is aloof from life. This is the sort of art that

Stephen Dedalus propounds in *A Portrait of the Artist as a Young Man*—"The artist, like the God of the creation, remains within or behind or beyond or above his handiwork, invisible, refined out of existence, indifferent, paring his fingernails"[16]—a concept that Humbert alludes to in his search, in the Briceland *Gazette*, for "a portrait of the artist as a younger brute" (p. 264). In this tradition the artist imitates God, creating a unified, ordered, artistic world, such as the world of Lolita, but being himself removed from it. This is the point at which most critics of Humbert founder. As Beebe says, "Critics of fiction often confuse the 'I' of the story teller with the person who wrote the work."[17] In Humbert's case the problem of differentiating the creating and created aspects of his divided self is quite complex.

Beebe points out that "an underlying assumption in the artist novel is that creative man is a divided being, man *and* artist." The man, a human being with normal appetites and needs, lives a fairly normal life, while the artist is "a free, detached spirit" looking down on the man and removed from him and trying to transcend life through art. The man must die, but the spirit survives by uniting itself with its works and "thus escaping the bonds of time."[18] When Humbert is performing the actions of the novel, creating fantasies in his own mind and then creating his work of art in Lolita, he is split between the artist who plays with his imagination on the world and transforms it and the pervert who attempts to imprison the object of his carnal desires but eventually destroys her. Hum cannot maintain such a split, though, as he cannot maintain the objectivity necessary to create; his only lucid moments, the "icebergs in paradise," are brief, destroyed by his constant lust.

Patricia Merivale sees this as the assertion of reality against Hum's fantasy, so that "the real nature and needs of the person, Lolita, will not be denied." For her, Hum's life is a failure, as he has tried to make his life "book-shaped." At the end he has left "only" his novel, clearly for Merivale a less "real" or important aspect of life than the actual living of it.[19] Hum's diseased imagination depletes itself in realizing in artistic goal, its misapplied energy flowing from Humbert to Quilty, who becomes Hum's doppelgänger[20]—shadowing him, luring away the object of his desires, and becoming the objectification of the evil Humbert must kill in order to become a successful artist. (Interestingly, Quilty displays the dangers of the "Ivory Tower" artistic pose, just as Humbert does of the "Sacred Fount"; Quilty's detachment is too complete. He lacks any emotional involvement either with his work of his life. As he himself admits, "I'm the author of fifty-two successful scenarios. I know all the ropes" [p. 300]. And his feelings for Lolita end when she refuses to participate in pornographic movies—again, sex detached from contact and feeling [pp. 278–79]. As a result, his art is as sterile as he is impotent.) Humbert also writes the book, however, so he must split again, into character and narrator. This time he is almost totally drained of life, locked in a prison cell with a failing heart, and here, where his physical self can do nothing, his artistic self can flourish, creating a work of art: *Lolita*.

C. G. Jung states that "we can only understand [the artist] in his capacity of artist by looking at his artistic achievement."[21] and Humbert must be judged doubly. As an artist immersed in life and creating his art from his life, he is a failure, for Lolita deserts him and thinks the whole affair trivial, and the artistic self of his active life ends with his killing of Quilty. As an artist removed from life, sitting in his cell creating *Lolita*, however, he succeeds admirably, writing a story which gives him and Lolita admittedly limited immortality while affording him solace. At the beginning of the book, when he exists most artistically in a world of fantasy, he nonetheless requires the palliative of flesh. As his dreams and fantasies solidify, though, the flesh ceases being a refuge and becomes another torture of dreams come true, and he requires the "palliative of articulate art" (p. 285). Humbert's failure as an artist of the flesh requires him to try again, so his journey through the book from pure fantasy (before Lolita) through a mix of fantasy and reality making failed art (with Lolita) to a period of undisturbed reality (with Rita) finally leads to successful art (*Lolita*).

If John Ray, Jr. is also a creation of Humbert's, as similarities in their prose styles suggest,[22] then the levels of authority in Lolita are again multiplied: Humbert has created his life's story as art, acting as character and then author in his self-created existence, but if, as seems likely, he has also created Professor Ray, psychopathologist and critic of the novel, then he has distanced himself yet further from his narrative, revealing himself as yet another character lurking behind his construct as "author" and so imitating Nabokov himself, who is correspondingly more distant from his creation. This increased distance is necessary to avoid the apparent incongruity, pointed out by Appel, between the intricacy of the text and its supposed speedy composition. Appel insists that the book's intricacy is "beyond the capacities of any 'point of view' in the book," arguing that the complexity cannot be the product of a man writing furiously in prison.[23] This view is undercut by Ray's being a fiction of Humbert's, for the prison and its time span, like everything else in the novel, is then part of Humbert the narrator's work of art—not of Humbert the character's "real" existence. Humbert, then, like Nabokov, sits like God, paring his fingernails, leaving only obscure clippings to indicate his presence.[24]

Critics sometimes confuse the Humberts, narrated failed artist and narrator and successful artist. Harold, for one, confuses Humbert's description of events with those events and in doing so neglects Hum's control over the artistic narrative. When he says that throughout Part Two Humbert feels like a character in someone else's book,[25] he forgets that Humbert the character is indeed a character in a book written by Humbert the narrator. Julia Bader, too, confuses the two Humberts, criticizing the narrator as if he were writing the events as they happened, rather than in the retrospect of artistic creation and transformation.[26] Strangely, she notes the clues hinting at Quilty and reasons from them either that Hum pretends ignorance of Quilty for "novelistic purposes" or that the clues allude to an author behind Humbert.[27] Similarly, Stegner asserts that Humbert converts his vulgar life into "a thing of beauty," but goes on to argue that Hum's imprisonment demonstrates his final victimization by and "imprisonment in art," suggesting that "art eventually perverts him because his life *becomes* art." [28] Stegner here separates character and narrator but then unites them again, failing to take into account an important early statement by Humbert the narrator.

> And now take down the following important remark: the artist in me has been given the upper hand over the gentleman. It is with a great effort of will that in his memoir I have managed to tune my style to the tone of the journal that I kept when Mrs. Haze was to me but an obstacle. . . . I have considered it my artistic duty to preserve its intonations no matter how false and brutal they may seem to me now. . . . I can cease insulting poor Charlotte for the sake of retrospective verisimilitude.   (p. 37)

"Retrospective verisimilitude" explains his (feigned) ignorance of Quilty in the early stages of the novel and maintains the careful split between the actor on the stage and writer feeding him his lines. He maintains that he was brutal in the name of truth—yet this truth may now be false. Where, then, can we find truth, if despite its realistic aura the book's events, as Field notes,[29] maintain at times a "very dubious reality," especially when Humbert specifically reserves his right to falsify for art's sake (p. 265)? Bader says that the search for a basis of reality is hopeless, for the question is simply not answered by the book. Humbert's fantasy life, she asserts, "is indistinguishable from his 'real' life." [30]

I believe her observation to be correct, although not due to a lack of answers. The question of the reality or non-reality of events in *Lolita* cannot be answered because, Humbert being an artist, it is irrelevant: the entire book, an artistic construct, is fantastic and realistic at once. As Bader states, " 'verisimilitude' exists only in relation to imaginative landscapes, and . . . the fictional and unique 'truth' about a novel lies in the artist's self-contained fictional construct." [31] Moreover, Charles Kinbote, Nabokov's narrator in *Pale Fire,* also affirms that " 'reality' is neither the subject nor the object of true art which creates its own special reality. . . ." [32] The profound "message" of Quilty's play is that "mirage and reality merge in love," but Humbert demonstrates in *Lolita* that in truth, fantasy and reality merge in art (which Nabokov defines as "curiosity, tenderness, kindness, ecstasy").[33]

This profoundly important unification of two realms reverberates throughout Lolita's pregnancy and brings the entire novel into sharp focus. In being pregnant Lo echos Hum's assertion that he is "with Lolita" as a woman is "with child" (p. 109). Thus, the sexual act, a merger comparable to the artistically creative act, is in this novel at once incestuous and solipsistic, for if Lolita (and, by extension, *Lolita*) is in Humbert, Humbert is also in *Lolita,* and in spiralling from questionable narrative into unquestionable work of art and in forming a series of inward-turning spirals and circles the novel becomes, as Nabokov ostensibly sees his own life, "a colored spiral in a small ball of glass." [34] Within that ball, in the memories of Humbert translated into art, "nothing will ever change, nobody will ever die." [35] Humbert's "poor immortality" is assured, for in creating *Lolita* as a work of art compounded in his own life, he unites physical and fantastic in the artifact and does the same in his very being, existing in the work as both artist and artifact, cause and effect.

The world of *Lolita*, then, is a world in which the duality of mind and body, creation and creature, ideation and sensation, fantasy and reality merge eternally in the spiralling progress of the narrative, and along its way the novel makes important statements about what art is, what it is not, and what it can do. As Nabokov would wish his perfect novel to end, the book's close "is a sensation of its world receding in the distance and stopping somewhere there suspended." [36] Humbert acknowledges the fragility and tenuousness of this very local and melancholy palliative for life in the world; still, the timelessness and immortality such a palliative offers are worth the effort of doing it, for it is the only "way out." For Nabokov as well as Humbert, the work of art is "the only immortality you and I may share," for both "only have words to play with" (p. 34), and it is with words and their controlling that each artist acts within his world as "precise fate, that synchronizing phantom" (p. 105), abolishing time and creating palpable shadows by creating a timeless world. When we return to the first lines after finishing the novel, then, "Lolita" reverberates with meaning, signifying fact, fantasy, and their magical transformation into art, and "Lolita" is now not only a girl, a fantasy, and a book, it is the constitutive element of all three: a word. The first line now bespeaks not a moldy passion, but rather an expansive, embracing totality, the outer pair of phrases framing and subsuming the inner: "Lolita. Light of my life . . . my soul."

NOTES

[1] Alfred Appel, Jr., ed. *The Annotated Lolita*, by Vladimir Nabokov (New York: McGraw-Hill, 1970), p. 11. All subsequent references to the novel itself will be given in the text of the paper.

[2] This concept is explained in E. D. Hirsch, Jr., *The Philosophy of Composition* (U. of Chicago Press, 1978), pp. 30–31.

[3] See Appel, pp. 322 and 372, for more.

[4] Andrew Field, *Nabokov: His Life in Art* (Boston: Little, Brown & Co., 1967), p. 326.

[5] Field, p. 341.

[6] Field, p. 343.

[7] *Escape into Aesthetics: The Art of Vladimir Nabokov* (New York: Dial Press, 1966), pp. 34–35.

[8] A possibility also denied by Stegner in his assertion that Quilty represents a "worn convention" to be parodied and dispensed with (p. 35).

[9] Douglas Fowler, *Reading Nabokov* (Cornell U. Press, 1974), p. 158.

[10] Brent Harold, "*Lolita*: Nabokov's Critique of Aloofness," *Papers on Language & Literature* 11 (1974): 80–81.

[11] As Fowler points out, pp. 155–56.

[12] Maurice Beebe, *Ivory Towers and Sacred Founts* (New York U. Press, 1964), p. 13. The many similarities between *Lolita* and the archetypal artist novel outlined by Beebe are grist for numerous studies; they also suggest that Nabokov may have been writing the artist novel to end all artist novels by incorporating as many features of that genre into *Lolita* as he could.

[13] Beebe, pp. 13–17.

[14] "Nabokov's Dialectical Structure," in L. S. Dembo, ed., *Nabokov: The Man and His Work* (U. of Wisconsin Press, 1967), p. 180.

[15] Appel notices the problems Hum the character has with language at the points of greatest intensity in his life ("What's the katter with misses?" [p. 122]), again demonstrating his inability to control successfully his life in art. ("*Lolita*: The Springboard of Parody," in Dembo, p. 137.)

[16] James Joyce, *A Portrait of the Artist as a Young Man* (New York: Modern Library, 1928), p. 252, quoted in Beebe, p. 13.

[17] Beebe, pp. 9–13. Kathleen Tillotson makes the same point in *The Tale and the Teller* (London: Rupert Hart-Davis, 1959), p. 22.

[18] Beebe, pp. 6–7.
[19] "The Flaunting of Artifice in Vladimir Nabokov and Jorge Luis Borges," in Dembo, p. 221.
[20] As Appel notes, *Annotated Lolita*, pp. 330–33.
[21] C. G. Jung, *Modern Man in Search of a Soul*, trans. W. S. Dell and Cary F. Barnes (London: Kegan Paul, Trench, Trubner, and Co., 1945), pp. 194–95, quoted in Beebe, p. 10.
[22] Carl Proffer, *Keys to Lolita* (Indiana U. Press, 1968), p. 82.
[23] Appel, *Annotated Lolita*, p. 329, and "Springboard," in Dembo, p. 118.
[24] See again Appel's note (*Annotated Lolita*, pp. 327–29) for evidence of Nabokov's "phosophorescent fingerprints."
[25] Harold, p. 78.
[26] Julia Bader, *Crystal Land: Artifice in Nabokov's English Novels* (U. of California Press, 1972), pp. 76–77.
[27] Bader, p. 75.
[28] Pp. 114–15, italics his.
[29] Field, pp. 327–28.
[30] Bader, p. 80.
[31] Bader, p. 63.
[32] (New York, 1966), p. 94, quoted in William Woodin Rowe, *Nabokov's Deceptive World* (New York U. Press, 1971), p. 73.
[33] Nabokov, "On a Book Entitled *Lolita*," in Appel, *Annotated Lolita*, p. 317.
[34] Nabokov, *Speak, Memory* (New York: G. P. Putnam, 1966), p. 275.
[35] Nabokov, *Speak, Memory*, p. 77.
[36] "An Interview with Vladimir Nabokov," in Dembo, p. 28.

Jeffrey Berman

NABOKOV AND THE
VIENNESE WITCH DOCTOR

With its false scents, clever ambushes, and multiedged ironies, *Lolita* (1955) is the supreme parody of the psychiatric case study. The novel brilliantly puts into practice the strategy Nabokov uses in the forewords to his other stories: It lures in the unsuspecting Freudian and then springs the trap upon him. *Lolita* mocks the psychopathological approach to literature and taunts the reader to solve the mystery of Humbert's obsession with his nymphet. As Elizabeth Phillips remarks, "Nabokov's ironic version of the 'psychopathological' case history ridicules both the method and the content of the formula by which the inspiration of art has been Freudianized."[1] The intensity of the novel's attack on the talking cure is unrivaled in literature. Calling himself "King Sigmund the Second," Humbert belittles Freud at every opportunity, daring anyone to tell him something about himself he does not already know. At times it seems that Freud, not Quilty, is the secret antagonist in *Lolita*. In this novel, the Viennese witch doctor is revealed for what he really is, less a mad doctor than Nabokov's white whale, a shadowy symbol of satanic proportions who must be killed again and again lest the universe go awry. Nothing less than the purity of literature and the survival of the imagination are at stake in *Lolita* and, if both Humbert and his maker become monomaniacal in their pursuit of evil, that is incidental to the outcome. The battle lines are drawn.

The irony begins with the mock "Foreword" to *Lolita* by John Ray, Jr., Ph.D., whose training in clinical psychology qualifies him as a Fraudian. In his role as editor of Humbert's confessional manuscript, Ray confirms Nabokov's belief that the difference between the rapist and therapist is but a matter of spacing. Ray's introduction to Humbert's story lends the appearance of clinical authenticity, which is precisely what Nabokov parodies. Ray asserts that literature should elevate and inculcate, that human nature can be improved, that art functions as a warning of the dangers of abnormalcy and perversion. ". . . for in this poignant personal study there lurks a general lesson; the wayward child, the egotistic mother, the panting maniac—

From *The Talking Cure: Literary Representations of Psychoanalysis* (New York: New York University Press, 1985), pp. 222–38.

these are not only vivid characters in a unique story: they warn us of dangerous trends; they point out potent evils" (*The Annotated Lolita*, pp. 7–8). Ray assumes, furthermore, that Humbert is a pervert, that his case study should alert us to future Humberts lusting for our daughters, that the chief value of literature lies not in aesthetic beauty but in social and ethical import, and that psychopathology menaces us to the same extent that communism does. (His language at the end of the introduction evokes the breathless rhetoric of McCarthyism.)

The irony, then, is that Ray is editing a story whose literary meaning remains beyond his understanding. Nabokov introduces the novel to us through an unreliable narrator and then proceeds to wrest *Lolita* out of Ray's clinical grasp. Oddly enough, Ray is not without a degree of insight into Humbert's story. He wisely refrains from editing or altering the manuscript apart from the correction of "obvious solecisms." He preserves the anonymity of the author by telling us that "its author's bizarre cognomen is his own inventions." The psychologist surprisingly rejects the charge of pornography, arguing that what is "offensive" in a story is frequently a synonym for "unusual." A great work of art, he realizes, is always original and shocking. Although he remains horrified by the author, he can appreciate the power of the manuscript. "But how magically his singing violin can conjure up a tendresse, a compassion for Lolita that makes us entranced with the book while abhorring its author!" (Which author is Ray referring to here—Humbert or Nabokov? If the latter, then Nabokov is poking fun at Ray even as the psychologist is disparaging the novelist!) Ray also concedes a point that Nabokov's other therapists would have missed: "that had our demented diarist gone, in the fatal summer of 1947, to a competent psycho-pathologist, there would have been no disaster; but then, neither would there have been this book" (p. 7). In short, there is a ray of truth in the psychologist's introduction, although Nabokov would remind us that a "competent psychopathologist" is a contradiction in terms.

One must wonder, however, whether Dr. Ray is aware of Humbert's sadistic delight in foiling his psychiatrists. Given Nabokov's delight in deception, Humbert maintains a poker face in analyzing his "symptomatology" and bouts of insanity. In his contempt of Freud, Humbert is Nabokov's faithful son. "At first, I planned to take a degree in psychiatry as many *manqué* talents do; but I was even more *manqué* than that . . ." (p. 17). Wooed by psychoanalysts with their "pseudo-liberations of pseudolibidoes," Humbert claims to have suffered several major psychological breakdowns which have caused him to be hospitalized in expensive sanatoriums where he perfects his maker's art: psychiatry-baiting:

> I discovered there was an endless source of robust enjoyment in trifling with psychiatrists: cunningly leading them on; never letting them see that you know all the tricks of the trade; inventing for them elaborate dreams, pure classics in style (which make *them*, the dream-extortionists, dream and wake up shrieking); teasing them with fake "primal scenes"; and never allowing them the slightest glimpse of one's real sexual predicament. By bribing a nurse I won access to some files and discovered, with glee, cards calling me "potentially

homosexual" and "totally impotent." The sport was so excellent, its results—in *my* case—so ruddy that I stayed on for a whole month after I was quite well (sleeping admirably and eating like a schoolgirl). And then I added another week just for the pleasure of taking on a powerful newcomer, a displaced (and, surely, deranged) celebrity, known for his knack of making patients believe they had witnessed their own conception. (pp. 36–37)

Not for a moment does Nabokov consider Humbert's anti-Freudianism an example of clinical resistance to therapy. Questions of transference and counter-transference seem as alien to Nabokov as they would to B. F. Skinner. Humbert's criticisms of psychoanalysis coincide exactly with Nabokov's position, and both use the identical parodic attack to demolish the foe. The reader cannot take seriously Humbert's declarations of past insanity, and there is nothing that ever threatens his lucidity or verbal power. The psychiatrists fail to uncover his deception. "I love to fool doctors," he confides merrily. In his role of "Jean-Jacques Humbert," he fabricates the most histrionic confession. He can play the role of analyst or patient. "The child therapist in me (a fake, as most of them are—but no matter) regurgitated neo-Freudian hash and conjured up a dreaming and exaggerating Dolly in the 'latency' period of girlhood" (p. 126). Never deviating from his anti-Freudianism, he expects the reader to share his point of view. "Mid-twentieth century ideas concerning child-parent relationship have been considerably tainted by the scholastic rigmarole and standardized symbols of the psychoanalytic racket, but I hope I am addressing myself to unbiased readers" (p. 287).

How much psychoanalytic theory does Humbert—and Nabokov—actually know? The question is difficult to answer, if only because the novelist may be assimilating more Freudian theory than he cares to parody. Humbert's mocking allusion to the "dream-extortionists," and Van's equally contemptuous reference in *Ada* to "Sig's epoch-making confession," suggest that *The Interpretation of Dreams* (1900) forms the cornerstone of Nabokov's understanding or misunderstanding of psychoanalytic theory. Nearly all of the parodist's comments focus on id psychology, which represents historically the beginning of psychoanalysis, the emphasis upon biological drives. Nabokov strongly objects to the biologizing of psychology, especially the Oedipus complex. He also attacks the "theatrical" side of psychoanalysis: the primal scene, the death wish, the birth trauma. Nabokov's fictional psychiatrists undertake the most preposterous research, with predictable conclusions. In "Ultima Thule," Dr. Bonomini is studying the "dynamics of the psyche," seeking to demonstrate that "all psychic disorders could be explained by subliminal memories of calamities that befell the patient's forbears . . ." (*A Russian Beauty and Other Stories*, p. 161). If a patient were suffering from megalomania, for example, it would be necessary to determine which of his great-grandfathers was a power-hungry failure. In *Pale Fire*, an old psychiatrist warns the Prince of Zembla that his vices had subconsciously killed his mother and would continue to kill the mother in him until he renounced sodomy. Otto Rank's theory of birth trauma also comes under attack. The narrator of *Pnin* refers to a "phenomenon of suffocation that a veteran psychoanalyst, whose name escapes me, has explained as being the sub-consciously evoked shock of one's baptism which causes an explosion of interven-ing recollections between the first immersion and the last" (p. 21). Pnin refers disapprovingly to Dr. Halp's "theory of birth being an act of suicide on the part of the infant."

A list of the books written by Nabokov's psychiatric researchers reveals a world gone mad over the mind-curing industry. Psychiatry, progressive education, the self-help business, how-to books, and psychobabble are exposed as the shams of shamans. Once again, Nabokov attacks the biologizing of psychology and the comic nature of psychoanalytic theory. Betty Bliss, one of Pnin's former graduate students, writes a paper on "Dostoevski and Gestalt Psychology," which nicely expresses Nabokov's deprecation of his nineteenth-century Russian predecessor. Before her marriage to Eric Wind, Liza Bogolepov works at the Meudon sanato-rium directed by a destructive psychiatrist called Dr. Rosetta Stone. Psychotherapy, implies Nabokov, generates arcane hieroglyphics. The Winds' delightful son Victor proves to be a "problem" child because of his disturbing lack of pathology. The boy contradicts his parents' deeply held belief that "every male child had an ardent desire to castrate his father and a nostalgic urge to re-enter his mother's body." The father is so alarmed by his son's normalcy that he has him tested by the leading prognosticators of psychological health: the Gudunov Drawing-of-an-Animal Test, the Fairview Adult Test, the Kent-Rosanoff Absolutely Free Association Test, and the Augusta Angst Abstract Test. Unfortunately, Victor's interpretation of Ror-schach ink blots proves of little interest to the psychologists, and the poor boy is finally left to struggle through life on his own. His parents, though, remain com-mitted to their professional training and collaborate to write an essay on "Group Psychotherapy Applied to Marriage Counseling" for a psychiatric journal. In "Ultima Thule," Dr. Bonomini writes a book called *The Heroics of Insanity*. In *Lolita*, John Ray receives the Poling Prize for a modest work entitled "Do the Senses Make Sense?" in which certain morbid states and perversions are discussed. Nabokov has the last word, however, to this proliferating psychological literature. Near the end of *Ada*, Van grows disgusted with the "Sig" school of psychiatry and writes a paper entitled *The Farce of Group Therapy in Sexual Maladjustment*. The epigraph to the study contains a passage from Sig's epoch-making confession: "In my student days I became a de*flowerer* because I failed to pass my botany examination" (p. 577). This is a reference to a letter Freud wrote to Wilhelm Fliess in 1899.[2] Van's paper proves to be devastating to the psychiatric establishment. "The Union of Marital Counselors and Catharticians at first wanted to sue but then preferred to detu-mify."

Nabokov demonstrates that he can out-psychologize the most orthodox Freudian, and Humbert is less interested in proving the psychoanalyst incorrect than in casting him into Hell. Both novelist and narrator ransack the psychoanalytic canon and then load their own cannon or torpedoes with enough explosives to sink the deepest depth reading. Humbert would have us believe that his tragic passion for Lolita springs from an unhappy love affair with Annabel Leigh, a lovely child of 13 who is only a few months younger than he. Humbert falls madly in love with her, and they meet surreptitiously to carry on their youthful romance. Fate intervenes and within a few months she dies of typhus, their love unconsummated. Humbert remains convinced that "in a certain magic and fateful way Lolita began with Annabel." The physical similarities between the two girl-children seem to support his statement. He emphasizes the Poesque quality of the doomed love, and he is highly conscious—self-conscious—of the parallels between Annabel Leigh and Poe's Annabel Lee. Humbert marries Charlotte Haze to be near her daughter, just as Poe marries his child-cousin to be near his beloved aunt. But the parallel to Poe is misleading, as Andrew Field points out. "The historian of literature knows, however, that Poe married his child bride primarily to tighten his rather strange and neurotic ties to her guardian aunt. If *Lolita* were indeed modeled on the life of Poe (as at least one article has tried to maintain), Humbert would marry Lolita in order to be closer to her mother Charlotte!"[3] The possibility that Humbert's love for Lolita is a repetition of his thwarted love for another nymphet, Annabel Leigh, thus turns out to be a dead end.

Another psychiatric dead end is the "Daddy's Girl" theme. Just as Humbert never tires of referring to Lolita as his daughter, so does Nabokov exploit all the ironies implicit in the apparently incestuous relationship. "Be a father to my little girl" (p. 70) Charlotte writes to Humbert, and he proceeds to carry out her wish. He marries the detestable mother only to be near her desirable daughter whom he is happy to help raise. "Lolita, with an incestuous thrill, I had grown to regard as *my* child" (p. 82), he adds parenthetically. After Charlotte's death, he informs Lolita that "For all practical purposes I am your father" (p. 121). This is the relationship he announces to others, particularly to motel owners. His lecture on the history of incest is truly impressive: No one can question his devotion to research. When he finally catches up with Quilty, he introduces himself as Lolita's father and insists that the playwright stole his child. Quilty denies the kidnapping and maintains that he rescued the girl from a "beastly pervert."[4] The reader's response to this Oedipal play is that Humbert protests too much. There are simply too many Freudian "clues" for us to take seriously and, like Roth's Portnoy, Humbert is too comfortable in his posture of lying on the analytic couch. It is possible, of course, that there are Oedipal implications of Humbert's relationship to Lolita, but not the interpretation he deceptively offers.

Similarly, Nabokov parodies the subjects of homosexuality and impotence. Humbert refers gleefully to the psychiatrist's diagnosis of him as "potentially homosexual" and "totally impotent." He recalls a dream that seems to be culled from *The Interpretation of Dreams.* "Sometimes I attempt to I ill in my dreams. But do you know what happens? For instance I hold a gun. For instance I aim at a bland, quietly interested enemy. Oh, I press the trigger all right, but one bullet after another feebly drops on the floor from the sheepish muzzle. In those dreams, my only thought is to conceal the fiasco from my foe, who is slowly growing annoyed" (p. 49). The limpness of the unmanly bullets foreshadows the comic killing of Claire Quilty, Humbert's "evil double." Lest we miss the deep symbolism of the shooting,

Humbert pointedly tells us that "we must remember that a pistol is the Freudian symbol of the Ur-father's central forelimb" (p. 218). Fingering his gun in the presence of the man who has married Lolita, Dick Schiller, Humbert imagines shooting his sexual rival. But one wonders whether murder or detumescence is Humbert's goal. He conjures up a scene in which he "pulled the pistol's foreskin back, and then enjoyed the orgasm of the crushed trigger: I was always a good little follower of the Viennese medicine man" (p. 276). On another occasion, Humbert psychoanalyzes the symbolism of the fountain pen, the anatomical relative of the pistol. The fact that Quilty does not use a fountain pen clearly indicates, "as any psychoanalyst will tell you," that the patient was a "repressed undinist" (p. 252). Quilty obligingly admits that he had no fun with Dolly because he is "practically impotent," and he then implores Humbert to postpone the killing so that he can nurse his impotence. The actual shooting of Quilty parodies the ineffectuality of Humbert's bullets and the incomplete sexual gratification of the act. As the phallic bullets penetrate Quilty, his face twitches in an absurd clownish manner and he emits a "feminine 'ah!' " as if the bullets were tickling him.

Nabokov parodies the Daddy's Girl theme in *Lolita* and the impotence motif, but he remains more serious about traumatic loss. In the beginning, Humbert discloses cryptically that his mother died in a freak accident—"picnic, lightning"—when he was three years old. He returns to the theme of maternal loss near the end of the story, telling us that "in retrospect no yearnings of the accepted kind could I ever graft upon any moment of my youth, no matter how savagely psychotherapists heckled me in my later periods of depression" (p. 289). Apart from the question why sadistic therapists would want to heckle him, Humbert fears a similarly tragic death awaiting Lolita. Nabokov teases us with the names of Quilty's plays, such as *The Lady Who Loved Lightning*. Lolita dies not from lightning but during childbirth, as does Humbert's first wife, Valeria. Is there a link between pregnancy and death? Is there a significance in the premature deaths of Humbert's women: his mother, Annabel Leigh, Valeria, Lolita? Is Nabokov parodying the theme of traumatic loss, or is he using parody to conceal the overwhelming pain of death?

In other words, to what extent does Nabokov's use of parody invalidate a psychological interpretation of *Lolita?* If parody is viewed as a protective shield, against what is the novelist defending? No writer poses a greater threat or challenge to psychoanalytic criticism than Nabokov, who is not only the most virulently anti-Freudian artist of the century but one of the greatest literary figures of our time, unquestionably a genius—and a genius at deception. His duplicity, James R. Rambeau has observed, places his readers in a defensive position: "they must first prove they understand what Nabokov is *doing* before they can judge the final effects of his fiction."[5] Most readers have concluded that Nabokov's fiction is psychoanalytically impenetrable. Curiously, Nabokov's condemnation of psychoanalysis derives from his belief that it perpetrates a cruel hoax or deception on an unsuspecting public. "Freudism and all it has tainted with its grotesque implications and methods appears to me to be one of the vilest deceits practiced by people on themselves and on others" (*Strong Opinions*, pp. 23–24). One would assume that Nabokov is irrevocably opposed to deception and that everything deceptive is evil. Not true. He consistently affirms the quality of deception within art and nature. "I discovered in nature the nonutilitarian delights that I sought in art. Both were a form of magic, both were a game of intricate enchantment and deception" (*Speak, Memory*, p. 125). And in *Strong Opinions* he reveals that "all art is deception and so is nature; all is deception in that good cheat, from the insect that mimics a leaf to the popular enticements of procreation" (p. 11). How, then, does the deception of the psychoanalyst differ from the artist's duplicity? Cannot the analyst be a good cheat, as the insect and artist are, inventing strategies that unlock hidden truths?

Obviously not, for Nabokov. He praises the artist as an encoder of fictional reality, while he condemns the analyst as a false decoder of psychic reality. The issue for Nabokov is not the question of deep reality—his novels are as multi-layered as onions and as difficult to peel—but the principle of freedom and control. Anything that impinges upon the artist's ability to create a self-enclosed and self-determined world becomes a threat to his autonomy. And the major threat lies in the Freudian assertion that man is neither fully aware nor in control of his fears and desires. Nabokov's reality is generated and sustained by the artist, not the reality unlocked by the analyst. Nothing could be further from Nabokov's assumptions than a world in which dreams follow psychic, as opposed to artistic, laws and which contain meanings discoverable through the tools of psychoanalysis. Nabokov insists that only the artist can create magical reality; only the artist can lie truthfully. In *Pale Fire*, Kinbote mentions that " 'reality' is neither the subject nor the object of true art which creates its own special reality having nothing to do with the average 'reality' perceived by the communal eye" (p. 130). The artist's deceptions lead to freedom and independence; the psychoanalyst's deceptions lead to slavery. For Nabokov, the artist is married to creation, the analyst wedded to destruction.

Behind Nabokov's explicit rejection of psychology lies an implicit psychology of art: the belief that art and psychoanalysis exist at opposite poles of the imagination; the conviction that art, not analysis, is the last defense against suffering and injustice; the affirmation of the artist's autonomy amidst deterministic forces. Art and psychoanalysis represent good and evil, respectively, in Nabokov's world. Thus, Humbert begins his story in a psychopathic ward and drives his doctors crazy. One of Nabokov's earliest and most perceptive critics, Vladislav Khodasevich, wrote in 1937 that the basic theme to which the novelist returns is the "life of the artist and the life of a device in the consciousness of the artist." The artist or writer is never shown directly, however, but always behind a mask.[6] Art becomes a refuge or sanctuary, with the artist, not the therapist, as the real healer.

Contrary to Humbert's assertions, there is an implicit psychology underlying *Lolita*, and it involves Humbert, a lyrical writer, whose theme is the creation and preservation of his beloved nymphet as a delicately wrought object of art. Critics have noted the two Lolitas in the novel: the real Dolores Haze, whose coarse mannerisms and speech betray a satirical and often unflattering portrait of innocence and experience; and the symbolic or mythic Lolita, the creation of Humbert's imagination. There is an almost Platonic need to subordinate the real Dolly Haze to the alluring manmade fantasy of Lolita, to transmute fleshy reality into artistic purity. "What I had madly possessed was not she, but my own creation, another, fanciful Lolita—perhaps, more real than Lolita; overlapping, encasing her; floating between me and her, and having no will, no consciousness—indeed, no life of her own" (p. 64). Humbert loves the gum-chewing, comic-book-reading, hardened bobby-soxer, juvenile clichés and all; but he is more enchanted with his own autoerotic creation, the product of his febrile imagination. He cannot help rendering her into an object of art, a fictional love object in his own image. His imagination animates Lolita; without him, she cannot exist. Insofar as Lolita is created by Humbert, a diarist whose heroic faith in the power of language endows her with immortality, he becomes, like his own creator—Vladimir Nabokov—a rescuer and redeemer of beauty and truth.

It is Humbert's imagination, not his phallus, that is the vital energizing spirit behind his artistic creativity. "It is not the artistic aptitudes that are secondary sexual characters as some shams and shamans have said; it is the other way around: sex is but the ancilla of art" (p. 261). Yet, whichever theory of creativity one accepts, the psychoanalyst's or novelist's, Humbert's devotion to Lolita resides less in her body or sex than in his imaginative recreation of her. "I am not concerned with so-called 'sex' at all. Anybody can imagine those elements of animality. A greater endeavor lures me on: to fix once for all the perilous magic of nymphets" (p. 136). Whether or not we take seriously his self-proclaimed nympholepsy, his fascination for girl-children arises from a paradoxical union of "tender dreamy childishness and a kind of eerie vulgarity," a fusion of chaste and profane love. For all its eroticism, *Lolita* remains curiously suspicious of the biological components of sexuality. Like Pygmalion, Humbert demonstrates that the artist can rival God as the creator of life; but unlike the Greek sculptor, Humbert remains more infatuated with the inner artistic vision, the ravished bride of stillness whose flight and pursuit are forever frozen into marble immobility. Humbert inevitably loses Lolita, as all people must lose their loved ones; but through the creation of the manuscript, the writer preserves a merged relationship with her, a union that will never dissolve, not even after the deaths of Dolly Haze and Humbert Humbert. Artistic creation unites artist and subject in an ecstatic oneness suggestive of the mother-child relationship. Humbert's devotion to art may be seen as an attempt to master the inevitability of death and to recreate a new reality that will defy the ravages of time. The artist thus pursues a rescue fantasy in which the nymphet's unformed beauty is given shape and preserved from change.

At the risk of succumbing to clinical black magic, we may invoke briefly the voodooism of the Viennese witch doctor to explain Humbert's rescue fantasy. In "A Special Type of Choice of Object Made by Men" (1910), part of Freud's contributions to the psychology of love, the analyst discusses the phenomenon of rescue fantasies and the family romance. He lists four necessary preconditions for this type of object choice. First, there must be an injured third party, such as a husband, fiancé, or friend, who claims possession of the girl or woman in question. Second, the woman's fidelity or reliability must be open to question—either the faint hint of scandal attached to a married woman or the implication of an openly promiscuous way of life. This is often termed "love for a prostitute." This precondition is necessary, Freud says, because the man experiences jealousy toward the third party. "What is strange is that it is not the lawful possessor of the loved one who becomes the target for this jealousy, but strangers, making their appearance for the first time, in relation to whom the loved one can be brought under suspicion."[7] Third, instead of the woman's value being measured by her sexual integrity and correspondingly reduced by promiscuous behavior, as it is in "normal" love, the situation is reversed. A woman becomes more desirable as she approaches the behavior of a prostitute. The final precondition is that a man of this type expresses the need to rescue the woman he desires from ruin. "The man is convinced that she is in need of him, that without him she would lose all moral control and rapidly sink to a lamentable level" (p. 168).

The psychical origins of this type of love derive from the infantile fixation of tender feelings on the mother, Freud claims, and represent a consequence of that fixation. The love objects usually turn out to be mother surrogates, and the object from which he is rescuing the mother surrogate usually is the father. "It is at once clear that for the child who is growing up in the family circle the fact of the mother belonging to the father becomes an inseparable part of the mother's essence, and that the injured third party is none other than the father himself" (p. 169). To defend himself against the realization of incestuous attachment to the mother, the son divorces spiritual from sensual love. The split reveals the antithetical image of woman: the madonna and the prostitute. Freud links the rescue motif to the Oedipus complex (he uses the term for the first time in this essay) and relates it to the idea of the family romance he had discussed in the preface to Otto Rank's well-known book, *The Myth of the Birth of the Hero.* In the family romance the son exalts one or both of his parents in an effort to recreate the happy, vanished days of his childhood when his parents seemed to be the noblest and dearest of all people. In one of his most daring imaginative leaps in "A Special Type of Choice of Object Made by Men," Freud asserts that the son's need to rescue his mother acquires the significance of giving her a child in his own image:

> His mother gave him a life—his own life—and in exchange he gives her another life, that of a child which has the greatest resemblance to himself. The son shows his gratitude by wishing to have by his mother a son who is like himself: in other words, in the rescue-phantasy he is completely identifying himself with his father. All his instincts, those of tenderness, gratitude, lustfulness, defiance and independence, find satisfaction in the single wish *to be his own father.* Even the element of danger has not been lost in the change of meaning; for the act of birth itself is the danger from which he was saved by his mother's efforts (p. 173).

Without presuming to illuminate the mystery of *Lolita,* we may suggest that Humbert's rescue fantasy affirms the refuge of art, the only immortality he can bequeath upon his beloved Dolly. Just as the rescue fantasy implies a splitting of the mother image into the sacred and profane, so does Humbert see Lolita and all nymphets as a paradoxical fusion of tender dreamy childishness and eerie vulgarity. From a legal point of view, he kidnaps and corrupts an innocent adolescent; yet from the novelist's point of view, he attempts to rescue her from sordid reality and to worship her to the point of Mariolatry. There are several ironies surrounding Lolita's identity and Humbert's treatment of her. The innocent girl turns out to be far more sexually experienced than Humbert ever imagined, and it is she who seduces him. Although Humbert does not know this in advance, her desirability to him only increases when she is stolen by Quilty, the "injured third party" and the object of Humbert's rage. Humbert is less guilty of sexually violating Lolita than of attempting to control omnipotently her life and smothering her independence. Gladys M. Clifton is certainly correct when she argues that readers have tended to overvalue Humbert's perspective and to undervalue Lolita's.[8]

Ironically, although Humbert brutally thwarts Lolita's natural wishes for separation and independence, thus depriving her not only of her childhood but her right to choose her own adult life, he also unconsciously attempts to save her from the life experiences, particularly marriage and motherhood, that will eventually destroy her. The world of reality proves deadly to the doomed Lolita, not because Humbert is trying to extinguish her autonomy, but because the novel insists upon her premature crucifixion by time and the biological trap. Risking life and liberty for the pursuit of a cruel mistress, Humbert is the classic unrequited lover, betrayed by a woman who is unaware of his heroic sacrifice. This too is one of the preconditions Freud talks about in his analysis of the rescue fantasy. "By her propensity to be fickle and unfaithful the loved one brings herself into dangerous situations, and thus it is understandable that the lover should be at pains to protect her from these dangers by watching over her virtue and counteracting her bad inclinations" (p. 172). This is what Humbert does: He is an all-controlling father.

The little we learn about his own father is inconclusive evidence on which to speculate Humbert's relationship to the family romance. Besides, Nabokov is probably setting another trap for the psychoanalytic reader who is seeking a connection between the father and son. Humbert insists he adored his father, a strong, virile man. It may be that Humbert's attraction to the tomboyish quality of nymphets contains a bisexual element related to his identification with the father. "The specific psychological character of Humbert's perversion is very close to homosexuality," Andrew Field writes, emphasizing, however, that Humbert is not in fact homosexual.[9] By contrast, Quilty is homosexual and represents Humbert's perverse alter ego. Nabokov's parody of the double has been extensively explored.[10] Psychoanalytically, the phenomenon of the double affirms the ability to split off part of the self to maintain a cohesive identity. Quilty may be interpreted in several ways: a narcissistic extension of the self, a mirror image of Humbert's bad self, the human tendency toward duplication. Otto Rank's conclusion in his pioneering study, *The Double,* has interesting relevance to the Humbert-Quilty relationship. "So it happens that the double, who personifies narcissistic self-love, becomes an unequivocal rival in sexual love; or else, originally created as a wish-defense against a dreaded eternal destruction, he reappears in superstition as the messenger of death."[11] Compared to perverted Quilty, Humbert seems wondrously normal. Humbert refers to him as his brother, but he may also be the bad father in his unloving treatment of Lolita. Hence Humbert's need to murder him. Both men are artists, one an enormously prolific playwright, the other a lyrical-confessional novelist. Significantly, neither Quilty nor Humbert is procreative.

Lolita is a novel of passion but not procreation. The distinction is worth pursuing. The link among love, pregnancy, and death identifies the novel with fatal passion, destructive to the childbearing mother and aborted offspring. Lolita's death seems to be a punishment for her illicit love, illicit not from society's point of view but from Humbert's, the broken-hearted lover. The deaths of his first wife, Valeria, and eternal wife, Lolita, reveal a sterility associated with reality that sharply contrasts the fecundity of the artist's imagination. Lolita's creativity turns out to be literally a figment of Humbert's imagination. Feeling her warm weight in his lap, he remarks that he was "always 'with Lolita,' as a woman is 'with child' " (p. 109). As man and artist, Humbert embodies all the roles in the Freudian family romance. He is the loyal son devoted to the muse of invention; the mature lover or enchanted hunter in quest of his Mission Dolores; the spiritual father hovering over his child in an effort to protect her from inartistic lovers and from the mortal enemy of the nymphet, time; and the mother creator, always pregnant with Lolita, begetting and immortalizing her through the novelist's act of labor, the creation of art.

The Freudian interpretation of Humbert's rescue fantasy suggests an underlying Oedipal level of meaning, but, in light of more recent psychoanalytic research in the areas of ego psychology, identity formation, and separation and individuation, other meanings emerge from Lolita. Although, in his attack on psychoanalysis, Nabokov does not seem to be aware of ego psychology, the shift in emphasis away from instinctual drives to the defensive and adaptive functions of the autonomous ego, Humbert's commitment to art reveals an attempt to master fears of death and to preserve forever Lolita's beauty. This agrees with Phyllis Roth's conclusion that "despite his asseverations to the contrary, Nabokov, like others, employed his art to master fears, anxieties, and unacceptable desires, transforming them into a transcendent fiction which is acceptably 'aesthetic.' "[12] Paradoxically, the fear of death leads to the strongest affirmation of immortality, thus demonstrating Nabokov's triumphant assertion of individuality and free will. One of the mysteries of the novel is how Humbert can continue to idealize Lolita even after she repeatedly rejects him. But Nabokov also shows how the creative process resolves the dualistic tension between unity and separation. Before Humbert writes the manuscript, he is separated from Lolita; yet he fuses with her during the creative act to achieve a new union. And insofar as his story is intended for others to read and participate in, Nabokov affirms once again the paradox of separation and oneness that defines all interactions. Humbert's merging with a higher ideal that will outlive him has an undeniably therapeutic effect on him. "I see nothing for the treatment of my misery but the melancholy and very local palliative of articulate art" (p. 285). Humbert is the only therapist Nabokov celebrates, the creative artist, who rescues life from death, form from chaos, triumph from defeat.

Lolita also has interesting implications for Kohut's emerging self-psychology. Although Humbert sees Lolita with painful clarity, he also idealizes her and mirrors her self-love.[13] The act of writing resembles the mirroring and idealizing transference relationship that Kohut speaks about in the treatment of narcissistic personality disorders, though it is not necessary to label Humbert in pathological terms. Kohut's psychology, in fact, can be extended to normal personality development.[14] Viewed from this perspective, the creation of the manuscript allows Humbert to restore his damaged self by transmuting the object (or in Kohutian terms the self-object) of his autoerotic love, Lolita, into new internalizations. Through art he achieves a restoration of the self.

Lolita, then, is not exempt from its own unique subterranean mythic system and psychology. Curiously, Nabokov's story is a reversal of the fairy tale of the wolf and Little Red Riding Hood that Kinbote dismisses in *Pale Fire*. Fromm's interpretation, we recall, suggests that the wolf is made ridiculous in the attempt to imitate a pregnant woman by having a living being in its belly. Humbert does not eat Lolita, though he would like to. "My only grudge against nature was that I could not turn my Lolita inside out and apply voracious lips to her young matrix, her unknown heart, her nacreous liver, the sea-grapes of her lungs, her comely twin kidneys" (p. 167). Humbert first incorporates her into his imagination and then into the body of his art. Interestingly, in Nabokov's fairy tale the roles of the huntsman and wolf are reversed. Instead of rescuing the innocent teenager, the huntsman marries her, impregnates her, and fills her belly with the living thing that will eventually destroy her. As lover and husband, Dick Schiller is the unenchanted hunter. Life without art is sterile and meaningless. By contrast, the poetical wolf is the good father in his attempt to rescue his beloved daughter from Quilty's maltreatment and Schiller's artificial insemination. Despite the wolf's tyrannical control over her, neither his voracious appetite nor his deceptive identity has harmed the little girl. Fromm's interpretation of the classic fairy tale emphasizes the man's defeat in the Oedipal battle, but in Nabokov's transformation the wolf has the last word. He has swallowed the delicious girl and then given birth to a new Lolita who will outlive all the participants in the magical drama.

Given their differences over sex, love, psychoanalysis, and art, it is impossible to believe that Freud and Nabokov could ever agree on anything; yet, in the final analysis, there are surprising similarities between the two. The voodooism or black magic of the Viennese witch doctor parallels the marvelous spells and wiles of the novelist, who remains a trickster. In Nabokov's view, Freud is more of an artist (albeit a bad one) than a social scientist, and the Russian is always attempting to prove that his magic is more potent than the Viennese's. Indeed, Nabokov's sorcery may be viewed as an elaborate "disappearing act" to cast the psychoanalyst into the void, yet in a curious way he needed to keep Freud alive, if only to make him appear upon command in his forewords and fictions. Nabokov's criticisms of Freud may also be turned against the novelist. Rejecting Freud's labyrinthine symbolism and mythology ("something like searching for Baconian acrostics in Shakespeare's works"), Nabokov himself became, next to Joyce, the supreme fabulous artificer of twentieth-century literature. He has devised a fictional system of Baconian acrostics that has confounded a generation of literary critics eager to decipher hidden patterns and wicked word puzzles in his writings. Moreover, both men adapted their obsessional personalities to creative purposes. Freud's quest for knowledge and faith in his intellectual powers were matched by Nabokov's complete mastery and omnipotent control of his fictional universe. Freud's case studies probably contain no greater assortment of mad and eccentric characters than those found in Nabokov's stories, which present a dazzling array of psychopaths, sadists, perverts, paranoids, and suicides. Freud wrote like a novelist (when his name was mentioned for the Nobel Prize, it was more often for literature than for medicine), and Nabokov had the insight of a shrewd clinician. Both geniuses changed their professions in ways we are only beginning to understand. Each was fascinated by the other's field but also deeply ambivalent toward it. Although Freud's admiration for the artist is well known, he also disparaged him, reducing the man of letters to a neurotic[15] or a narcissist[16] and claiming that unlike the scientist, which he considered himself to be, the artist is incapable of abstinence[17] or renunciation.[18] Nabokov reciprocated these feelings with a vengeance.

Finally, both men had strong prejudices and, in affirming the autonomy of their separate disciplines, erred in ways that are not dissimilar. Not only does Freud equate art with the pleasure principle and science with the reality principle, he makes the astonishing statement that "We may lay it down that a happy person never phantasies, only an unsatisfied one."[19] The psychoanalyst can be guilty of the most outrageous pronouncements: "The 'creative' imagination, indeed, is quite incapable of *inventing* anything; it can only combine components that are strange to one another."[20] The assertion is no less startling than Nabokov's insistence that the artist's fictional universe remains fiercely independent of reality. "Literature was born not the day when a boy crying wolf, wolf came running out of the Neanderthal valley with a big gray wolf at his heels: literature was born on the day when a boy came crying, wolf, wolf and there was no wolf behind him" (*Lectures on Literature*, p. 5). Future scholars will no doubt explore the extent to which Nabokov's celebrated Wolf Man, Humbert Humbert, echoes the unheard cries of the young artist. Nor should this distress Nabokov's faithful readers. It is inconceivable that biographical knowledge will diminish the greatness of his achievement or the mystery of his art. As Freud prudently wrote, "Before the problem of the creative artist analysis must, alas, lay down its arms"—a truth and truce not even Nabokov would fail to heed.[21]

NOTES

The following editions by Nabokov are cited in the text. All references are to these editions. *Ada or Ardor: A Family Chronicle* (New York: McGraw-Hill, 1969); Alfred Appel, Jr., ed., *The Annotated Lolita* (New York: McGraw-Hill, 1970); Fredson Bowers, ed., *Lectures on Literature* (New York: Harcourt Brace Jovanovich, 1980); *Pale Fire* (New York: Putnam, 1962); *A Russian Beauty and Other Stories*

(New York: McGraw-Hill, 1973); *Speak, Memory: An Autobiography Revisited*, rev. ed. (New York: Putnam, 1966); *Strong Opinions* (New York: McGraw-Hill, 1973).

[1] Elizabeth Phillips, "The Hocus-Pocus of *Lolita*," *Literature and Psychology*, Vol. 10, No. 4 (Autumn 1960), p. 101. Phillips argues that in *Lolita* Nabokov is satirizing Marie Bonaparte's psychoanalytic study of Edgar Allan Poe.

[2] Van is referring to Freud's letter to Wilhelm Fliess, 19 February 1899, in which he alludes to an individual with a fantasy of being a "deflowerer" of every person he comes across. See Sigmund Freud, *The Origins of Psycho-Analysis* (New York: Basic Books, 1954), p. 278. After returning home from a trip to the Rockies, Nabokov wrote a letter to Edmund Wilson in August 1956 in which in a bemused tone he quotes from Freud's correspondence. "Incidentally, in one of his letters to Fliess the Viennese Sage mentions a young patient who masturbated in the w. c. of an Interlaken hotel in a special contracted position so as to be able to glimpse (now comes the Viennese Sage's curative explanation) the Jungfrau" (Simon Karlinsky, ed., *The Nabokov-Wilson Letters* [New York: Harper and Row, 1979], p. 300). Karlinsky misdates Freud's letter to Fliess to which Nabokov alludes. Interestingly, in *Lolita* there is a three-page account of Humbert's ecstatic masturbation in the presence of his "Jungfrau," the maiden Dolly Haze.

[3] Andrew Field, *Nabokov: His Life in Art* (Boston: Little, Brown, 1967), p. 338.

[4] See L. R. Hiatt, "Nabokov's *Lolita*: A 'Freudian' Cryptic Crossword," *American Imago*, Vol. 24 (1967), pp. 360–370. Hiatt argues that despite Nabokov's antipathy to psychoanalysis, he endows Humbert with the classic symptoms of an Oedipus complex. "Nabokov has given him an Oedipus complex; he has also given him a set of defences against self-understanding. He has, in addition, thrown up a smoke-screen to hide his hero's secret from public gaze. It is a strange game for an author to play. If he wins, the reader loses the point of the book" (p. 370).

[5] James R. Rambeau, "Nabokov's Critical Strategy," J. E. Rivers and Charles Nicol, eds., *Nabokov's Fifth Arc* (Austin: University of Texas Press, 1982), p. 30.

[6] Vladislav Khodasevich, "On Sirin," in Alfred Appel, Jr. and Charles Newman, eds., *Nabokov: Criticism, Reminiscences, Translations, and Tributes* (Evanston: Northwestern University Press, 1970), p. 100.

[7] Sigmund Freud, "A Special Type of Choice of Object Made by Men" (1910), *Standard Edition* (London: The Hogarth Press, 1957), Vol. XI, p. 167. All references are to this edition.

[8] Gladys M. Clifton, "Humbert Humbert and the Limits of Artistic License," J. E. Rivers and Charles Nicol, eds., *The Fifth Arc*, op. cit., p. 164.

[9] Field, *Nabokov: His Life in Art*, op. cit., p. 339. It is appropriate to mention here, as Field does in *Nabokov: His Life in Part* (New York: Viking, 1977), the "remarkable gallery of homosexual characters in Nabokov's writing" (p. 63). Psychoanalytic biographers may wish to explore the relationship between Nabokov's artistic preoccupation with homosexuality and his keen distress over his brother Sergei's homosexuality. Nabokov's maternal uncle, Vasily Ivanovich, was also homosexual. Field records Nabokov's inordinate difficulty in speaking about his brother's homosexuality despite the fact, as the biographer observes, that "I know well and with no possibility of error that Sergei's homosexuality was a subject about which his brother himself spoke with the greatest frankness and naturalness, even to his sisters and his mother" (*Nabokov: His Life in Part*, p. 13). Nabokov's father was an expert on the legal and social ramifications of homosexuality. According to Field, Vladimir Nabokov shared his father's belief that homosexuality was an illness transmitted by heredity. By contrast, a contemporary view would suggest that gender identity arises from psychological and interpersonal factors. In *The Nabokov-Wilson Letters*, Karlinsky mentions that Sergei died in a German concentration camp as a consequence of Hitler's campaign to exterminate homosexuals (p. 157, n. 4).

Nabokov's interest in homosexuality almost certainly derives from autobiographical concerns and, given his fascination with identical twins as well as his physical resemblance to Sergei (as suggested by a photograph of the two brothers in *Nabokov: His Life in Part*), it may be that his parody of the homosexual theme in the Humbert-Quilty *Doppelgänger* relationship and elsewhere is a defense against submerged bisexual drives and an effort to transform fears and anxieties into art.

[10] To cite but a few works: Claire Rosenfeld, "The Shadow Within: The Conscious and Unconscious Use of the Double," *Daedalus*, Vol. 92 (1963), pp. 326–344; Robert Rogers, *A Psychoanalytic Study of the Double in Literature* (Detroit: Wayne State University Press, 1970); Phyllis A. Roth, "The Psychology of the Double in Nabokov's *Pale Fire*," *Essays in Literature*, Vol. 2 (1975), pp. 209–229.

[11] Otto Rank, *The Double*, Harry Tucker, Jr., ed. and trans. New York: Meridian, 1979), p. 86. For an excellent study of Rank's importance as an unacknowledged forerunner of ego psychology and modern developmental theory, see Esther Menaker, *Otto Rank: A Rediscovered Legacy* (New York: Columbia University Press, 1982).

[12] Phyllis A. Roth, *The Fifth Arc*, J. E. Rivers and Charles Nicol, eds., op. cit., p. 44.

[13] Clifton points out in *The Fifth Arc*, J. E. Rivers and Charles Nicol, eds., op. cit., that the most convincingly erotic passage in the novel "is not one in which Humbert actually possesses Lolita but one which involves masturbation" (p. 167).

[14] See, for example, Robert D. Stolorow and Frank M. Lachman, *Psychoanalysis of Developmental Arrests* (New York: International Universities Press, 1980) and Arnold Goldberg, ed., *Advances in Self Psychology* (New York: International Universities Press, 1980).

[15] Sigmund Freud, *Introductory Lectures on Psycho-Analysis*, Part III (1916–1917), *Standard Edition* (London: The Hogarth Press, 1963), Vol. XVI, pp. 375–376.

[16] Stanley A. Leavy, trans., *The Freud Journal of Lou Andreas-Salomé* (New York: Basic Books, 1964), p. 109.

[17] Sigmund Freud, " 'Civilized' Sexual Morality and Modern Nervous Illness" (1908), *Standard Edition* (London: The Hogarth Press, 1959), Vol. IX, p. 197.

[18] Sigmund Freud, "Formulations on the Two Principles of Mental Functioning" (1911), *Standard Edition* (London: The Hogarth Press, 1958), Vol. XII, p. 224.

[19] Sigmund Freud, "Creative Writers and Day-Dreaming" (1908), (London: The Hogarth Press, 1959), *Standard Edition*, Vol. IX, p. 146.

[20] Sigmund Freud, *Introductory Lectures on Psycho-Analysis*, Part II (1915–1916), *Standard Edition* (London: The Hogarth Press, 1961), Vol. XV, p. 172.

[21] Sigmund Freud, "Dostoevsky and Parricide," (1928), *Standard Edition* (London: The Hogarth Press, 1961), Vol. XXI, p. 177.

John Haegert

THE AMERICANIZATION
OF HUMBERT HUMBERT

That is the true myth of America. She starts old, old, wrinkled and
writhing in an old skin. And there is a gradual sloughing off of the old
skin, towards a new youth. It is the myth of America.
— D. H. Lawrence, *Studies in Classic American Literature*

"**I** am an American writer, born in Russia and educated in England where I
studied French literature, before spending fifteen years in Germany."[1] Thus Vladimir
Nabokov described the circuitous process, begun twenty-four years earlier, of
evolving a new American identity and adapting it to his European past. Readers
of *Lolita* (1955) have long noted a comparable effort of assimilation in the creation of his only "American" novel and of its émigré protagonist, Humbert Humbert.
Despite his persistent disclaimer that "There is nothing autobiographic in *Lolita*,"[2]
Nabokov's critics have repeatedly stressed the many striking affinities between
Humbert's uneasy life in Ramsdale and Beardsley and his creator's early émigré
years in the northeastern United States.[3] It has often been observed that Humbert's
fervid desire for the eternal nymphet is similar to, if not actually derived from, the
many quests for some imperishable ideal embodied in Poe and Hawthorne and,
indeed, in much subsequent American fiction.[4] Humbert's energetic pursuit of his
"ultraviolet darling" across the American dreamscape has also received pointed
attention, and, of course, Nabokov's own Homeric attempts to master the *poshlost*
and dreary Philistinism of middle-class American life have become all but legendary
in our time.[5]

Questions spring to mind when so overt an appeal is made to American
themes and sources. In what ways may *Lolita* be expressive not only of Nabokov's
perennial concerns (namely, art and the aesthetic imagination) but of a new and
pressing interest in securing an American identity? What does that vague term
American Novel mean after all, and of what use is it when applied to the work of

From *ELH* 52, No. 3 (Fall 1985): 777–94.

a writer so conspicuously international in outlook? In light of Nabokov's concerted attempt to reclaim America for his own creative purposes, it may prove fruitful to reexamine *Lolita,* both as an American novel and as a work of émigré fiction, in an effort to see how its celebrated theme of the wayward artist is imbued with a characteristically American resonance.

It is a commonplace, and rightly so, that *Lolita* underscores the enduring conflict between the claims of the imagination—especially when it is drawn to some aesthetic ideal—and the obligations and infringements of everyday reality.[6] Exploring this tension in depth, the novel deals centrally with Humbert's fantastic attempt to revive the past and incarnate an impossible vision of imperishable bliss. That the vision thus embodied is actually a human child, and an all-American one at that, is for Humbert only a minor obstacle in an otherwise all-consuming passion: the gradual absorption of Lolita into a changeless realm "where nothing mattered, save the infusion of joy brewed within my body."[7] So conceived in the novel, Humbert's crazed obsession with Lolita is less a matter of physical desire than of aesthetic compulsion, and less a matter of either than of metaphysical envy. As Alfred Appel has argued, Humbert's insatiable need to "fix once for all the perilous magic of nymphets" (136) is not merely cause for amusement, it is an occasion for Nabokov's "devastating criticism of the reflexive attempt to move out of time."[8] The novel traces his farcical attempt to thwart time, then, but also his developing sense of doom before time's irresistible encroachments. The countermovement to its theme of "nympholeptic" bliss is Humbert's growing awareness, throughout part two, that his idealizing efforts have been both aesthetically futile and morally transgressive, insofar as they have led him to inflict his desires on Lolita and thus deprive her of her childhood and her status as an independent being.[9]

Whether Humbert really achieves such awareness has been widely contested, of course. Some would have it that for once John Ray, Jr.—the fictitious pedant who "preambulates" the narrative—is reliable when he describes the book as "a tragic tale tending unswervingly to nothing less than a moral apotheosis" (7), while others would see Humbert's "confession" as nothing more than a virtuoso performance: an artfully contrived *apologia* designed to stimulate his readers' sympathies and recast his misdeeds as the aberrations of genius. My aim here is not to resolve this issue, but to point out that the perplexing ambiguities inherent in Humbert's motives are not confined to his "aesthetic" interests, properly so-called, nor even, strictly speaking, to his relationship with Lolita; insofar as they define his character they arise as well from his ambivalent role as an émigré hero: that of a wandering, ill-fated exile uneasily suspended between two conflicting sets of cultural values. For in the final analysis, as has been said, *Lolita* is not only or even primarily " 'about' literary originality, creative language, art in general, or *any* similar abstraction."[10] As a novel of character (rather than a self-reflexive fiction like *Pale Fire*), it is chiefly concerned to demonstrate the complexities of human behavior and experience in a particular time and space; including, it should be noted, the very American space to which Humbert Humbert feels himself condemned.

Behind all the familiar oppositions of the book—the conflict between Lolita as daemonic temptress and Lolita as prepubescent brat, the conflicts between art and nature and between imagination and reality—looms the greatest and most potent of American polarities: the legendary conflict between New World possibilities and Old World sensibilities. And Humbert himself is the pivotal figure in Nabokov's interpretation of this most fundamental of American myths. Humbert does not of course "represent" Europe any more than Lolita "embodies" America: as Nabokov insists in his afterword to the first American edition, nothing is more alien to the spirit of the novel than the "idiotic" imposition of such allegorical equivalences. As an émigré protagonist, on the other hand, Humbert serves to qualify the equally allegorical view that *Lolita* is essentially a timeless fable of the artistic life. Recent criticism, for example, stressing the psycho-autobiographic sources of Humbert's story, has often contended that in the portrayal of his feckless hero, Nabokov was in part attempting to exorcize an unwanted "double": the solipsistic artist who is indifferent to human needs and human suffering.[11] In this view, Humbert's molestation of Lolita is symptomatic of the artist's own voyeuristic velleities and desires, his "unnatural" tendency to preempt and transform reality, to arrest it—as we have seen—at a moment of imaginative perfection. My own consideration of the text as an exemplary work of émigré fiction is meant to offer a complementary argument: namely, that Humbert's evolving attitude toward Lolita reflects (to use no stronger a word) his creator's changing and generally much-improved estimate of American life. Viewed from this perspective, as we shall see, Humbert's ambivalent search for "his" lost Lolita in the last third of the book enacts an émigré's quest for a truer vision of his host environment—an America no longer seen as a nubile, nymphet in need of European refinement, but as an estimable independent spirit requiring (and deserving) a national identity of her own.

To specify the émigré character of Humbert's life does not, of course, give a complete account of *Lolita;* but it can help to illuminate the novel's unique and in many ways anomalous position in American literature. There is a Humbert Humbert in all of us, a capacity for pride and its consequence, damnation. And this pride is of the most inviting and seductive kind—not pride of place or position or wealth, but pride of the intellect: the beguilingly insidious idea that we know more than others and are somehow wiser and better than they are. Other people should automatically admire us, and our inner life should likewise be a kind of pleasing dream, without the prehistoric monsters or the modern gargoyles always looming up in the shadows behind us or around us. Pride and its deceptiveness are, of course, the subject of all serious literature from *Oedipus Rex* through *Faust* to *Remembrance of Things Past.* But in *Lolita* this legendary theme acquires a unique cultural importance through its association with the other great legend, Humbert and Lolita's, which is in part the legend of America as a whole and of its historical relationship to Europe.

Again it would be a mistake to oversimplify the Old World–New World antithesis in *Lolita,* as if the novel were an extended vindication of American vulgarity (Lolita) over European gentility (Humbert), or vice versa. As Nabokov pointedly remarked in refuting the charge of anti-Americanism leveled against the book: " . . . [I]n regard to philistine vulgarity there is no intrinsic difference between Palearctic manners and Nearctic manners. Any proletarian from Chicago can be as bourgeois (in the Flaubertian sense) as a duke" (317).[12] I would add, however, that the complex issue of Humbert's intellectual pride and moral depravity is often simplified by regarding it as a purely "aesthetic" problem, to be pondered apart from the peculiar historical and cultural circumstances underlying it. To understand the cause of his obsessive behavior toward Lolita, we must consider his character not only as a self-conscious "poet"—the usual view—but as a cultural exile: an American ethnic hero, albeit a very sorry one, whose ignoble fate it is to wander aimlessly with Lolita along the margins and byways of American society, *sans* roots, *sans* family, *sans* anything save his glorious memories of an older European world.

In that shimmering Riviera world, the splendid Hotel Mirana owned by his father "revolved as a kind of private universe, a whitewashed cosmos within the blue greater one that blazed outside" (12). To be sure, the privileged world of the Mirana—with its wealthy American ladies leaning toward him "like Towers of Pisa"—does not represent Europe, pure and simple, for, obviously, all the other characters and places associated with his youth are European as well. Yet it represents one of its most distinctive features, and since it constitutes Humbert's earliest and fondest memory, it is also the most plainly evocative one. There is also a recurring perspective in the novel as a whole through which the circumstances and events of Humbert's early life become generalized and at which level Europe is not merely a "salad of racial genes" (like his Franco-Austrian father) but an integration, any one of whose parts is representative and typical. For example, when Humbert recounts the sad story of his Annabel "phase," he reflects, somewhat pompously even for him: "Our brains were tuned the way those of intelligent European preadolescents were in our day and set, and I doubt if much individual genius should be assigned to our interest in the plurality of inhabited worlds, competitive tennis, infinity, solipsism and so on" (14). Presumably "individual genius" is not required of such preadolescents because an archetypal genius, European and upper class, animates their various nationalities, knitting them together in their knowledge of things like infinity and solipsism, to which their brains are precociously "tuned."

The importance of Europe in *Lolita*, however, is not merely that it provides a unified perspective on Humbert's early life. It also underlies and informs all of his subsequent impressions of America. In explaining the origin of his incurable "nympholepsy," for example, Humbert argues that his infatuation with Lolita was prompted by an earlier "prototype"—the half-English, half-Dutch Annabel—whose tragic and untimely death had introduced him to the idyllic raptures of unrequited love and impelled him to "incarnate" her being in another: "All I want to stress is that my discovery of [Lolita] was a fatal consequence of that 'princedom by the sea' in my tortured past. Everything between the two events was but a series of gropings and blunders, and false rudiments of joy" (42). The argument may well be specious, not to say self-serving, as some have suggested; but it underscores a tendency toward narrative repetition and reconstruction which is entirely characteristic of

Humbert and which, in its own way, is premonitory of that wider pattern of Nabokovian parody and coincidence for which the novel itself has been alternatively celebrated and condemned.[13] Culturally speaking, the argument suggests what is obvious enough in other ways throughout the book—that Humbert regards his new American life as a mere succession of "gropings and blunders," and America itself as a pale imitation or parody of "prototypical" Europe.

Thus America is generalized and an an "American character" is adduced in the "horrible hybridization" of the Haze household. Humbert is prospecting for suitable lodgings in Ramsdale and wondering how, in heaven's name, he can elude the predatory Charlotte. He then recapitulates the hopeless decor of her home:

> I could not be happy in that type of household with bedraggled magazines on every chair and a kind of horrible hybridization between the comedy of so-called "functional modern furniture" and the tragedy of decrepit rockers and rickety lamp tables with dead lamps. I was led upstairs, and to the left—into "my" room. I inspected it through the mist of my utter rejection of it; but I did discern above "my" bed René Prinet's "Kreutzer Sonata." And she called that servant maid's room a "semi-studio"! (39–40)

For Humbert, the "hybridization" here is an ordeal which his "old world politeness" obliges him to endure. In its way it is expressive of that wider hybridization—of past and present, Old World and New, Europe and America—that for Nabokov typifies American middle-class life (especially in the East) and that so accurately defines the deracinated condition of his hero.

Thus when Humbert, the émigré scholar, first arrives in New York, he is compelled to pursue two incommensurable jobs—one devising and editing perfume ads for his uncle's company, the other composing a comparative history of French literature for English-speaking students. "As I look back on those days," he reflects, "I see them divided tidily into ample light and narrow shade: the light pertaining to the solace of research in palatial libraries, the shade to my excruciating desires and insomnias of which enough has been said" (34). It is as if the incongruities of his émigré life serve to objectify the inner divisions of his psychic life. Still later, in the wake of a nervous breakdown, he sets out with an expedition into the Canadian wilderness, attaching himself as a "recorder of psychic reactions." (The decisively American caste of the expedition is enhanced by the site of their weather station, based on "Pierre Point in Melville Sound"!) Even under the "translucent" Arctic sky there would seem to be no reprieve from the horrible hybridization of his new life. Notwithstanding the sexual favors of the camp nutritionist, Humbert is alternately bemused and appalled by the motley conditions of the camp itself, where, among other staples of American life, supplies are said to include "the Reader's Digest, an ice cream mixer, chemical toilets, and paper hats for Christmas" (35).

By the time he reaches Ramsdale and his "fate," therefore, Humbert's initiation into the hybrid texture of American life is well under way, if by no means complete. What it has taught him can be readily surmised not only from his reaction to

Charlotte's home, already cited, but from his early descriptions of Lolita herself. More than anything else, we are told, she is a maddening "mixture" of discordant qualities. On the one hand, she is all "tender dreamy childishness" and innocence; on the other, she is said to embody an "eerie vulgarity" which combines "the blurry pinkness of adolescent maid servants in the Old Country" with the harsh corruption of their counterparts—the "very young harlots disguised as children in provincial brothels." And these qualities in turn, of course, get all "mixed up" in Humbert's mind with the immemorial memory of Annabel, his "Riviera love," "so that above and over everything there is—Lolita" (46–47).

It would appear, in fact, that Humbert's so-called portrait of Lolita—her alleged individualization of "the writer's ancient lust"—is itself a highly hybridized affair, one that mixes an equal and abundant measure of cant, hypocrisy, egotism, and willful self-delusion. Moreover, it is as much a cultural statement as an aesthetic one, and constitutes an extended variation on Humbert's view of America as a whole. Encoded in his attempt to portray her fatal attractiveness and daemonic charm, therefore, is an émigré perspective that laments the insubstantiality of American society and, by implication, apostrophizes Europe. Thus in emphasizing "what is most singular" about Lolita, he in fact does just the opposite; that is, he treats her "twofold nature" as a transcendental type or category—the enigmatic "nymphet"—to the exclusion of anything materially concrete about her, including her own national identity, In such a perspective even her quintessentially American vulgarity, so amusing to most readers, is only an analogue of an earlier European decadence. Hence Humbert's exclusive reliance upon continental prototypes and precursors ("adolescent maid servants in the Old Country") as a means of mitigating her corruption and of reattaching it to that saturnalia of "nymphic" symptoms by which Lolita and her like are separated from their ordinary, earthbound sisters. In the middle-class world of Ramsdale, evidently, American vulgarity is an excusable offence only when accompanied by a European pedigree.

From Humbert's point of view, it might be said, all regions of America are necessarily middle class, in the sense that they seek to mimic in a makeshift and thoroughly middling way the ostentatious splendors of Europe. (Consider his description of Pavor Manor, for example, Quilty's home in Parkington: a combination brothel, pleasure palace, and medieval castle.) Seldom in his account, therefore, is American life shown to be a distinct if variable experience, worthy of sustained exploration and discovery. More often than not, it is portrayed as a ghostly and degenerate version of his European past—as when, for instance, he strives to create "a morning illusion of Venice when actually it was Pennsylvania and rain" (147), or when, attempting to replicate "the crisp charm, the sapphire occasion and rosy contingency of my Riviera romance" (169), he is confounded by the foul weather and "matter-of-fact mist" of the New England coast. Indeed, every time that Humbert tries to recapture some memorable moment of his European "phase," he invariably encounters obstacles and disappointments that come as a series of abrasive shocks to his émigré sensibility and make him feel like the displaced person that he is. Thus in his relationship with Lolita—Nabokov's stric-

tures notwithstanding—we see European culture and experience trying to sup-
press and "solipsize" American otherness, the Old World expressing its incestuous
disdain for the New. So fervent is Humbert's desire to recast Lolita in the role of
her European predecessor, complete with stage props and dramatic settings, that
there is something faintly onanistic in his efforts. After wresting her away from
Ramsdale, for example, he deliberately intensifies his lust by resorting to imaginary
reconstructions and reminders of his original "Riviera romance." In his own words:
my "search for a Kingdom by the Sea, a sublimated Riviera, or whatnot, far from
being the impulse of the subconscious, has become the rational pursuit of a purely
theoretical thrill" (169).

Rational or not, Humbert's energetic embrace of Old World stereotypes in
preference to native American realities inspires fierce and prolonged resistance,
not only from his nubile quarry but from the hybrid culture of which she is a part.
For in a very real sense, it is not Lolita or even Quilty who is his chief antagonist and
"nemesis" (as Humbert would have us believe). Rather, the agent of his undoing is
his own inability—cultural as well as aesthetic—to participate in the plenitude of
American life on its own terms, without some mediating vision of Europe to direct
and control it. In the light of such visions, not only American culture is anomalous
and disordered. Seemingly, the enormous continent itself—with its immense profusion of forests, deserts, and mountains ("altitudinal failures as Alps go")—is but a
grotesque distortion of a more serene and civilized European ideal. Recalling his
"hopeless hauntings of public parks in Europe," for example, Humbert expresses his
dismay at the difficulty of ravishing nymphets in the "never Arcadian" American
wilderness:

> But in the wilds of America the open-air lover will not find it easy to indulge
> in the most ancient of all crimes and pastimes. Poisonous plants burn his
> sweetheart's buttocks, nameless insects sting his; sharp items of the forest
> floor prick his knees, insects hers; and all around there abides a sustained
> rustle of potential snakes—*que dis je,* of semi-extinct dragons!—while crablike
> seeds of ferocious flowers cling, in a hideous green crust, to gartered black
> sock and sloppy white sock alike. (170)

In the spectral glow of memory, even his immediate impressions of the land prove
disconcertingly surreal.

Inevitably, then, the New World that emerges in *Lolita* is a world already
mired in *poshlost* and suffused with satire. For Humbert, obviously, it is the middle-
class world of Ramsdale and Charlotte Haze, with her passion for "culture" and
exotic books. Less obviously but more generally, it is the rootless American world
at large, represented by the myriad motor courts, movie theaters, public parks, and
roadside restaurants that litter the landscape throughout part two, and whose
purely commercial culture embraces both the pornography of a Clare Quilty and
the "progressivism" of a Miss Pratt—headmistress of the Beardsley School for Girls,
where America's future mothers are forever instilled with the utilitarian value of
"the Four D's: Dramatics, Dance, Debating and Dating" (179). Although Nabokov
often expressed delight in its creation, it should be emphasized that the New

World so hilariously and savagely evoked in the novel is a world directly presided over by Humbert, not his creator.[14] (Sensitive to this point, Nabokov will often underscore the discrepancy between his own and Humbert's views by having the latter repeatedly avow either the vagueness or the artfulness of his recollections.) In so far as we have a vision of America in the book, it is a vision not once but twice removed from reality—a Nabokovian rendering of a character's reminiscence. And like so many other elements in Humbert's self-serving account, it is largely a fictionalized projection, the effect of which is to enhance his émigré memories and legitimize his émigré desires.

Whatever the precise degree of Humbert's unreliability, there can be no doubt that his denigration of America is designed, at least in part, to rationalize his relationship with Lolita and endow his criminal conduct with a sense of high heroic purpose. So committed is he to the monumental task of self-exoneration that he comes to see himself—and so to portray himself—as a kind of émigré quester in an alien wasteland, seeking the coveted Grail of his European past amid the resplendent ruins of America. Traveling with Lolita during their first cross-country odyssey, he recalls how "Treasured recollections of my father's palatial hotel sometimes led me to seek [in vain] for its like in the strange country we traveled through" (149). Later "that mad year" (August 1947 to August 1948), as Lolita's mutinies grow more frequent and ferocious, he tries to improve her temper by teaching her tennis; in the process he is able to forget his troubles and, for a few halcyon moments, "relive the days when in a hot gale, a daze of dust, and queer lassitude, I fed ball after ball to gay, innocent, elegant Annabel ..." (164). Such moments of self-forgetfulness are admittedly few and far between, but they point to a persistent pattern of his émigré life. As its more or less circular movement attests, Humbert's vertiginous flight with Lolita across America (beginning with "a series of wiggles and whorls in New England" and "petering out in the college town of Beardsley" [156]) brings him not renewal but regression, not a new beginning but only another return—the eastward arc of their travels describing a journey back to America's New England origins when Europe still exerted an irresistible hold on American life. Consequently, Humbert's extensive and often-quoted account of their itinerary (156–68) is not, properly speaking, a description at all. For all its vaunted accuracy and amplitude, it amounts to little more than an exotic clutter of American names spanning the continent in featureless profusion, like the faded entries in a collection of "ruined tour books." Only in retrospect—after his nymphet has departed—does America slowly begin to impress itself on his consciousness as a distinct cultural presence with a coherent sense of place independent of his émigré dreams of an earlier world. Until then, its only apparent function in his wandering life is to provoke his fantasies and increase his homelessness. "We had been everywhere. We had really seen nothing," Humbert sadly recalls. "And I catch myself thinking today that our long journey had only defiled with a sinuous trail of slime the lovely, trustful, dreamy, enormous country that by then ... was no more to us than a collection of dogeared maps, ruined tour books, old tires, and her sobs in the night ..." (177–78).

Thus in comparing himself throughout the book to Poe as well as to much greater artists such as Virgil, Dante, and Petrarch ("nympholepts" all), Humbert is not merely establishing ample erotic precedent for his own misconduct. He is also identifying himself as one of a noble company of spiritual explorers whose illustrious peregrinations throughout human history he can liken to his own. Humbert as pilgrim, in fact, embodies a crucial dimension both of the New World experience and of his own illicit relationship with Lolita. Imprisoned in the present indicative of his new American life, he is nonetheless driven, as we have seen, to repeat the past, to search for some supreme, unutterable consummation whose final object lies far beyond and above the nubile, mortal clay of Lolita, who is its ostensible object. Lolita, it has often been said, is valuable to Humbert not only as sexual object but as aesthetic possibility: her "nymphetage" and inexperience allow her to be "safely solipsized" by Humbert's haunted imagination. This is certainly true; yet even here, in the "umber and black Humberland" of their private and secluded world, Nabokov has rung in his own characteristic cultural complexities. For at the center of their relationship proper lies not only the relationship between Europe and America, but also the ambiguous interaction between the contradictory impulses of Europe that led to the original settling of America: commercialism and transcendentalism. The contradictory nature of the two impulses has been described by Van Wyck Brooks (who could well have been Humbert's philosopher in these matters) in his *The Wine of the Puritans* as follows:

> You put the old wine [Europeans] into new bottles [American continent] . . . and when the explosion results, one may say, the aroma passes into the air and the wine spills on the floor. The aroma or the ideal, turns into transcendentalism and the wine or the real, becomes commercialism.[15]

Throughout American history, Van Wyck Brooks suggests, the two impulses have a way of being both radically exclusive and mutually confusing, the one melting into the other: the human faculty of wonder, on the one hand, and the power and beauty of things, on the other. Perhaps no one better understood these competing drives of the American psyche than William Carlos Williams, who in his imaginative reconstruction of America's colonial past, *In the American Grain,* accords them definitive expression in two antithetical figures of American life and legend: Benjamin Franklin and Daniel Boone. For Williams, Franklin's deification of "industriousness" and "frugality" expresses a purely commercial desire to dominate and improve the environment, to render it amenable to practical use; whereas Boone's near-mystical attachment to the Kentucky wilderness suggests a purely "aesthetic" perception of the land in all its wondrous plenitude and otherness: "The beauty of a lavish, primitive embrace in savage, wild beast and forest rising above the cramped life about him possessed him wholly. Passionate and thoroughly given he avoided the half logic of stealing from the immense profusion."[16] While Williams's sympathies as a poet are obviously with Boone, the historical perspective generated by his book compels a conclusion quite similar to Brooks's: as the country grew older and as Americans themselves became more conscious of their national identity, these once archetypal attitudes toward the New World became blurred and indistinct, often manifesting themselves at the same time, indeed in the same person.

Lolita dramatizes this continuing ambiguity directly in the life of Humbert and retrospectively by a glance at rural America at the end of the novel. It does so especially in the once-notorious chapter 13 (part one), which describes Humbert's first—and conceivably last—ecstatic moment with Lolita, a moment when his imagination seems on the verge of entering an earthly paradise. As Lolita sits squirming in his berobed lap in the Haze living room, Humbert triumphantly reflects:

> I entered a plane of being where nothing mattered, save the infusion of joy brewed within my body. What had begun as a delicious distension of my innermost roots became a glowing tingle which *now* had reached that state of absolute security, confidence and reliance not found elsewhere in conscious life. With the deep hot sweetness thus established and well on its way to the ultimate convulsion, I felt I could slow down in order to prolong the glow. Lolita had been safely solipsized.   (62)

The emphasis in the passage of Humbert's "joy" and "security" hardly needs comment, or the sexuality, immature in Lolita's case and illicit in Humbert's—or the solipsizing process whereby Humbert seeks to enter an ideal realm "where nothing mattered." For these are the central symbols of his émigré life: the cultured European imagination trying to transfigure the as-yet-unfinished, though potentially beautiful American object. But, of course, Lolita can be neither solipsized nor transfigured completely, any more than the North Atlantic coast can be transformed into a "Sublimated Riviera" or the American wilderness into an "Arcardian" paradise. Behind the rhetorical rapture of his prose Humbert's moment of ecstasy remains a purely onanistic act, a solitary indulgence in which Lolita herself is both idealized and ignored, elevated and exploited.

The conflicting impulses at work in Humbert's "moment" accurately identify his character and condition in the New World. Confronted with the raw material and "immense profusion" of the land, he is impelled to reconstruct them in his own image—to impose his outworn idealizations upon them; in the process, as the novel makes clear, he robs them of their native beauty and individual identity. (Thus he may scoff at the protective mimicry and hybridization of American life; but have not his own idealizations of Lolita been at bottom a form of mimicry, a way of replicating his European past—as exemplified by Annabel—and grafting it to his American present?) The ambiguities inherent in Humbert's motives derive then not merely from his contradictory attitudes toward art, sex, fate, or even the moral implications of his "confession"—important as these are to any overall estimate of his character. As much as anything, the ambivalence of his behavior reflects a self-conscious attempt to reconcile the equal but divergent interests of his émigré heart: the commercial impulse to dominate and exploit things, on the one hand, and the transcendental impulse to idealize and transform them, on the other.

This ambidextrous attempt is inscribed on nearly every page of Humbert's narrative, complexly mixed with intermittent recognition of failure. Early in his "confession" we hear of the exalted artistry and sublime madness required to appreciate the nonhuman nature of nymphets; two pages later he alludes to that "incomparably more poignant bliss" (20) unceasingly bestowed by the ardors of nympholepsy; and on the next page he solemnly salutes Virgil, Dante, and Petrarch as his illustrious predecessors in the privileged art of pedophilia. Yet only two pages after that we find him sternly rebuking himself for his "degrading and dangerous desires" (23). Indeed, in the very passage devoted to the poignant bliss of nympholepsy, he also refers to "the dimmest of my pollutive dreams" (20). Midway through the book he is describing his sexual appetites as "monstrous," yet within thirty pages he reiterates his contention that "there is no other bliss on earth comparable to that of fondling a nymphet" (168). These are not isolated examples, either, for almost every page reveals Humbert's maddening ambivalence toward his own behavior, as well as his conflicting attitudes toward Lolita. As the incarnation of his émigré dreams, Lolita is nothing less—and ultimately nothing more—than his adored enchantress, an "ultraviolet darling" made miraculously manifest to his unworthy and unsuspecting eye; this Lolita must be carefully preserved and protected. But as a flesh-and-blood child, she is little more than the wayward daughter of Charlotte Haze, an all-American brat of dubious taste and even more dubious virtue; this Lolita must be carefully suppressed and controlled. "To the wonderland I had to offer," Humbert complains of this other Lolita, "my fool preferred the corniest movies, the most cloying fudge. To think that between a hamburger and a humburger, she would—invariably, with icy precision—plump for the former. There is nothing more atrociously cruel than an adored child" (168). The conflict that Humbert is vainly attempting to resolve, in other words, consists in his contradictory impulses toward the idealization of Lolita (which he achieves only in fantasy or in the quiet "refuge of art") and the subjugation of her to the practical imperatives of adult experience and consciousness. These impulses are, in an important respect, the same impulse: they both imply the repudiation of Lolita as an autonomous being, and they are both symptomatic as well of his perennial inability to adopt a consistent posture toward his new American life.

To the extent that Humbert's passion for Lolita embodies an unstable union of spirit and substance, of dream and reality, his relationship to her represents a dramatization of the basic thesis proposed by Brooks and Williams: that America had produced an idealism so impalpable that it had lost touch with reality and a materialism so intractable that it became corrupt. (Hence Humbert's endless ambivalence toward his own obsessions, and hence too his curious identification with Clare Quilty, whom he regards first with aversion as his "nemesis" and then with affinity as his "brother.") The novel as a whole offers another elaboration on this American legend, with the impossible idealism trying to actualize itself, to its utter destruction, in the gross materiality. As Humbert acknowledges, in one of his most impressive moments of self-analysis in the book: "It had become gradually clear to my conventional Lolita during our singular and bestial cohabitation that even the most miserable of family lives was better than the parody of incest, which, in the long run, was the best I could offer the waif" (289). Yet he imagines still—so resilient is his passion, so enduring are his delusions—that even in death, if only in death, they will find eventual union in the consoling eternality of art: "I am thinking of aurochs and angels, the secret of durable pigments, prophetic sonnets, the refuge of art. And this is the only immortality you and I may share, my Lolita" (311).

Thus Nabokov multiplies the ambiguities and ironies of Humbert's life, but does so in a way that deeply implicates his aesthetic obsessions with his temporal fate as an émigré in an unsettled, expanding, traditionless culture. No one knows better than Humbert, of course, that nothing could finally match the splendors of his own imagination—least of all a churlish and wily nymphet determined to resist him—and the novel would suggest finally that not only had his aesthetic vision of Lolita been corrupted but that it was, in part anyway, necessarily corrupted, for it asked too much. Nothing of this earth, even the most beautiful of earthly objects, could be anything but a perversion of it. *Lolita,* it is often said, is a powerful demonstration of this idea and constitutes a severe and fundamental challenge to the aesthetic ideal. Yet even here, in portraying his hero's downfall, Nabokov may properly be said to generate an essentially émigré perspective on events. After Lolita runs off, therefore, Humbert slowly begins to reconstruct her true and quintessentially American worth. He recalls her moments of unguarded inwardness and grace, her untutored sensitivity and depth—as well as his own tyrannical authority and possessiveness. Too late, he reflects that there was in her "a garden and a twilight, and a palace gate—dim and adorable regions which happened to be lucidly and absolutely forbidden to me, in my polluted rags and miserable convulsions" (286). But perhaps most significant of all, it is in the context of his newly awakened affection for the "lovely, trustful, dreamy, enormous" American continent that Humbert's dramatic reappraisal of Lolita begins—a point symbolically strengthened by the fact that she makes good her escape from him on the Fourth of July. The terms of that emerging affection may be best suggested by a final quotation, one of Nabokov's recorded favorites, taken from the conclusion of the novel. Having just murdered Quilty—his "nemesis" and his "brother"—Humbert recalls the time, soon after Lolita's disappearance from his life, when he had stopped along a mountain road in Colorado. Looking into "its friendly abyss," he heard a "melodious unity" of children's voices emanating from the valley town below:

> What I heard was but the melody of children at play, nothing but that, and so limpid was the air that within this vapor of blended voices, majestic and minute, remote and magically near, frank and divinely enigmatic—one could hear now and then, as if released, an almost articulate spurt of vivid laughter, or the crack of a bat, or the clatter of a toy wagon, but it was all really too far for the eye to distinguish any movement in the lightly etched streets. I stood listening to that musical vibration from my lofty slope, to those flashes of separate cries with a kind of demure murmur for background, and then I knew that the hopelessly poignant thing was not Lolita's absence from my side, but the absence of her voice from that concord. (310)

Worthy of comparison with Huck Finn's "lonesome" eloquence on the river or even with Nick's imaginative reconstruction of the legendary Dutchmen at the end of *Gatsby,* the passage comprises one of those rare aboriginal moments—usually pastoral and invariable elegiac—of which modern American literature is so fond and whose recurrent expression runs from Hawthorne and Melville through Twain and Faulkner, Hemingway and Bellow. In *Lolita,* as in the works of these other classic American writers, the primary purpose of this narrative moment is to provide a counter-movement to the main events, a journey back to man's Eden-like beginnings in the American landscape.[17] While its lyric poignancy and power have often been noted, its true significance seems to me preeminently cultural, deriving from Humbert's unfettered awareness, at last, of a native American reality "unsolipsized" by his émigré imagination. Indeed, it is as though, having divested himself of his Old World pretensions and preconceptions, he can finally see Lolita—and America—for the slightly tawdry, hybrid beauties they have always been.

NOTES

[1] Vladimir Nabokov, *Strong Opinions* (New York: McGraw-Hill, 1973), 26.

[2] *Strong Opinions,* 77.

[3] See, for example, Alfred Appel, Jr., "Backgrounds of *Lolita,*" *TriQuarterly,* no. 17 (1970): 17–40. Appel's essay appears in somewhat different form as part of his introduction to *The Annotated Lolita* (New York: McGraw-Hill, 1970), xxxiii–lviii.

[4] Several critics have remarked the affinities between Humbert's legendary "nympholepsy" and the visionary element in classic American literature, but see especially Martha Banta, "Benjamin, Edgar, Humbert, and Jay," *Yale Review* 60 (Summer 1971): 532–49; also, Lucy Maddox, *Nabokov's Novels in English* (Athens: University of Georgia Press, 1983), 66–85.

[5] Nabokov's fascination with *poshlost* ("Corny trash, vulgar clichés, Philistinism in all its phases," etc.) is ventilated at length both in his study of Gogol (*Nikolai Gogol* [New York: New Directions, 1944]), 63–74, and in a *Paris Review* interview of October 1967, reprinted in *Strong Opinions,* 100–101. On Nabokov's imaginative mastery of American *poshlost,* see Alfred Appel, Jr., "The Road to *Lolita,* or the Americanization of an Émigré," *Journal of Modern Literature* 4 (1974): 3–31.

[6] See, for example, Andrew Field, *Nabokov: His Life in Art* (Boston: Little, Brown and Company, 1967), 323–51; Alfred Appel, Jr., "*Lolita:* The Springboard of Parody," in *Nabokov: The Man and His Work,* ed. L. S. Dembo (Madison: University of Wisconsin Press, 1967), 106–43; and Brent Harold, "*Lolita:* Nabokov's Critique of Aloofness," *Papers on Language and Literature* 11 (1975): 71–82.

[7] *Lolita* (New York: G. P. Putnam's Sons, 1955), 62. Subsequent references to this edition will be incorporated in the text.

[8] Alfred Appel, Jr., *Nabokov's Dark Cinema* (New York: Oxford University Press, 1974), 251.

[9] The moral vision of *Lolita* is persuasively discussed by Martin Green, "The Morality of *Lolita,*" *Kenyon Review* 28 (June 1966): 352–77, and by Robert J. Levine, "'My Ultraviolet Darling': The Loss of Lolita's Childhood," *Modern Fiction Studies* 25 (1979): 471–79.

[10] Robert Merrill, "Nabokov and Fictional Artifice," *Modern Fiction Studies* 25 (1979): 454.

[11] See in this connection Douglas Fowler's discussion of *Lolita* in his *Reading Nabokov* (Ithaca: Cornell University Press, 1974), 147–75, and Ellen Pifer's chapter "Singularity and the Double Pale Ghost: From *Despair* to *Pale Fire,*" in her *Nabokov and the Novel* (Cambridge: Harvard University Press, 1980), 97–118.

[12] As is well known, Nabokov always regarded with disdain and suspicion the idea that art—least of all *his* art—could ever survive as a creature of cultural affiliation or national identity. "The writer's art is his real passport," he suavely asserted. "I have always maintained . . . that the nationality of a worthwhile writer is of secondary importance" (*Strong Opinions,* 63). In describing the essence of his own achievement therefore, Nabokov always carefully refrained from using ethnic labels or cultural stereotypes, as if to portray himself as a defiantly global artist endowed with gifts of imagination and language far exceeding the nourishing traditions of any particular soil or society.

[13] Favorable and unfavorable reactions to Nabokov's extensive use of parody and artifice in *Lolita* are represented, respectively, by Appel's several articles on the work incorporated in his introduction to *The Annotated Lolita* and by Max F. Schulz, "Characters (Contra Characterization) in the Contempo-

rary Novel," in *The Theory of the Novel: New Essays*, ed. John Halperin (New York: Oxford University Press, 1974), especially 144–47.

[14] As Nabokov humorously quips in his afterword: "Humbert is a foreigner and an anarchist, and there are many things, besides nymphets, in which I disagree with him" (317). Too often an unintended consequence of the few cultural analyses of Humbert's American experience is the collapse of this elementary distinction—as in Appel's otherwise illuminating essay, "The Road to *Lolita*, or the Americanization of an Émigré."

[15] Van Wyck Brooks, *The Wine of the Puritans* (London: Sisley's Ltd., n.d.), 17–18.

[16] William Carlos Williams, *In The American Grain* (New York: New Directions, 1925), 136.

[17] On the ideological development of this theme in American literature and culture, see R. W. B. Lewis's still valuable study, *The American Adam: Innocence, Tragedy, and Tradition in the Nineteenth Century* (Chicago: University of Chicago Press, 1955).

Trevor McNeely

"LO" AND BEHOLD: SOLVING THE *LOLITA* RIDDLE

One of my dreams is that someday, somewhere, someone will find, hidden perhaps behind the butterflies in a forgotten display case in the entomological museum of Harvard or Montreux, and in the master's own hand, his "elegant solution" to what he called the "riddle" of *Lolita*. These terms are used by Nabokov in an interview he gave to the B.B.C. in 1962;[1] and remembering also his insistence that every public utterance of his, including interviews, was written by him in advance, the element of deliberation in his choice of such terms cannot be in question. If it could be in question, there is, as it happens, a second very similar reference in a 1964 *Playboy* article, and here he introduces a further wrinkle, equating the *character* of Lolita with the *book:* "I shall never regret *Lolita*," he says, "she was like the composition of a beautiful puzzle—its composition and its solution at the same time, since one is a mirror view of the other."[2]

Now if it can be inferred from these remarks that the element of riddle or puzzle is central to the book's conception, at least from its author's point of view, this inference obviously has important hermeneutic implications. A riddle has usually a single solution; in a satisfying riddle the solution is at once simple yet subtle; a number of apparently unrelated or contradictory elements are shown to have an occult relationship, one as precisely calculated, and ultimately as logical, as a mathematical equation. It is my contention that such a key exists for *Lolita,* that the book was in fact written with this point in mind, and that Nabokov went to his grave enjoying the fact that almost a full generation of readers had failed to find him out. And what is the basis, then, of the *Lolita* riddle? Like the typical good riddle just described it involves the resolution of an apparent contradiction; it also provides a single elegant answer to a, superficially at least, rather complex set of questions. And a third characteristic of this particular riddle, exactly as Nabokov's comment said, is that riddle and solution are bound together: that is to say, when you understand the riddle, you also and at the same time *have* the solution. Criticism of *Lolita* has been busy for years trying to find the book's real theme. It has been an

From *Studies in the Novel* 21, No. 2 (Summer 1989): 182–99.

interesting if inconclusive chase, whose primary value, however, viewing the book as a "riddle" again, has been largely as a confirmation of Nabokov's conjuring skill. And what I mean by this is that criticism has faithfully performed the task he set it to perform in *Lolita*, that of pursuing its own phantom, duping itself into believing that *Lolita* exists for some other, and presumably more significant, reason than mere deception. It does not. The true theme of this novel, or at any rate its true Nabokovian theme, may be stated as a parody of a famous American maxim—or rather a combination of two famous maxims, one from the pen, the other from the legend of one of America's most illustrious sons, and an unexpected inspiration for such a book, Abraham Lincoln. Mocking American values even as it pretends to respect them, *Lolita* is "dedicated to the proposition" not of equality, with Lincoln, but of its exact opposite—inequality, Nabokov setting himself up deliberately as the intellectual master of his perennially innocent, not to say contemptibly naive, American readers. After fifteen anonymous years in the American academy, in spite of a European reputation of no small note and a string of English titles already behind him, finding himself at 53 the perfect model for his own Timofey Pnin—that is to say, ignored, forgotten as a writer, occasional butt in all probability of coffee-room jibes by patronizing colleagues of more fashionable critical persuasions—he is getting his revenge, like Malvolio, on the whole pack of them: the Freudians, the New Critics, the Existentialists, the Structuralists, and all their bastard progeny; and along with them, "lovely, trustful, dreamy, enormous" American society as a whole, all in one fell swoop, as it were. Lincoln said that you can't fool all of the people all of the time? Nabokov will prove in *Lolita* that you can.

Hints and clues to the *Lolita* riddle abound—not only in the book itself, of course, but in comments Nabokov made on it, like those we have already looked at. Some of the most revealing of these clues, again deliberately, are found in the Afterword he appended in his own name to the American edition of 1958, and which is now always printed with the book. Mentioned there, for example, is a certain anonymous "American critic" who is said to have called *Lolita* "the record of my love affair with the romantic novel," which Nabokov, after first noting this as an "elegant formula," then corrects by inserting the words "[the] 'English language' " in place of "the romantic novel." By emphasizing this particular passage in this unusual way, quoting and then changing it, Nabokov has in effect done two things—he has made the statement stand out as important, and second, and critically, he has directed the reader, clearly the academic reader, to approach *Lolita* not as a novel but as an aesthetic poem. Many critics have called *Lolita* a love story; and it is one, but as this comment of Nabokov's emphasizes, it is not a love story in the conventional novelistic sense. I noted earlier that in one of his other comments on *Lolita* Nabokov referred to the book and the character as a single entity. That reference constitutes a clue to the *Lolita* riddle very close to the "love story" idea we are considering here. Lolita as a *character*, in other words, means nothing; as a *book*, however, she is an altogether different matter. And the "love" theme of the book works the same way. The *true* love theme is an aesthetic, not a novelistic one at all, and thus has nothing to do with either "Humbert" or "Lolita," neither one of whom, as we shall shortly see, has any reality or significance anyway; what they are, both of them, are mere conjurer's diversions, the hocus pocus gestures the magician uses to distract the audience, while the real manipulation goes on unseen before its very eyes. *Lolita* is a love story, yes, but the lover/hero of the story is Vladimir Nabokov, and the love, just as his comment says, his lifelong affair with language.

While it may not be immediately clear how these observations bring us any closer to knowledge of even the existence, let alone the solution, of a *Lolita* "riddle," they are necessary background to the appreciation of the subtlety of Nabokov's thinking as regards the real meaning of *Lolita*. Most of these are not new ideas about Nabokov, of course; quite the contrary, they are critical common-places—that his intellectual biases are aesthetic,[3] that his is a "Conjurer's Art," as Page Stegner said,[4] or that his "heroes," like Sebastian Knight's, are only " 'methods of composition' ";[5] but no commentator on *Lolita* including Appel has to my knowl-edge ever taken these ideas to their logical conclusion, and thus put himself in a position actually to track Nabokov all the way to his lair. To do this requires recognizing first that the *only* meaning the novel has to Nabokov is as an exhibition of his own verbal skill, his linguistic and literary sophistication, nothing more—to accept this is to be positioned to solve the *Lolita* riddle. Now as a proposition this seems straightforward, but in reality it is not an easy thing to grasp, requiring as it does a voluntary act of absolute intellectual nihilism on the part of the reader—a Kierkegaardian leap, as it were, not of faith, in this case, however, but of despair, into a world, Nabokov's world, where the concepts of purpose and value lose all meaning, and even such fundamental existential guideposts (as we think them) as love, truth, morality, and beauty, become mere verbal stratagems, powerful but ultimately sterile tokens of that intrinsically value-neutral semiotic system known as language, out of which all our illusory worlds are constructed. Knowing that few will follow him down this dark road, Nabokov knows also that power lies in the ability to manipulate these tokens consciously and with skill, a power of which he will give a demonstration in *Lolita,* and at the same time and as a corollary, trap his readers in the emptiness of their own intellectual futility. I have been suggesting that as well as the "contemptibly naive" general reader being the intended victim of Nabokov's wiles in *Lolita,* he has a particular target in the modern literary establishment—the "Teachers of Literature" as he addresses them specifically in his Postscript. The intellectual thrust of *Lolita* is directed especially towards this group, to prick the balloon of ivory-tower arrogance and complacency that holds them above the world of ordinary humanity. While his own experience in the academy may ac-count in part for his bitterness, it is more the contempt of the nihilist that galvanizes his spirit into goading them—what to him after all can their schools of criticism be but so much empty posturing, they whose whole existence is built on the fraud of reason and whose writings for the most part exhibit all the creative energy of a corporation's annual report? As an academic veteran himself, literary trickster par excellence, and master of a Joycean range of intellectual resources and materials, Nabokov is uniquely qualified to perpetrate the perfect novelistic hoax, knowing that the scholarly community, with its penchant for symbol- and allusion-hunting and its terror of the void of unmeaning, will fall like sheep into his trap. With this preparation, we may now finally expose the *Lolita* riddle itself. As promised, it has the inspired simplicity that is a quality of children's thinking; the very obviousness of the whole thing has no doubt contributed to the ease with which it has duped a generation of the subtlest adult readers; while at the same time it penetrates the mists of academic obfuscation that surround the book with the clarity and power of a laser. *Lolita* was written to prove a simple point in a complex way. The point is that style can do anything. The subject of the novel, the sexual slavery and abuse of a twelve-year-old orphan girl by a mature and diabolically clever man, who continues his abuse until the girl finally escapes from him into the arms of an even more perverted second man, and for which not a single word of regret or remorse is once expressed, is an integral, indeed *the* essential element giving the riddle its focus and point. This subject is deliberately chosen as being of all human activities the most universally despised, in its nature the most inexcusably and uncompro-misingly vile, beyond all dispute or discussion evil. By choosing pedophilia as his subject, then, Nabokov is setting himself the ultimate challenge as a stylist, as well as setting himself up for the ultimate triumph as a jokester—to present this inher-ently repellent activity in such a way that the public will not only read and enjoy a book about it, but also that the scholarly community again will work it into a *cause célèbre* like *Ulysses*, championing its author and even committing the ultimate absurdity of condoning the activities of its hero—finding "legitimate" scholarly grounds for judging him innocent. Indeed, swallowing the bait deeper into their entrails than probably even Nabokov dared hope they would, pillars of the American critical establishment as substantial as Lionel Trilling and Leslie Fiedler actually began the official romantic apotheosis of Humbert Humbert almost as soon as the book appeared.[6]

In a way, perhaps, it is understandable that, appearing in the United States in 1958, *Lolita* might be surprisingly *less* of a scandal than if it appeared in 1988. Untalked and undreamed of in main stream cultural circles in the inhibited intel-lectual climate of that era, pedophilia as a subject has shock value sufficient to dull, nay, paralyze the collective mind, making it impossible to grasp it in its full serious-ness and viciousness. It might be said that we understand pedophilia today in a way that the '50s could not: the fact that it has taken thirty years to solve Nabokov's riddle is both testimony to the extent of the evolution of culture over that period, and tribute also to the prescient intellect of an author that it has taken the rest of us thirty years to catch up to. Be that as it may, however, the point remains that Nabokov conceived *Lolita* strictly as a game, an intellectual game, in which all the advantage of playing his counters to maximum effect is Nabokov's, through his knowledge of his opponent's mind. It helps also, of course, that the opponent does not even know that a game is going on. Is *Lolita* on a scandalous subject? Good! Then he can count on the academic and literary establishment's enthusiastic support for the book on the grounds of its knee-jerk instinctive anti-philistinism alone— Heaven forfend that a professor should ever be found in the same camp morally or intellectually as a mere ignorant bourgeois! And already he has his opponent in a false position. To defend this work, as critics have done, requires, plainly and simply, that the moral issues it raises must be ignored.[7] It is perhaps the cleverest of Nabokov's devices so to have structured his book that the reader is forced into a moral/aesthetic dilemma by it from which there is no escape—or rather there is only one possible escape, and that is by the method I am outlining here, in effect to reject totally both book and author for the frauds they are, even though one may still admire the author's language skill and intellect. Every other approach to the book victimizes the reader, leading him necessarily into one form or another of obfuscation, as he tries desperately (and unconvincingly) to make something out of nothing—to find meaning where none exists. I said earlier that a good riddle finds a clever way of resolving an apparent contradiction. The contradiction here, of course, would be the obvious one the reader is made to feel immediately between the hero's perversion—which he admits and makes very clear *is* a perversion (his obsession, to the exclusion of all other interests, with the bodies of prepubescent girls)—and the gorgeous cover of romantic language in which he cloaks these desires, bilking the reader of his sympathy thereby, and undermining his awareness of the evil. There are two possible ways, then, of resolving this conflict, only one of which is authentic, the other constituting the trap Nabokov has set for his readers. The first one is by recognizing that in the "poetic" side of the hero's personality we are meeting Nabokov the fraud and the joker, deliberately dressing up an evil, with one sole end in view—to dupe the reader, by the spell of language, into the false position of condoning perversion. The other is to fall into his trap, to take the hero's "love" as real, as something that somehow mitigates the evil and makes perversion acceptable. And while the latter course is the route that, in their different ways, all the commentators take, the interesting thing about this option, as I suggested earlier, is that in fact it does not work—*this* contradiction cannot be resolved; to pretend to do so is to do as Nabokov himself does in the book, it is to lie. It is thus not merely a matter of the reader being taken in by Nabokov; his diabolic cleverness runs much deeper than that; the joke is that we take *ourselves* in with this novel. To suggest that their hero's "love" is somehow real, or that the cult of beauty he worships outweights in importance all over considerations, is simply to pervert the truth, and to do so knowingly and willfully. Nabokov wins his game by proving that his readers are not only fools, but liars to boot—at heart, indeed, the same kind of Hitlerian nihilists that he himself is.

There are basically two opposite ways that commentators use to try to get around the moral/aesthetic dilemma the book creates, both of which involve a contradiction. The critic Merrill calls these two approaches the "fabulistic," based on the theory that Nabokov is writing not traditional fiction in *Lolita,* but "metafiction," his real subject being "nothing less than 'form itself' "; and his version of the opposite approach to this, the one he himself favors, the view that *Lolita is* traditional fiction and therefore "primarily devoted to the creation of character."[8] The fabulistic or aesthetic approach to Nabokov has been the dominant one over the years; again, this is familiar territory to students of Nabokov, but for my purposes these issues have to be emphasized, because they bear directly on the understanding of the *Lolita* riddle. Space considerations preclude detailed discussion of the "aesthetic" approach to *Lolita,* but there are at least three obvious reasons why it has been the most popular one. One is that critical fashion in this generation favors it; the second, closer to our territory, is that Nabokov explicitly encourages this approach—and there is a strong element of tricksterism in this encouragement—and third, and by far the most important for our purposes, the aesthetic approach is convenient for critics of *Lolita* because it enables them, or at least they think it does, to evade the moral issue entirely in dealing with the book. The latter two criteria go hand in hand, of course; in his Afterword to the book Nabokov sets the academic reader up for the copout he needs by pretending to take it himself: the "accusation of immorality" leveled at *Lolita,* he says, is "idiotic"; his only goal is "art": "for me a work of fiction only exists insofar as it affords me what I shall bluntly call aesthetic bliss."[9] Here again I cannot go into the literary background to these ideas; the territory is a very familiar one in any case, but the principles of Nabokov's aestheticism are represented historically perhaps most characteristically in the work and the legend of Oscar Wilde, with his professed contempt for bourgeois values and his belief that "through art, and . . . art only . . . we can realize our perfection." Nabokov's rejection in his Afterword of the moral criterion for judging *Lolita* is a virtual paraphrase of Wilde's famous pronouncement from *Dorian Gray* that "there is no such thing as a moral or an immoral book. Books are well written, or badly written. That is all."[10] Actually, there is probably no writer in history whom it is more correct to characterize as a purely literary creature than Nabokov—it is one of his strangenesses as well as one of the sources for his fascination for the critics, but what it is primarily is a recognition of the fact that *all* of his material is literary. Oscar Wilde is thus not just a vague or general influence in the conception of *Lolita,* but a specific and direct one, an influence that runs all the way from the book's neo-"Reading Gaol" narrative frame (with a pun of course on "Reading"), to the costume of "silk shirt . . . transparent taupe socks . . . waistcoat with nacreous buttons . . . pale cashmere tie and so on," Nabokov gives Humbert to wear when he sends him off to kill Dick Schiller near the end. As a further example of *Lolita*'s "literariness," Martin Green, in an excellent 1966 article, points out correctly that the book can also be read as virtually a gloss on Tolstoy's famous essay *What Is Art?* Almost point by point the book can be read as a direct rebuttal of Tolstoy's didactic theory in that essay, the basis and precursor of socialist realism. And as a final example of the theoretical background to *Lolita* I would mention the writer with whose temperament of all artists Nabokov may well be most in sympathy, E. A. Poe. Poe's fictional "Annabel Lee" and factual child bride figure directly in *Lolita,* of course, but no less important in its contribution to Nabokov's professed aesthetic is Poe's treatise "The Poetic Principle," the statement that marks the actual beginning of the aesthetic movement in western literature, and the first to repudiate specifically any connection between the moral and the aesthetic realms. Freighted with this and much more literary baggage, *Lolita*'s critics swallow Nabokov's bait, and come to believe, or rather pretend to believe, what he himself pretends to suggest in his remarks on the book, that the pedophilia and sexual slavery it depicts actually *do not matter.* The model for this response to *Lolita,* which every academic critique of the book that I have seen fits perfectly, is John Ray, Jr., Ph.D.'s resolutely non-judgmental Foreword, in which he pleads the case for the mitigating values of Humbert's narrative and personality in spite of his perversion. John Ray, Jr., Ph.D., of course, is supposed to be a psychiatrist, one of the tribe that Nabokov delights in hating, but what is unstated though equally clear in Nabokov's attitude, is that the pretended scientific detachment and objectivity of the John Ray, Jr., Ph.D.'s, of this world is no different in fact from the pretended detachment of that other related tribe that have attached themselves to the book with even greater tenacity—that is, the literary tribe, the professorial Ph.D. tribe, who apply superficially different criteria to *Lolita* but whose analyses lead them in the end to the same position as John Ray, Jr., Ph.D., the basically nihilistic position of ignoring, and therefore condoning, the evil of pedophilia.

I said earlier that no critic of *Lolita* follows the logic of Nabokov's aestheticism far enough to catch him in his lair, because to do so requires an act of intellectual nihilism that few of us would be prepared to take. The Nabokov intellectual position, articulated in his Afterword and echoed by his commentators, is that *Lolita* is justified on aesthetic grounds alone, that no other criteria are relevant in judging it. I call this position nihilistic—that is to say, utterly meaningless, and known to be such by Nabokov—though masquerading as a reasonable and logical proposition. Its apparent authority is further enhanced by its resemblance to some of the things I have quoted from his sources like Wilde and Poe: the "sole arbiter" of Beauty, says Poe, for example, is "taste," which "unless incidentally . . . has no concern whatever with either Duty [—also called 'the Moral sense'—] or with Truth."[11] Quoted selectively and manipulated rhetorically, it can be made to seem that Poe's position is the same and Nabokov's, but that this is a distortion is evident in a more thorough reading of Poe, and indeed obvious to common sense anyway. For the truth of aestheticism is not that it abolishes the moral criterion in judging literature, but simply that it gives it a different label. The "good" is now equated with the "beautiful," the "evil" with the ugly or deformed. Wilde says this explicitly: books are "well written or badly written"—there they are, "good" and "bad," our old friends, right out front and in black and white terms. Poe says essentially the same thing: Taste "wag[es] war upon Vice solely on the ground of her deformity—her disproportion—her animosity to the fitting, to the appropriate, to the harmonious—in a word, to Beauty."[12] It is, as I say, simply common sense to recognize that the moral criterion is as indispensable to aestheticism as it is to any other form of thought or philosophy. Human discourse, and indeed the very concept of meaning, are tied to the dialectical principle—self-evidently nothing can be either "beautiful" or "good" except by comparison, implied or overt, with what is ugly or evil. To pretend to close off one half of this dialectic, as Nabokov does in *Lolita,* is simply to lie—not only does Nabokov know this, but so must his readers, and it is for this reason that no commentary on the book can carry Nabokov's pretended thesis all the way to its logical conclusion. To do so, to say that the beauty of *Lolita*'s form has *no* corollary or antithesis in the deformity of its content, the conclusion to which the logic leads, is to affirm meaninglessness—only to make such a statement is precisely to enter the nightmare world of intellectual nihilism Humbert Humbert inhabits.

That Nabokov is totally aware of his deception in this regard, implicit throughout in the novel's nightmarish plot—a pedophile's fantasy of what paradise must be like—is made explicit only once in the book, again I suggest deliberately on Nabokov's part, so as not to make the solution of his riddle too obvious, yet not to be so unsporting as to fail to provide at least one good clue. The passage to which I refer is the little bit of forgettable doggerel Humbert quotes from a source identified as "an old poet" at the end of II 31, a passage concerning which Appel for one has not a word to say:

> The moral sense in mortals is the duty
> We have to pay on mortal sense of beauty.

While the attempt at wordplay here is silly to the point of embarrassment, probably a deliberate distraction on Nabokov's part, one implication of the passage is deadly serious from the author's point of view, as it should be from that of the alert reader as well. This is his coupling in the passage of the concepts of "beauty" and "the moral sense," exactly as Poe does, and even using his very words. What this says in effect, is just what was suggested above, that the two are fundamentally inseparable—two sides of a single coin. One of the differences between life and literature is that in literature one controls one's creatures and their destinies totally—the writer can avoid, if he wishes, the confusion that sometimes overtakes the dialectic in real life; instead he can sharpen the dialectic, making it impossible for either character or reader not to know exactly what kind of a story they are involved in. If one has sufficient skill, indeed, one can do both this and its opposite at the same time—reveal the truth in black and white, yet through the magic of poetic language, and taking advantage of his reader's naivety, so transform that truth that while it tantalizes it still may not be seen. This is what Nabokov had done in *Lolita*. It is no accident that just at the point that he slips in for the first and only time this direct reference to the inseparable linkage of the moral and the aesthetic in life (and it should be noted that the reference is specifically to life, rather than literature), he simultaneously heightens the tension between his pleading for the reader's compassion and understanding for his creature Humbert, and the unmitigated grossness and brutality of that same creature's moral character and actions. Thus in the two pages immediately following the little poem quoted above he depicts the evil of pedophilia exactly as it is, in straightforward descriptions that come closer to the truth than probably any others in the book, while at the same time the special pleading for his character rises to a stylistic climax of Jamesian sophistication and Brontëan intensity. I have to quote from the book at a little more length at this point:

> There was the day, during our first trip—our first circle of paradise—when in
> order to enjoy my phantasms in peace I firmly decided to ignore what I could

not help perceiving, the fact that I was to her not a boy friend, not a glamour man, not a pal, not even a person at all, but just two eyes and a foot of engorged brawn—to mention only mentionable matters. There was the day when having withdrawn the functional promise I had made her on the eve (whatever she had set her funny little heart on—a roller rink with some special plastic floor or a movie matinee to which she wanted to go alone), I happened to glimpse from the bathroom, through a chance combination of mirror aslant and door ajar, a look on her face . . . that look I cannot exactly describe . . . an expression of helplessness so perfect that it seemed to grade into one of rather comfortable inanity just because this was the very limit of injustice and frustration—and every limit presupposes something beyond it—hence the neutral illumination. And when you bear in mind that these were the raised eyebrows and parted lips of a child, you may better appreciate what depths of calculated carnality, what reflected despair, restrained me from falling at her dear feet and dissolving in human tears, and sacrificing my jealousy to whatever pleasure Lolita might hope to derive from mixing with dirty and dangerous children in an outside world that was real to her. . . . I loved you. I was a pentapod monster, but I loved you. I was despicable and brutal, and turpid, and everything, *mais je t'aimais, je t'aimais!* And there were times when I knew how you felt, and it was hell to know it, my little one. Lolita girl, brave Dolly Schiller.

I recall certain moments, let us call them icebergs in paradise, when after having had my fill of her—after fabulous, insane exertions that left me limp and azure-barred—I would gather her in my arms with, at last, a mute moan of human tenderness (her skin glistening in the neon light coming from the paved court through the slits in the blind, her soot-black lashes matted, her grave gray eyes more vacant than ever—for all the world a little patient still in the confusion of a drug after a major operation)—and the tenderness would deepen to shame and despair, and I would lull and rock my lone light Lolita in my marble arms, and moan in her warm hair, and caress her at random and mutely ask her blessing, and at the peak of this human agonized selfless tenderness (with my soul actually hanging around her naked body and ready to repent), all at once, ironically, horribly, lust would swell again—and "oh, *no,*" Lolita would say with a sigh to heaven, and the next moment the tenderness and the azure—all would be shattered.   (*TAL,* pp. 285–86, 287)

The absurdity of praising Nabokov solely on the basis of his style is manifest through a careful reading and consideration of passages such as these. Separation of form and content is as meaningless in literature as it is in life, and Nabokov has so arranged his material here as not only to make that meaninglessness absolutely manifest, but even more importantly, to show the emptiness of a criticism based solely on technique, in which the question of mimesis is not considered. Organizations in our society that lobby for the rights of pedophiles, organizations like the "British Pedophile Information Exchange," who are campaigning to have the age of consent in England lowered to four, or the René Guyon Society of Los Angeles, whose motto is "sex before eight or else it's too late," could not ask for more eloquent boosters and friends than those Professors who praise *Lolita* as a great work of literature, in the naive belief that they can somehow do this without necessarily supporting pedophile rights at the same time.

For those who take the alternative approach to the moral/aesthetic dilemma of *Lolita,* what Merrill calls the character approach, treating the book as a romantic novel, and justifying its hero's actions on various grounds of character and plot, the blatancy of the manipulation to which these readers subject themselves approaches the laughable when the movements of the magician are slowed down and dissected. It is an interesting observation also that while these two approaches are logically contradictory, most commentators, again including Appel, find themselves having to use both, as they scramble to find some basis for including *Lolita* in the pantheon of major works of literature. It is clear enough, I should hope, that the two approaches *are* contradictory: that if one says, on the one hand, that Nabokov is a trickster and his characters are sham, and that the value of his work lies in his prodigious language skill and cleverness, then one cannot also draw thematic lessons and meanings out of those same characters that one has just dismissed as pawns in a linguistic game. The dilemma here, however, is that the aesthetic approach, as we have seen, is nihilistic; it has no meaning; a great work of literature cannot be just verbal trickery; beautiful patterns of words in themselves mean nothing. The trick, then, for the commentator, is to base his indifference to the moral issue on the aesthetic argument, but to make selective use of the character argument at the same time in a desperation attempt to wring some meaning—any meaning—out of what Nabokov is doing. Thus Appel, for instance, duly swallows the aesthetic bait, recognizing (accurately enough) that "if one responds to the author's . . . 'specious lines of play' . . . and believes, say, that Humbert's confession is 'sincere' . . . or that a Nabokov book is an illusion of reality proceeding under the natural laws of our world—then one has . . . lost the game to the author"; but having disposed so neatly of any engagement with the "reality" of Humbert's activities, he returns immediately to find the meaning he has just rejected in Humbert's search for "ineffable bliss," or, quoting Humbert himself, his aesthetic quest, "to fix once for all the perilous magic of nymphets" (*TAL,* pp. xix, lvi). The pattern of *Lolita* criticism is actually a circular one—selective use of either the aesthetic or the character argument as a fall-back position when the other fails. The aesthetic argument *seems* to enable one to admire the book yet avoid condoning pedophilia, the character argument, once the pedophilia problem has been safely got round by a back-door application of the other argument, *seems* to justify the novel on traditional or romantic grounds. In neither case, however, can *seems to* be made into *does.* The argument from character in support of the book is as empty and meaningless in fact as is the argument from aesthetics. And once again it is Nabokov's triumph as a trickster so to have designed his book that one can praise it at all only at the cost of going heels up into its author's trap. It is as self-evidently impossible, for example, to separate form from content in terms of character and plot in the novel as it is in terms of structure and style. To claim to admire Humbert's poetic sensibility, say, or his vision of "ineffable bliss," while passing over the perversion of which these are parts, is at the very least a distortion, if not an outright lie—notwithstanding the fact that this is the interpretation Nabokov expects us to make. Listen for a moment to Humbert plead with the reader for understanding of his deviance, in a passage that might have come directly from a real-life case history, indeed from the notes of Krafft-Ebing himself:

> Ladies and gentlemen of the jury, the majority of sex offenders that hanker for some throbbing, sweet-moaning, physical but not necessarily coital, relation with a girl-child, are innocuous, inadequate, passive, timid strangers who merely ask the community to allow them to pursue their practically harmless, so-called aberrant behavior, their little hot wet private acts of sexual deviation without the police and society cracking down upon them. We are not sex fiends! We do not rape as good soldiers do. We are unhappy, mild, dog-eyed gentlemen, sufficiently well integrated to control our urge in the presence of adults, but ready to give years and years of life for one chance to touch a nymphet. Emphatically, no killers are we. Poets never kill. (*TAL*, pp. 89–90)

This is slick, it's very authentic, it's even appealing in its way, but to swallow it is to choke. The pervert and the poet are forever one in Humbert, his pedophilia a stark and unforgivable fact that makes horror of everything he is and does. I suggested earlier that readers who praise this work put themselves by that act into the camp of "Hitlerian nihilists" along with the book's author. If the seriousness of those terms was doubted in any way, or if they were not understood, the aspect of the novel presently under consideration should serve to clarify as well as remove any doubt about the appropriateness of that expression. Some critics have called this a "love story"; the twisted rationalizing that it takes to confuse the emotions described above with the emotion of love is identical in kind, certainly, if not quite in degree, perhaps, to the rationalization of Nazi racial policies by which many Germans deceived themselves for years.

Not only does Humbert's style serve to trap the naive reader and at the same time implicate him in Humbert's crime, exactly as his creator has calculated, but the whole plot of the book is put together with the same care and for the same purpose. And here again is where the aesthetic argument comes unfailingly to the floundering critic's rescue when his defence of the book on character grounds begins to collapse. The aesthetic argument holds that plot and character are irrelevant, in fact phony; the whole thing is a literary game—and that argument is absolutely correct. The plot has one justification and basis only—to trap the reader. Thus Humbert's evil is easily rationalized and lessened by the convenient fact that Lolita was already "utterly and hopelessly depraved," in Humbert's words, *before* he got to her, seduced by Charlie Holmes at the summer camp. Also, when their first intercourse takes place it is she, as everyone knows, who seduces him; another convenient trap set by Nabokov to catch the Humbertians—and it does catch them, even though the context makes perfectly clear that to her what they were doing was innocent—the naughty but romantic "game she and Charlie had played." This whole episode, indeed, is formulaic, a confirmation of the plot's actual pho- niness and insignificance, for it is nothing more than an ingenious reversal of the ancient pornographic device, as old as Venus and Adonis, of having the innocent young male introduced to the glories of debauchery by the voluptuous older woman. Lolita's age, again, is also significant in Nabokov's eyes, not for any tradi- tional novelistic reasons of character or anything of that sort, of course; that means nothing, but simply because if he had made her any younger her own innocence could not be in question, whereas at 12, and experiencing the menarche the very morning of the great seduction, as he has her conveniently do, she can be manipu- lated into an apparent share of the guilt with "innocuous, inadequate, passive, timid" Humbert. And one could go on in the same vein about the plot almost indefinitely— the great climax, the killing of Quilty, like Lolita's age, is there for one sole purpose, to manipulate the reader into a romantic vindication of the hero—he *must* have loved Lolita truly; in an interpretation of the novel based on character the murder can have no other meaning. And that vindication is achieved, moreover—this is Nabokov's really diabolical cleverness—while all the time both character and plot are being literally waved in the reader's face as phony from start to finish. Getting Humbert to America, for example, takes only two quick maneuvers—get him some money (his *oncle d'Amérique* can die, bequeathing him an income—shades of Pixerécourt!), and get rid of Valeria, his first wife—not, however, without giving her one hilarious moment on stage (the sole purpose of having her in the book in the first place) to burst the limits of "the stock character she was supposed to impersonate," and not forgetting either the suitably humiliating punishment that is in store for her for her disloyalty to our hero. Charlotte's death too is likewise a novelistic parody of the same order, occurring excactly on cue and with an op- portuneness that is as impossible to miss as it is to take seriously.

The ultimate artificiality of the plot, however, comes in the creation of the two central characters, Lolita and Humbert, both of them figures of parody, deliberately created absurd in their exaggeration, the one the very embodiment of '50s teeny- bopper pop (though it took the term twenty-five more years to catch up to the concept), the other a literary pastiche, a composite of some dozens of the heroes from a whole range of nineteenth-century romantic sources. The Lolita conception is shallower as a parody, of course, as it must be; a shallow culture produces shallow archetypes; not a "stock character" like Valechka, she may be characterized instead as a walking cliché, the literal incarnation of a culture based on image:

> Mentally, I found her to be a disgustingly conventional little girl. Sweet hot jazz, square dancing, gooey fudge sundaes, musicals, movie magazines, and so forth—these were the obvious items in her list of beloved things. The Lord knows how many nickels I fed to the gorgeous music boxes that came with every meal we had! I still hear the nasal voices of those invisibles serenading her, people with names like Sammy and Jo and Eddy and Tony and Peggy and Guy and Patty and Rex, and sentimental song hits, all of them as similar to my

ears as her various candies were to my palate. She believed, with a kind of celestial trust, any advertisement or advice that appeared in *Movie Love* or *Screen Land*—Starasil Starves Pimples, or "You better watch out if you're wearing your shirttails outside your jeans, gals, because Jill says you shouldn't." If a roadside sign said: VISIT OUR GIFT SHOP—we *had* to visit it, *had* to buy its Indian curios, dolls, copper jewelry, cactus candy. The words "novelties and souvenirs" simply entranced her by their trochaic lilt. If some café sign proclaimed Icecold Drinks, she was automatically stirred, although all drinks everywhere were ice-cold. She it was to whom ads were dedicated: the ideal consumer, the subject and object of every foul poster.   (*TAL*, p. 150)

Nabokov at his most arch and his most characteristic, however, emerges in the figure of Humbert Humbert. Simultaneously a pastiche, a parody, and a labor of love, Humbert epitomizes Nabokov's total commitment to literary rather than real-life models in his work, though put together with an attention to detail and a degree of care that is almost Joycean in its richness and scope. Without writing a book on *Lolita* it would be impossible to trace all the sources that have been consciously sifted to provide touches for our hero, but they encompass almost the whole romantic tradition, including several of the Don Juans of literature, satiric and serious, as well as a wide range of other very specific romantic characters—Rousseau's Saint Preux, Pushkin's Onegin, and Emily Brontë's Heathcliff to name only three. The romantic novelist to whom Nabokov undoubtedly owes the most is Dostoevsky, several of his works having provided very direct inspiration for *Lolita*. Raskolnikov is one model, physical as well as moral, with his "strikingly handsome [yet 'delicate features,'] . . . fine dark eyes, and . . . well-knit figure, taller than the average"; while the nameless narrator of *Notes from Underground*, with his penchant for "[sinking] deeper into [his] slime . . . just when . . . most keenly aware . . . of everything 'lofty and beautiful,' " is spiritual father not only to Humbert, but to his creator, this "man of breadth and scope, our [Russian] romantic," who is at the same time "the greatest fraud of all our frauds."[13] One specific Dostoevskian allusion in *Lolita* that should be mentioned is one that has not previously been caught, but which precisely illustrates both the care with which Nabokov adapts his sources, while at the same time mocking the conventions they represent. The episode in *Lolita* to which the allusion relates is Humbert's reference, itself an egregious parody of every instance of solemn preaching that turns up in literature from the Bible through to T. S. Eliot, to the "distasteful task [he is at one point] . . . faced with . . . of recording a definite drop in Lolita's morals," (*her* morals, yet!) when she discovers that her cooperation in their bedroom activities is necessary to Humbert's satisfaction, and that she can sell that cooperation for money. He pays her, but later of course contrives to steal her little hoard back again, allowing the housekeeper, "honest Mrs. Holigan," to be blamed for the theft. The episode in Dostoevsky that is parodied here is the famous "Stavrogin's Confession" from *The Possessed*, which involves both a theft, for which though guilty Stavrogin because of his power is never blamed, and the deliberate abuse, again at Stavrogin's hands, and subsequent suicide of a helpless and destitute twelve-year-old girl. If it were not already self-evident in the *Lolita* episode itself that it is a joke, a mockery of reason and reality, the clear connection it has with this classic of literary sentimentality makes the parodic intention absolutely unmistakable.[14]

There are other touches to the characterization that make the portrait of Humbert one of near slapstick exaggeration of its romantic origins. Not just "striking" in his good looks like Raskolnikov or Count Vronsky, Humbert with his "exceptional virility," "soft dark hair and . . . gloomy but all the more seductive cast of demeanor" has long since had to learn the "habit," as he says, "of not being too attentive to women lest they come toppling, bloodripe, into my cold lap" (*TAL*, p. 27). Exaggeration as fantastic as this, I suggest, can only be overlooked by a skillful application of the same kind of intellectual acuteness that distinguishes regular readers of the Harlequin romance genre.

The final example I will cite of Nabokov's deliberate trickery that has deluded readers from the 1950s to the present about this book, is his clever use of the technique of false analogy in building the case for both Humbert and himself as legitimate inheritors of the romantic literary tradition. In Humbert's famous opening rhapsody in praise of nymphet love one of the ways Nabokov pretends to justify him is by associating his case with that of two of the western world's most celebrated literary lovers, Dante and Petrarch, both of whose eternal loves first flowered when the objects of their passion were of nymphet age. The blatant falsehood in this comparison, known perfectly well to Nabokov even as he makes it, is first that Dante and Petrarch did not fall in love with Beatrice and Laura *because* they were children as Humbert does, but *when* they were children—the difference of course is crucial; as crucial as the second deliberate omission in his making the analogy, the fact that *chastity* is a fundamental condition of the relationship in both the classical instances. And a similar falsification is again attempted by Nabokov, this time in his own voice, in his Afterword, when he refers to the "three themes which are utterly taboo as far as most American publishers are concerned," one by implication being the pedophilia of *Lolita*, the "two others" said to be "a Negro-White marriage which is a complete and glorious success resulting in lots of children and grandchildren; and the total atheist who lives a happy and useful life, and dies in his sleep at the age of 106." It is a slick but wholly unacceptable maneuver to gain credit for the repulsive and despicable act of pedophilia by associating it with such liberal principles as racial and religious tolerance.

I might conclude with a final note about one more literary source for *Lolita*, perhaps the single most important of all its literary antecedents, Charles Dodgson's *Alice in Wonderland*. The photography motif in the opening pages of *Lolita*, for example, has an obvious tie-in with Dodgson, both biographically and thematically—as Dodgson and Nabokov both know, in their photographs the Alice Liddells of the world remain perfect children forever. But perhaps the most interesting element of the Carroll connection to *Lolita* is its implication in the area of modern thought—specifically Freudian thought. Affecting a total contempt for Freudian ideas throughout his works, Nabokov could nevertheless never have written *Lolita* had not both Freud and Dodgson written before him. For of all the things Nabokov attempts to do in *Lolita*, what the book perhaps most clearly is is

Nabokov's version of the *Alice in Wonderland* Dodgson would have written had he lived 100 years later than he did; in addition to being, what Dodgson would probably have appreciated even more, a perfect piece of linguistic nonsense.

NOTES

[1] Vladimir Nabokov, *Strong Opinions* (New York: McGraw-Hill, 1973), p. 16.

[2] Ibid., p. 20.

[3] Cf., for example, his tribute to his own pseudonym V. Sirin, in *Speak, Memory*, he of the "unusual style, brilliant precision, [and] functional imagery," and "the real life of [whose] books flowed in his figures of speech" (Nabokov, *Speak, Memory* [New York: G. P. Putnam's, 1968], pp. 212, 213); or Martin Green, among many critics, notes Nabokov standing "in immediate and intimate relationship to [the] symbolist tradition . . . He belongs to that branch of the tradition sometimes called decadent." See Martin Green, "The Morality of *Lolita*," *Kenyon Review* 28 (1966): 352.

[4] The title of Chapter 2 of Stegner's *Escape into Aesthetics: The Art of Vladimir Nabokov* (New York: Dial Press, 1966).

[5] Nabokov, *The Real Life of Sebastian Knight* (New York: New Directions, 1941), p. 95.

[6] See Lionel Trilling, "The Last Lover," *Encounter* 11 (October, 1958): 9–19. His title gives Trilling away, of course, but he is guilty of sentiments in the article that Nabokov might almost have dictated: "In recent fiction no lover has thought of his beloved with so much tenderness, no woman has been so charmingly evoked, in such grace and delicacy, as Lolita; it is one of the few examples of rapture in modern writing [etc.]." Fiedler to his credit exhibits less naivety than Trilling; he sees that there is an irony in the book's being a best-seller "despite its endorsement by eminently respectable professors," though unable at the same time to penetrate that irony's deepest level; and while he does not quite concede full heroic status to Humbert, his view of him as victim—"raped, driven to murder, and left to die . . . in jail," as well as his comparison of him with Prince Amerigo of James' *The Golden Bowl*, leave no doubt where his sympathies lie. See Leslie Fiedler, *Love and Death in the American Novel* (Cleveland: World Publishing Company, 1960), p. 327.

[7] Trilling again, for example, calls the "subject matter" of the book "outrageous"—an unconsciously deft evasion of any moral judgment on it. Professor Robert T. Levine perhaps speaks for all his tribe when he professes almost to be shocked that "the captivity of Dolores Haze was taken so seriously by certain unimaginative segments of the reading public, when *Lolita* first appeared, that the novel was branded as immoral, decadent." See Robert T. Levine, " 'My Ultraviolet Darling': The Loss of Lolita's Childhood," *Modern Fiction Studies* 25 (1979): 478.

[8] Robert Merrill, "Nabokov and Fictional Artifice," *Modern Fiction Studies* 25 (1979): 439–62, particularly pp. 439, 440, 443.

[9] Vladimir Nabokov, *The Annotated Lolita*, ed. Alfred Appel, Jr. (New York: McGraw-Hill, 1970), p. 316. Subsequent references *TAL*. Page numbers in *TAL* correspond to those in G. P. Putnam's Sons original 1958 American hardcover edition of *Lolita*.

[10] Oscar Wilde, *The Artist as Critic: The Critical Writings of Oscar Wilde*, ed. Richard Ellmann (New York: Random House, 1968), pp. 380, 235.

[11] Edgar Allan Poe, "The Poetic Principle," in *Selected Poetry and Prose of Poe*, ed. T. O. Mabbott (New York: Modern Library, 1951), pp. 388–89.

[12] Poe, p. 388. Given Nabokov's background in Poe, is it, incidentally, I ask, likely to be an accident that my interpretation of *Lolita* exactly fits, for example, C. Auguste Dupin's solution to the mystery of "The Purloined Letter," which, it will be remembered, escapes the Prefect's observation "by dint of being excessively obvious; [where] the physical oversight is precisely analogous with the moral inapprehension by which the intellect suffers to pass unnoticed those considerations which are too obtrusively and too palpably self-evident?" (Poe, p. 306).

[13] The description of Raskolnikov, above, is from Feodor Dostoevsky, *Crime and Punishment* (New York: W. W. Norton & Company, Inc., 1975), p. 2. See also Feodor Dostoevsky, *Notes from Underground* (New York: Bantam Books, 1974), pp. 6, 54.

[14] Melvin Seiden ("Nabokov and Dostoevsky," *Contemporary Literature* 13 [1972]: 423–44) discusses this episode in *The Possessed* as an illustration of a pedophiliac tendency in Dostoevsky that Nabokov was aware of, but does not relate it to anything specific in *Lolita*. The quotation above is from *TAL*, p. 185.

Linda Kauffman

FRAMING LOLITA:
IS THERE A WOMAN
IN THE TEXT?

Like Shklovsky's *Zoo*, Vladimir Nabokov's *Lolita* (1955) combines lyric and satire, love and scholarship. Like *Zoo, Lolita* is a patchwork of fragmentary genres. Poems, jingles, advertisements, plays and filmscripts, literary criticism, newspaper articles, psychiatric and legal reports are mixed with vestiges of the diary, confessional, journal, and memoir. Nabokov follows Shklovsky in consciously dramatizing literary production. Just as Elsa Triolet's letters undermine Shklovsky's, Lolita's words and letters undermine Humbert's. Lolita's voice, however, is far more muted than Elsa's, despite the fact that an astonishing amount of writing, epistolary and otherwise, takes place in *Lolita:* Humbert writes "tortuous essays in obscure journals" on quixotic topics like "The Proustian Theme in a Letter from Keats to Benjamin Bailey,"[1] willfully distorting chronology as well as plausibility. Humbert reads endless psychiatric reports on his neuroses; composes behavioral studies of fellow expeditionists in arctic Canada; writes, copies, then reconstructs a diary about his fifty days of connubial bliss with Charlotte. Letters are crucial to the plot: Charlotte confesses her love for Humbert in a letter; she dies while rushing to the mailbox with letters exposing Humbert's treachery; Mona Dahl's cryptic letter to Lolita contains vital clues to Quilty's identity; Lolita's letter enables Humbert to track her to Gray Star. The cumulative effect of this voluminous writing, particularly that of the specialists, is to impress upon us how little we know. Manuals and manuscripts, authorities and authors ranging from St. Augustine to Judge Woolsey are cited, but there seems to be an inverse relationship between writing and wisdom, as if the more specialized our language becomes, the less we perceive. That is especially true of Humbert's perception of Lolita: from beginning to end, she remains an enigma to him. For her, the rest is silence.

Specific letters are embedded in a larger generic framework that has often been overlooked, for Humbert's entire narrative owes much to epistolarity. Initially

From *Special Delivery: Epistolary Modes in Modern Fiction* (Chicago: University of Chicago Press, 1992), pp. 53–79. An earlier version of this paper appeared in *Refiguring the Father: New Feminist Readings of Patriarchy,* edited by Patricia Yaeger and Beth Kowaleski-Wallace (Carbondale: Southern Illinois University Press, 1989), pp. 131–52.

composed for use in his murder trial, it is a confession and an appeal. Legal language, direct addresses to the jury, invocations of legal precedents and case studies all reaccentuate one of the most ancient strains of epistolarity: the trial motif. In the *Heroides,* for example, the victimized heroine laments her fate, exposes her lover's treachery, exhorts the law to prosecute him, and dedicates herself to revenge. Héloïse invokes the trial motif when she presents her grievances to Abelard, provides evidence of her wrongs, abjures Abelard to recognize the justice of her grievances and the allegiance he owes to her. Throughout, she remains defiantly unrepentant. The trial motif extends from *Clarissa, Jane Eyre,* and *The Turn of the Screw* to *Absalom, Absalom!,* where Rosa Coldfield obsessively weighs Sutpen's sins and finds him wanting.[2] Humbert's discourse is contested and contesting; he is the most eloquent witness for the defense and (occasionally) for the prosecution. It is he who reminds us that "you can always count on a murderer for a fancy prose style"; it is he who condemns himself to prison, not for the murder of Quilty but for the murder of Lolita's childhood.

Despite such self-indictments, Humbert identifies with the poet and the madman; he thinks his excesses place him beyond the pale of ordinary society. His heightened sensitivity and refinement distinguish him from the vulgar multitudes. In this respect, it is significant that his closet analogue is another epistolary "hero": Werther. Werther, too, glorifies heart over head, passion over intellect, spontaneity over prudence, the individual over society. For Humbert as for Werther, the female object of adoration scarcely emerges as anything but a hazy abstraction, the mirror of the hero's narcissism as well as his desire. (Nabokov evokes Goethe's Lotte not only in the name Lolita but parodically in Charlotte Haze.) Werther reveals his narcissism when he confesses, "I coddle my heart like a sick child and give in to its every whim."[3] Humbert insists that acute sensitivity (rather than pedophilia) is what sets him apart from other people. He repeatedly reminds us of the "gentleness of my nature" (67); "the doe in me" (119); "my shyness, my distaste for any ostentation, my inherent sense of the *comme il faut*" (226). Both heroes claim that they yearn to be satisfied, as most people are, with modest contentment; both complain of the burden of having an exalted sensibility. "To be misunderstood," Werther observes, "is the miserable destiny of people like myself" (27).

That lonely destiny is what drives both Werther and Humbert to letter writing, but epistolary production, always a solitary endeavor, only increases their solipsism, a paradox of which both novelists are well aware. That paradox is what led Goethe to use the epistolary technique:

> When it came to the point ... of my wishing to describe the weariness with which people often experience life without having been forced to such a dismal outlook by want, I hit upon the idea, as author, of expressing my feelings in letters. For this weariness, this disgust with life, is born of loneliness, it is the foster child of solitude. He who gives himself up to it, flees from all opposition. ... Thus he is thrust back upon himself by the very things that should serve to take him out of himself. If he ever does want to discuss it, then

surely only in letters, for a written effusion, whether it be joyous or morose, does not antagonize anyone directly, and an answer filled with counter-arguments gives the lonely man an opportunity to harden in his peculiarities and offers the inducement to become more obdurate.[4]

Goethe pinpoints the contestatory dialogic nature of epistolarity as well as its solipsism. Humbert "hardens in his peculiarities," using writing to become more "obdurate." Like Werther, Humbert composes himself as he writes, consciously creating a self and a prose style that blind as well as dazzle. "The artist in me has been given the upper hand over the gentleman." His rationale: "retrospective verisimilitude" (67–68). Werther's and Humbert's elegantly phrased celebrations of aesthetic and emotional excess disguise the most inordinate egotism. Each hero is infantile and vampiristic. Each sees his fate as unique and blames others for his failings, as when Werther asks, "Don't children try to grasp anything they can think of? And I?" (92). Humbert does not just lust after children, he identifies with them, even resorting to baby talk and using his childishness as an excuse for his crimes. The name Werther and Humbert each give to their egotism is Desire; the agent responsible for their actions is Fate. Each refuses to believe that he is culpable, despite the fact that Werther ruins Lotte's life by committing suicide (sadistically reminding her in his final letters that it was she who provided the weapons). Humbert kidnaps and drugs Lolita before having sex with her but excuses himself by complaining, "I was not even her first lover" (125). Werther tells himself that "my fate is unique. Consider all other men fortunate, I tell myself, no one has ever suffered like you. . . . I have to suffer much. Oh, has any heart before me ever been so wretched?" (95). Self-pity dominates Humbert's narrative, too: he insists that he "tried to be good," but "Never mind, never mind, I am only a brute, never mind, let us go on with my miserable story" (176).

The similarities between Goethe's novel and Nabokov's are structural as well as thematic. Like Goethe, Nabokov positions an obtuse editor as intermediary between the reader and the narrator. The editor's role is didactic. Unlike Werther and Humbert, William and John Ray are dull, practical men of common sense. (Ray even writes a scientific monograph on the topic, "Do the Senses Make Sense?") Structurally, in each novel two triangular relationships are superimposed: that of hero, editor, and reader *of* the text parallels that of hero, rival, and beloved *in* the text. The Werther-Albert-Lotte triangle structurally mirrors the triangle of Humbert, Quilty, and Lolita. Nabokov depicts reading as a process of transference: just as Werther identifies with every lost lover, Humbert identifies with Werther, Poe, and all other poets and madmen. (Similar identifications with Werther and Poe reverberate uncannily in Barthes and Derrida.)

By reinventing Werther in Humbert, Nabokov defamiliarizes not just the major codes of romantic love but the very roots of Romanticism. Yet, as with Goethe's gullible audience,[5] Nabokov's audience (unlike Nabokov himself) seems to have endorsed Humbert's self-presentation without a trace of irony. Lionel Trilling, for instance, proclaimed in reviewing the novel that "*Lolita* is about love . . .

not about sex, but about love. Almost every page sets forth some explicit erotic emotion or some overt erotic action and still it is not about sex. It is about love. This makes it unique in my experience of contemporary novels."[6]

Humbert's narrative is a Nabokovian trap for unwary readers like Trilling, for critics can celebrate Humbert's role as love only by minimizing his role as father. Yet paradoxically, only Humbert's role as father makes it possible to be Lolita's lover, since that is what gives him unmonitored access to the girl as her semi-legal "guardian."[7] Trilling is right to notice the overt erotic activity on every page, but wrong to conclude that the novel is about love, not sex. *Lolita* is not about love but about incest, which is a betrayal of trust, a violation of love. How have critics managed so consistently to confuse love with incest in the novel? My aim here is to show how—through a variety of a narrative strategies—the inscription of the father's body in the text obliterates the daughter's.

Literature as Social Change or Aesthetic Bliss

The first strategy involves the frame within which Humbert's narrative is placed between John Ray's foreword and Nabokov's afterword. John Ray, Jr., is the psychologist who reads Humbert's narrative for the message, the general lesson, the ethical impact: this cautionary tale "should," he pompously dictates," make all of us—parents, social workers, educators—apply ourselves with still greater vigilance and vision to the task of bringing up a better generation in a safer world" (7). Yet everything conspires against Ray's exhortation. The issue of child abuse is obscured by Ray's professional self-advertisement, his pompous literary allusions, and his high-blown literary style. Nabokov not only parodies such seeming erudition through Ray's preface but pokes fun at reachers who so simply correlate art with life. For " 'old-fashioned' readers who wish to follow the destinies of the 'real' people beyond the 'true' story" (6), we learn in the preface what became of both Humbert and Lolita after Humbert ceased writing: he died of a heart attack and she died in childbirth. But readers curious about such matters belong at the bottom of the class, along with other dreary moralists, Freudians, and feminists who may murmur against the brutality of Lolita's treatment. As parody, then, the foreward acts as an injunction against the kind of reading that foregrounds social issues like child abuse.

Such readers will always miss the appeal of "aesthetic bliss," which Nabokov proposes as the appropriate response in "his" afterword:

> After doing my impersonation of suave John Ray . . . any comments coming straight from me may strike one—may strike me, in fact—as an impersonation of Vladimir Nabokov talking about his own book. . . . I am neither a reader nor a writer of didactic fiction, and, despite John Ray's assertion, *Lolita* has no moral in tow. For me a work of fiction exists only insofar as it affords me what I shall bluntly call aesthetic bliss.   (282, 286)

Here, then, is the second strategy that explains why incest is overlooked: critics take Nabokov at his word. His wry disclaimer effectively throws sand in our eyes, for the fact is that the afterword is as thoroughly cunning an impersonation as John Ray's foreword. The "end," in other words, is as much a part of the fiction as the beginning. The afterword is a sham because it simply extends the Humbertian aesthetic manifesto, a detail that credulous readers fail to notice. The artifice of self-referential textuality extends through Nabokov's afterword: it is a trap for readers who pride themselves on their sophistication and their ability to distance themselves from "real life." It contributes as much to the text by way of irony and distortion as the spurious index at the end of *Pale Fire*.[8] Foreword and afterword are mirror images—distortions, displacements, impersonations that seduce us into reading Humbert's narrative in a way that minimizes the viewpoint of a bruised child and foregrounds Humbert's obsession. He is not obsessed with love but rather with his own body, as we shall see.

Foreword and afterword each direct us toward monologic readings that are mutually exclusive. The choice between John Ray's foreword (literature as a vehicle for social change) and Nabokov's afterword (literature as self-referential artifice) involve seemingly irreconcilable differences, and, since Ray is the butt of parody, readers seem willing to go to any length to avoid being identified with him. Parody thus acts as an injunction against a certain mode of referential reading.

The challenge for feminist criticism is thus to read against the grain, to resist Humbert's rhetorical ruses *and* Nabokov's afterword. Is it possible in a double movement to analyze the horror of incest by reinscribing the material body of the child Lolita in the text, and simultaneously to undermine the representational fallacy by situating the text dialogically in relation to other texts? Ironically, despite their commitment to using literature as a vehicle for social change, feminists also have a stake in dismantling the representational fallacy, for paradoxically the most misogynistic criticism of *Lolita* comes from critics who take the novel as a representation of real life. Trilling, for instance, begins by citing Humbert's "ferocity . . . his open brutality to women." Yet, Trilling continues:

> Perhaps [Humbert's] depravity is the easier to accept when we learn that he deals with a Lolita who is not innocent, and who seems to have very few emotions to be violated; and I suppose we *naturally* incline to be lenient towards a rapist—legally and by intention H.H. is that—who eventually feels a deathless devotion to his victim!   (14)

Yet far from finding rape and incest shocking, Trilling is only shocked that so few contemporary novels focus on "love." *Lolita*, he proclaims, is one of them, despite the fact that Humbert's greed is, in Trilling's own words, "ape-like."

Some feminist critics argue that only by reading referentially can one prevent the female subject from disappearing. By this logic, one would expect critics who read *Lolita* as a representation of real life to pay considerable attention to Lolita, but, in fact, few have imagined what her victimization is like. Instead, they identify with the sensations Humbert records about his body by uncritically adopting his viewpoint. Thomas Molnar is representative:

> The central question the reader ought to ask of himself is whether he feels pity for the girl. Our ethical idea would require that we look at Lolita as a sacrificial lamb, that we become in imagination, her knight-protector. Yet this is impossible for two reasons. One is very simple: before yielding to Humbert, the girl has had a nasty little affair with a nasty little thirteen-year-old. . . . Besides, she is a spoiled sub-teenager with a foul mouth, a self-offered target for lechers. . . . throughout, she remains an object perhaps even to herself.[9]

Molnar indicts Lolita for being a tease who "asks for it," and who deserves what she gets since she is "damaged goods." Both Trilling and Molnar castigate Lolita for being unknowable, but Humbert's failure to understand her demonstrates his obtuseness, not her inaccessibility. Indeed, despite his aggressive desire to know all, Humbert finally confesses that there are depths in her inaccessible to him (259).

Nor must one forget that Humbert is a notoriously unreliable narrator who lies to psychiatrists, deceives two wives, and otherwise takes elaborate precautions to avoid detection. In view of his unreliability, it is doubtful his claim that Lolita seduced him is true; more important, it is unverifiable, and credulous critics who read the novel as a reflection of life thus end up merely reifying codes that can be traced directly from literature, codes that—from the courtly love tradition to *Clarissa* to modern cinema—first idealize the woman loved from afar and then degrade her by blaming her for her own rape and humiliation.

My reservations about referential readings, however, do not imply that the opposite emphasis on self-referential artifice is any more enlightened. Parody can serve to defamiliarize habitual modes of perception, as in *Zoo,* but it can also disguise strategies of appropriation, an aggressive will to power. Yet critics invariably excuse Humbert. Take Alfred Appel, who describes the novel as a "springboard for parody," adding: "Humbert's terrible demands *notwithstanding,* Lolita is as insensitive as children are to their *actual* parents; *sexuality aside,* she demands anxious parental placation in a too typically American way, and affords Nabokov an ideal opportunity to comment on the Teen and Subteen Tyranny."[10] Such passages rupture the critical stance that self-referentiality demands; when it comes to women, Appel seems to forget his main point that the novel is *not* realistic! In a now famous statement, Appel goes on to assert: "By creating a reality which is a fiction, but a fiction that is able to mock the reader, the author has demonstrated the fiction of 'reality,' and the reader who accepts these implications may even have experienced a change in consciousness" (120).

But before one can analyze a fiction that mocks the reader, or results in a change in consciousness, one needs to examine the kind of reader one has in mind. Humbert is not only an avid writer, he is an avid reader: of motel registers, class rolls, road signs, comics, even movie posters. His reading of Lolita is the model on which male critics rely—wheher they read self-referentially *or* mimetically. And that is the source of their blindness: they fail to notice that Humbert is not only a notoriously unreliable narrator but that he is an unreliable reader, too. If he were not, he would have solved the mystery of Quilty's identity long ago. As it happens, he never does solve it; Lolita has to tell him. Like his heart, his powers of perception and his eyes are "hysterical unreliable organ[s]." A voyeur, he wants to see but not be seen. He wants to read, interpret, and write but not be analyzed by psychiatrists or "out-authored" by Quilty.

Despite his unreliability, feminist readers have the choice of either participating in their own "immasculation" by endorsing aesthetic bliss, or of demonstrating their humorlessness and frigidity. Judith Fetterly defines "immasculation" as the process by which "the female reader is co-opted into participation in an experience from which she is explicitly excluded; she is asked to identify with a selfhood that defines itself in opposition to her; she is required to identify against herself."[11] Consider the famous scene of Lolita on the couch with Humbert while he surreptitiously mastur-bates and enjoins the reader to respond:

> I want my learned readers to participate in the scene I am about to replay; I want them to examine its every detail and see for themselves how . . . chaste, the whole wine-sweet event is. . . . What had begun as a delicious distension of my innermost roots became a glowing tingle . . . not found elsewhere in conscious life. . . . Lolita had been safely solipsized. . . . Suspended on the brink of that voluptuous abyss (a nicety of physiological equipoise comparable to certain techniques in the arts). . . . I crushed out against her left buttock the last throb of the longest ecstasy man or monster had ever known.   (57–58)

This is a scene where the father's body is the site and the source of not only aesthetic bliss but literal orgasm; both come at the same time—if, that is, the reader is male. Lolita, however, is not so much "solipsized" as annihilated, as Humbert reveals while congratulating himself in the next scene:

> What I had madly possessed was not she, but *my own creation*, another, fanciful Lolita—*perhaps, more real* than Lolita; overlapping, encasing her; floating between me and her, and having no will, no consciousness—indeed no life of her own.
>
> The child knew nothing. I had done nothing to her. And nothing pre-vented me from repeating a performance that affected her as little as if she were a photographic image rippling upon a screen and I a humble hunchback abusing myself in the dark.   (59; emphasis added)

Thus physical as well as aesthetic *jouissance* for Humbert requires psychic anes-thesia or annihilation for Lolita. "Reader! Bruder!" Humbert exclaims, "I shall not exist if you do not imagine me" (119), is a man's appeal to male readers. The appeal disguises the fact that Lolita does not exist for Humbert precisely because he fails to imagine her except as a projection of his desire.

What the text mimes, then, is a bundle of relations between men, as clarified not only in the passage above but in the responses of critics like Trilling and Molnar. The incest taboo, as Lévi-Strauss (following Freud) reveals, has nothing to do with protecting the girl, and everything to do with ensuring that she functions as an object of exchange between men: "[I]t is the supreme rule of the gift ... which allows [the incest taboo's] nature to be understood."[12] The scene in which Humbert masturbates with Lolita on his lap is a good example of how what is male is made to seem "universal." As Patrocinio Schweickart explains in discussing the implied authorial contract:

> For the male reader, the text serves as the meeting ground of the personal and the universal.... the male reader is invited to feel his *difference* (concretely, from the girl) and to equate that with the universal. Relevant here is Lévi-Strauss's theory that woman functions as currency exchanged between men. The woman in the text converts the text into a woman, and the circulation of this text/woman becomes the central ritual that establishes the bond between the author and his male readers.[13]

That male bond and identification with the male body help to explain further how incest can be mistaken for love. From the opening words, Humbert's body is a palpable presence: "Lolita, light of my life, fire of my loins. My sin, my soul. Lo-lee-ta: the tip of the tongue taking a trip of three steps down the palate to tap, at three, on the teeth"(11). "Lolita" is a word; Humbert is flesh: loins, tongue, palate, teeth. Humbert's obsession with his body is not just narcissistic but infantile; it is he who is marked by a preoedipal fascination with his own bowels, his digestion, his heartburn, his headaches, his blood pressure—and of course, his penis, that "pentapod monster" that feels like a "thousand eyes wide open in my eyed blood" (41). As he masturbates, he "entered a plane of being where nothing mattered, save the infusion of joy brewed within my body" (57). Thus, while exploiting his role as guardian to enforce the Law of the Father, Humbert also reverses it. He turns oedipalization inside out, just as his "only grudge against nature was that I could not turn my Lolita inside out and apply voracious lips to her young matrix, her unknown heart, her nacreous liver, the seagrapes of her lungs, her comely twin kidneys" (151). She is the *femme morcélée par excellence.* The incestuous father-as-his-own-child: he feasts on the female body, sucking Lolita's flat breasts and "brown nose." In Lacanian terms, "Lolita" is little more than a signifier in Humbert's Image-repertoire, and Humbert's revealing allusion to her heart being "unknown" highlights how illusory his project (and his projections) are. Her sole function is to reflect and satisfy the body of the father. Initially, she has no reality for him except as the incarnation of his childhood love, Annabel Leigh; Lolita is little more than a replication of a photographic still. He wishes he had filmed her; he longs to to have a frozen moment permanently on celluloid since he could not hold her still in life. She is thus the object of his appropriation, and he not only appropriates her but projects onto her his desire and his neuroses. Significantly, she only serves as a simulacrum when her nicknames—Lolita, Lo, Lola, Dolly—are used, for her legal name, Dolores, points too directly toward another representation—Our Lady of Sorrows—and thus to a higher law than man's. An abyss lies between the "Lolita" who is purely imaginary product of Humbert's desire and the "Dolores" whose "guardian" is the source of her suffering.

Reading Dialogically: Lolita's Other Analogues

John Ray's foreword and Nabokov's afterword are diametrically opposed monologic readings. By exposing the weaknesses in such readings, one discovers what feminist criticism stands to gain by dismantling the representational fallacy. I should like to propose a dialogic reading, one that is both feminist and intertextual; one that releases the female body from its anesthesia and from Humbert's solipsism while simultaneously highlighting textual artifice. Nabokov, I would argue, is not writing in either the one mode or the other: he is writing a book that elides the female by framing the narrative through Humbert's angle of vision. He then comments indirectly on that framing device by references not to "real life" but to other literary texts. That the novel is an exercise in intertextuality, however, does not mitigate the horror of Lolita's treatment. Instead, it reinforces it. Among the multiple levels of intertextuality operating in the novel, four in particular deserve mention because they suggest the myriad ways in which the novel allegorizes Woman: the major poems in the courtly love tradition; certain stories and poems of Edgar Allan Poe, Henry James's *The Turn of the Screw*, and Charles Dickens's *Bleak House*.

The Handmaid's Tale ⟨. . .⟩ reveals that the effort to define Woman through binary oppositions (whore/madonna, victim/devourer, witch/angel, etc.) has been a popular pastime through the ages. *Lolita* is, among other things, a compendium of definitions of Woman, in texts ranging from *Know Your Own Daughter* and *The Little Mermaid* to *Carmen* and *Le Roman de la rose*. As in the courtly love tradition, Humbert moves from adoration to disillusionment when the beloved fails to measure up to his code of perfection. Like the knights who celebrated the chastity of the lady and the difficulty of their endeavors, Humbert boasts of his difficulties when he masturbates with Lolita on his lap. In contrast to his idealized "lady," "real" women are miserly, envious, fickle, loudmouthed, drunkards (like Rita, the drunk with whom Humbert lives after Lolita flees), or slaves to their bellies (like Valeria, the "brainless baba" who is Humbert's first wife). As he reveals when he insists that Lolita has no will or life of her own, Humbert denies not just what is womanly in Lolita—he denies what is human.[14] That is why he must insist that nymphets are demonic, and it is the myth of demonic children that ties the novel to James's *Turn of the Screw*.

Nabokov confesses, "My feelings towards James are rather complicated. I really dislike him intensely but now and then the figure in the phrase, the *turn* of the epithet, the *screw* of an absurd adverb, cause me a kind of electric tingle, as if some current of his was also passing through my own blood."[15] James said that he devised *The Turn of the Screw* as a trap to catch the "jaded, the disillusioned, the fastidious" reader—in other words, the reader who fancies himself or herself as being beyond sentimentality.[16] Similarly, sophisticated readers of *Lolita*, avid to align themselves with "aesthetic bliss," fall into precisely the same trap by ignoring the pathos of Lolita's predicament. James said his subject was "the helpless plasticity of childhood: that *was* my little tragedy."[17] For Nabokov as for James, "plasticity" is the medium enabling one to create aesthetic bliss. But "plasticity" has other connotations: to mold, to form, to fix. The governess in *The Turn of the Screw* tries to arrest the children's development; the desire to "fix" things indeed is one of her motives for writing her retrospective narrative. She wants to frame time itself, just as Humbert desires "to fix the perilous magic of nymphets." In both texts—indeed throughout Poe and Dickens as well as James—how and what you see depends on the frame: James's governess anticipates Humbert by resorting to a fancy prose style to frame a murder.[18] "Aesthetic bliss" is a frameup. In both the governess's narrative and in Humbert's, silence, exile, and cunning lie in that gap between past and present and determine what inflection will be given to the murder of childhood. As Poe asks in "Lenore," "How *shall* the ritual then be read?—the requiem how be sung/By you—by yours, the evil eye—by yours the slanderous tongue/ That did to death the innocence that died and died so young?"[19]

To recognize that violence, one must first defuse the charge that any lament for the murder of Lolita's childhood is sheer sentimentality, a willful misreading of a novel meant to parody such attitudes. Lecturing at Cornell, Nabokov himself defused the charge, noting that Dickens's *Bleak House* deals "mainly with the misery of little ones, with the pathos of childhood—and Dickens is at his best in these matters."[20] Nabokov emphasizes the astonishing number of children in the novel—he counts over thirty—and says that "one of the novel's most striking themes" is "their troubles, insecurity, humble joys ... but mainly their misery" (65). Their parents are either "frauds or freaks" (69). And then he says something that will surprise contemporary readers:

> I should not like to hear the charge of sentimentality made against this strain that runs through *Bleak House*. I want to submit that people who denounce the sentimental are generally unaware of what sentiment is. ... Dickens's great art should not be mistaken for a cockney version of the seat of emotion—it is the real thing, keen, subtle, specialized compassion, with a grading and merging of melting shades, with the very accent of profound pity in the words uttered, and with an artist's choice of the most visible, most audible, most tangible epithets.   (86–87)

His allusion to "grading and merging of melting shades, with the very accent of profound pity," echo a poignant and revealing sentence about Lolita's temperament—that temperament to which critics like Trilling and Molnar claim no reader has access. After he overhears Lolita commenting that "what is so dreadful about dying is that you are completely on your own," Humbert realizes that "[b]ehind the awful juvenile clichés, there was in her a garden and a twilight, and a palace gate—dim and adorable regions which happened to be lucidly and absolutely forbidden to me, in my polluted rags and miserable convulsions, ... living as we did, she and I, in a world of total evil" (259).

In his lecture on *Bleak House,* Nabokov goes on to contrast Skimpole, who *represents* a child, with the real children in the novel who are overburdened with adult cares and duties, like Charley, the little girl who supports all her little brothers and sisters. Dickens writes, "She might have been a child, playing at washing, and imitating a poor workingwoman." And Nabokov observes, "Skimpole is a vile parody of a child, whereas this little girl is a pathetic imitator of an adult woman" (86). The same is true of Humbert; like Skimpole, he imitates a child. It is Humbert, after all, who wants to play forever in his "pubescent park, in my mossy garden. Let them play around me forever. Never grow up" (22). It is Humbert who talks baby talk to Lolita—never she to him.[21] Thus, if parody serves as a "springboard," it can also be a "vile" screen for "total evil."

In contrast to Humbert's grotesque imitation of a child, Lolita is forced to imitate adult womanhood by performing "wifely" duties before she gets her coffee. In the very act of trying to fix her forever in childhood, Humbert not only stunts her growth but makes her old before her time. Her fate is presaged by Humbert's transactions with the whore Monique; he is briefly attracted to her nymphet qualities, but she grows less juvenile, more womanly overnight: only for a minute does "a delinquent nymphet [shine] through the matter-of-fact young whore" (24). The power of the image is one of the novel's dominant themes, for far from being in love with Lolita, Humbert is completely obsessed with the mental image he incessantly projects with random girls and women. From the moment he first masturbates on the couch, Humbert proceeds to turn Lolita into a whore, euphemistically alluding to her vagina as a "new white purse," and priding himself upon having left it "intact." By the time they reach the Enchanted Hunters Motel, he has begun paying her with pennies and dimes to perform sexually.

Father-daughter incest, as Judith Lewis Herman points out, is a relationship of prostitution: "The father, in effect, forces the daughter to pay with her body for affection and care which should be freely given. In so doing, he destroys the protective bond between parent and child and initiates his daughter into prostitution. This is the reality of incest from the point of view of the victim."[22] The victim's viewpoint in *Lolita* is elided, for rather than claiming any responsibility himself, Humbert defines his bribes as a "definite drop in Lolita's morals" (167). The fact that she ups the ante from fifteen cents to four dollars has been seen by misogynist critics as a sign that she was a whore all along. Humbert once again reveals his obsession with his own body and once again astutely sizes up readers' allegiances when he exclaims: "O Reader . . . imagine me, on the very rack of joy noisily emitting dimes . . . and great big silver dollars like some sonorous, jingly and wholly demented machine vomiting riches; and in the margin of that leaping epilepsy she would firmly clutch a handful of coins in her little fist" (168).

Humbert implicitly assumes that his (male?) readers will identify solely with his sexuality and sensibility. Since he presents himself as a schlemiel, the comic urge to identify with him is almost irresistible. The hilarity, however, is considerably undercut when we realize that Lolita is trying to accumulate enough money to run away—an escape Humbert thwarts by periodically ransacking her room and robbing her.

Nor can one ignore what materialist critiques of the novel expose: the rampant consumerism of postwar American society, a society that feeds on images rather than beliefs. Lolita is the ideal consumer: naive, spoiled, totally hooked on the gadgets of modern life, a true believer in the promises of Madison Avenue and Hollywood. Yet a materialist-*feminist* perspective enables one to see something seldom noted: Lolita is as much the object consumed by Humbert as she is the product of her culture. And if she is "hooked," he is the one who turns her into a hooker. She is the object of both his conspicuous consumption and concupiscence, as his voracious desire to devour her heart, liver, lungs, and kidneys demonstrates. When he sees a dismembered mannikin in a department store, Humbert comments vaguely that "it's a good symbol for something," and "Dolly Haze" (one of Lolita's many nicknames) comes more and more to resemble those mute, inanimate dolls on whose bodies consumer wares are hung. By the time of their final reunion in Gray Star, she has been so thoroughly prostituted that she assumes Humbert will only relinquish her rightful inheritance if she sexually services him in a motel.

What is most astounding about Ray's preface is that, despite his alleged interest in "reality," he says none of these things. He never once names incest; instead he refers to it as that "special experience" and insists that " 'offensive' is frequently but a synonym for 'unusual' " (7). While ostensibly reading Humbert's narrative as a "case history" and unctuously referring to its "ethical impact," he notes that, if Humbert had undergone psychiatric treatment, "there would have been no disaster; but then, neither would there have been this book" (7). Ray's disturbing statement reveals an utter disregard for Lolita's suffering. He effaces her entirely; "Lolita" is merely the title of a narrative by which he is "entranced." By thus focusing solely on Humbert's "supreme misery," Ray becomes Humbert's dupe. In charting Humbert's quest, he replicates his crime. Is Lolita anywhere to be found in the text?

Is There a Woman in the Text?

What effect does incest have on Lolita? The first act of coitus is rendered so poetically as to camouflage what is being described; importantly, it is one of the few passages depicting the sensations of Lolita's body rather than Humbert's. He describes it *as if* it were a painting: "a slave child [trying] to climb a column of onyx . . . a fire opal dissolving with a ripple-ringed pool, a last throb, a last dab of color, stinging red, smarting pink, a sigh, a wincing child" (124). Aesthetic form distances us from Lolita's pain, diverting our attention from content: Lolita is enslaved, bleeding, and in such pain that she cannot sit because Humbert has torn something inside her. Humbert's aesthetic response, however, cannot completely disguise the fact that with this act Lolita's aborted childhood is left behind forever: she learns that her mother is dead and realizes that she has nowhere else to go. In contrast to conventional criticism, which divides the first part of the novel from the second part in terms of such dichotomies as illusion/reality or dream/nightmare, all such framing devices invariably elide Lolita herself. Whether part one focuses on Humbert's body and part two on his misery, Humbert remains the focus: his suffering, his sensations, his sex and sensibility. The crucial dichotomy involves the shift in Humbert's role from Charlotte's lover to Lolita's father, from artful lodger to evil guardian. Perhaps the novel's most profound paradox is that Humbert cannot violate Lolita sexually until he assumes the societally sanctioned role of stepfather. The novel systematically exposes the relentless familialism of American behavioral science and psychology, with its obsessive insistence on "normalcy" in the nuclear family. By conflating that familialism with the literary clichés of romantic love, both ideologies are grotesquely defamiliarized.

John Ray's foreword is a parody of responses that might lead the reader to inquire about the relation of fictional representations of incest to clinical analyses. In that regard, it acts once again as an injunction, prohibiting the reader from inquiring into "reality." But readers who defy that prohibition discover that the novel is an uncannily accurate representation of father-daughter incest. Not surprisingly, the clinical literature reveals that step-fathers are guilty of incest as often as natural fathers are. Carol Lynn Mithers points out: "Researchers estimate that as many as twelve to fifteen million American women have suffered incestuous abuse; about half of these cases involves fathers or stepfathers."[23] The overwhelming majority of children experience no pleasure in the act; and even later in life, as mature women, they are seldom able to enjoy sexual relations.[24] The fact that Lolita similarly feels nothing for Humbert is repeatedly presented as a black mark against her: "Never," Humbert confesses, "did she vibrate under my touch," and for this "crime," he dubs her "My Frigid Princess." And he realizes that "she was ready to turn away from [me] with something akin to plain repulsion" (152). But her response is not *akin* to repulsion, it *is* repulsion, and the difference is one of Humbert's characteristic strategies of evasion. Elsewhere, he describes their existence as a "parody of incest," but within the fictional framework the incest is literal, not parodic. Nabokov's framing device parodies Ray's reading of the novel as a case history, but he also ensures that we only think of one kind of case—that of obsessional love. The fact that he never mentions incest is no accident. Parody, which prohibits inquiry into "real cases," also prohibits us from asking, "Whose case is it, anyway?"

Humbert's jealousy, his tyranny inside the home balanced by his ineffectuality and obsequiousness outside it, the threats of reform schools or punishment if Lolita reports him—these are all patterns of incest documented clinically as well as textually. To enjoy not Lolita but his fantasies, Humbert decides to "ignore what I could not help perceiving, the fact that I was to her not a boy friend, not a glamour man, not a pal, not even a person at all, but just two eyes and a foot of engorged brawn" (258). Humbert's exaggeration of the size of his penis may be male wish fulfillment or male penis envy, but in either case the exaggeration emphasizes male desire rather than the physical pain that the disparity between his physical proportions and Lolita's must cause her. The allusion to his eyes is revealing, for Humbert voyeuristically measures every aspect of Lolita's physical development. "Has she already been initiated by mother nature to the Mystery of the Menarche?" he asks (45).

Critics usually cite Humbert's obsessive scrutiny of Lolita's body as further evidence that the novel is a love story; instead, such obsessions are typical of father-daughter incest, signs not of overpowering love but of domination. Humbert spies on Lolita, monitors her every movement, subjects her to endless inquisitions about her whereabouts, her girlfriends, and potential boyfriends in a pattern common to incest. The father tyrannically controls the daughter's actions, is insanely jealous of boys, and strives to isolate her as much as possible from the rest of the world.[25] Humbert can only conceive of fatherhood tyrannically, as when he subjects Lolita to parental interrogations: Why has she missed two piano lessons? Who is she talking to when she disappears for twenty-eight minutes? His obsession with the names of all her schoolmates and acquaintances culminates in the crucial question he asks her in Gray Star about her rescuer/abductor's identity: "Where is he? . . . Come, his name?" (247). His dominant mode of discourse and of parenting is inquisitorial.[26]

Critics who condemn Lolita as wanton misunderstand the significance of Humbert's compulsion, for in philosophical terms it is he who is wanton rather than Lolita. As Harry K. Frankfurt explains, free will involves the freedom to have the will one wants. Those, like Humbert, who lack such freedom, are "wanton": "The essential characteristic of a wanton is that he does not care about his will. His desires move him to do certain things, without its being true of him either that he wants to be moved by those desires or that he prefers to be moved by other desires."[27] Humbert's sexual craving compels him to abuse Lolita, and while he insists that he does not want to be moved by such desires, he is never able to cease violating her sexually or psychically.

His mania for making Lolita reveal herself and respond to him demonstrates that she is not—nor was she ever—"safely solipsized." The word he uses most frequently to describe his violation of her is "operation," but an operation in which Lolita is never really completely anesthetized either psychically or physically: "The operation was over, all over, and she was weeping . . . a salutory storm of sobs after one of the fits of moodiness that had become so frequent with her in the course of that otherwise admirable year!" (154). Her "sobs in the night,—every night, every night" (160), the moodiness that Humbert finds unfathomable, her powerlessness to escape him when she says, "Oh no, not again!"—all point to a despair that surpasses his powers of description—or so he claims. But from *The Sorrows of Young Werther* to *The Turn of the Screw*, guilty narrators have taken refuge in the ineffable: whatever they want to evade they claim is impossible to describe. The ineffable—like the inevitable (nicknamed "McFate" by Humbert)—is invariably an evasion. In one such passage, Humbert says that Lolita has "a look I cannot exactly describe—an expression of helplessness so perfect that it seemed to grade into one of rather comfortable inanity just because this was the very limit of injustice and frustration" (258).

Does such a statement imply that Humbert finally perceives the enormity of his crimes against Lolita? Not until Humbert is entrapped by Quilty does he begin to comprehend his injustice, for as Thoreau said, "How much more eloquently and effectively he can combat injustice who has experienced a little in his own person."

Quilty "succeeded in thoroughly enmeshing me and my thrashing anguish in his demoniacal game. With infinite skill, he swayed and staggered, and regained an impossible balance, always leaving me with . . . betrayal, fury, desolation, horror and hate" (227). Quilty is the doppelgänger, the figure traditionally presented not just as a double but as a brother, with whom one has the usual rivalry of siblings, according to Freud. As doppelgänger, Quilty is the figure onto whom Humbert projects his guilt in an attempt to evade responsibility for the crime of incest. Freud suggests that the aim of the incest taboo is not to protect female children but to control male sexual rivalry. Lolita functions as the object of exchange between Quilty and Humbert, who are mirror images, locked in a Girardian triangle of mimetic desire.[28] Each wants what the other wants: "[Quilty's] condition," says Humbert, "infected me" (271).[29] In pursuing Lolita, Humbert plays three roles: avenging father, jealous lover, and rival scholar. The latter role torments him most, for as Humbert embarks on his "cryptogrammic paper chase," he is indignant that Quilty "challenged by scholarship" in motel registers across the country; furious that Quilty's anagrams "ejaculate in my face" (228). While that is an experience Lolita probably shared in Humbert's hands, her perspective has no place in this confrontation of rivals (That, indeed, is the problem with Girard's theory of mimetic desire: the female is always lost in translation.)[30]

In "The Springboard of Parody," Appel compared Lolita to Poe's "William Wilson," another "first-person confession by a pseudonymous narrator who fled in vain" from the Double who pursued him from school to school; like those doubles, "Humbert and Quilty are rivals in scholarship rather than love" (125). In their final confrontation, Humbert can no longer distinguish his own body from Quilty's: "I rolled over him. We rolled over me. They rolled over him. We rolled over us." Humbert describes the struggle as a "silent, soft, formless tussle on the part of two literati" (272). This competition between two second-rate talents disguises the fact that, even if they had been first-rate, their struggle would have been equally senseless, since it fails to undo the crimes against Lolita. Aesthetic bliss is not a criterion that compensates for those crimes; instead it is a dead end, meager consolation for the murder of Lolita's childhood. Conventional readings based on sin, confession, and redemption argue that Humbert exacts revenge because Quilty broke Lolita's heart. But Humbert's vengeance is more egotistic: Quilty out-authored him. Quilty turned Humbert into a character in his script, which is precisely what Humbert does to Lolita. Armed with the tattered totemic photograph of his childhood love, Annabel Leigh, he "reincarnates" her image and superimposes it on Lolita. In his avid pursuit of immortality through art, he studies Poe's dictum that the death of a beautiful woman is "the most poetical topic in the world—and . . . that the lips best suited for such topic are those of a bereaved lover."[31]

Indeed, even in his last scene with Lolita, Humbert continues to interrogate her as if she were his legal possession, to interpret her as if she were a frozen image, a blank page. He is still talking at her. When she says that she would sooner go back to Quilty than leave now with Humbert, he writes, "She groped for words. I supplied them mentally ("He broke my heart. You merely broke my life") (254).[32]

The narrative we read is an exercise in what Humbert calls "poetical justice"—but it is so only for himself, not for Lolita—although he never points this out. He writes simultaneously to set the record straight, to settle the score, and to ensure that the last word is his. But like all his other attempts to possess, to control, to fix, and to frame, this one, too, reveals his sterility and impotence—for while he has the last word on Quilty, John Ray has the last word on him. ("For better or worse, it is the commentator who has the last word," says Kinbote in *Pale Fire*.)[33] Humbert appropriates visibility, vulnerability, carnality for himself, and in so doing, he evacuates Lolita's body, turning it into a projective site for his neuroses and his narrative.

Humbert's notoriously poor circulation finally leads to coronary thrombosis; his heart proves to be as unreliable as his narrative is. His heart prompts him to declare that he has fallen in love forever, but he adds, "The word 'forever' referred only to my own passion, to eternal Lolita *as reflected* in my blood" (67; emphasis added). His is a closed circulatory system, solipsistic and narcissistic. Like Goethe, Nabokov perceived that epistolarity was the perfect vehicle to mirror that claustrophobia. Humbert fathers nobody. Lolita only exists insofar as she can reflect him, magnifying his stature. "The refuge of art" for Humbert is the mirror of castration for Lolita, a polarity clearly exposed in her tennis game. Humbert appreciates it aesthetically: "[H]er form was, indeed, an absolutely perfect imitation of absolutely top-notch tennis . . . it had . . . beauty, directness, youth, a classical purity of trajectory" (211). But her form lacks—as does she herself—feeling, force, conviction, for she has no will to win. Sex with Humbert has taught her too well merely to mime, without enthusiasm.

By thus inscribing the female body in the text, rather than consigning it to the hazy and dolorous realm of abstract male desire, or letting it circulate as the currency of exchange between male rivals, one discovers that Lolita is not a photographic image, or a still life, or a freeze-frame preserved on film but a damaged child. This is what Humbert's own humiliation at the hands of Quilty enables him finally to perceive: the "semi-animated, subhuman trickster who had sodomized my darling" (269) turns out to be not Quilty but himself. Quilty is not far wrong to insist that Humbert is "a beastly pervert" and that he, Quilty, is "not responsible for the rapes of others" (271).

One crucial distinction is between Humbert the focus, trapped in chronological time, and Humbert the voice,[34] writing from jail, composing his death sentences: "Had not something within her been broken by me—*not that I realized it then!*—she would have had on the top of her perfect form the will to win" (212). If in part one his sole obsession is with his lust, he is in part two still utterly self-absorbed: his guilt and his misery are his themes: "*my* heart and *my* beard, and *my* putrefaction" (258). Humbert challenges the reader to prove to him that "in the infinite run it does not matter a jot that a North American girl-child named Dolores Haze had been deprived of her childhood by a maniac . . . (and if it can, then life is a joke), I see nothing for the treatment of my misery but the melancholy and very local palliative of articulate art" (258).

The thirty-five-year sentence he imposes on himself for rape sounds harsh, but it actually lets him off the hook for other murders besides Quilty's: Lolita's death in childbirth and her stillborn baby's demise are anticipated as early as the first act of intercourse with Humbert when he feels "as if I were sitting with the small ghost of somebody I had just killed" (129). "Palliative," moreover, is yet another of Nabokov's Jamesian traps for the reader, for it can mean either to "lessen the pain without curing," or "to make appear less serious or offensive." Humbert is guilty on both counts, and while he takes refuge in the sham lyricism of articulating his shame, for Lolita the rest is silence.

Is there, then, a woman in this text—and in what sense is that question meant? For Shoshana Felman, it is allegorical:

> The allegorical question "She? Who?" will thus remain unanswered. The text, nonetheless, will play out the question to its logical end, so as to show in what way it *precludes* any answer, in what way the question is set as a trap. The very lack of the answer will then write itself as a different question, through which the original question will find itself dislocated, radically shifted and transformed.[35]

The feminist critic can expose the lack, the trap, and the frameup by reading symptomatically. She can dismantle the misogyny of traditional critical assessments of Lolita's "wantonness" by analyzing the precise nature of Humbert's craving. A feminist perspective thus shifts suspicion from Lolita to Humbert, for his organs— "heart," penis, eyes—expose his hysteria, treachery, and delusions. As Patrocinio Schwiekart explains, feminist criticism must pay attention to material realities in order to effect social change: "Feminist criticism . . . is a mode of *praxis*. The point is not merely to interpret literature in various ways; the point is to *change the world*" (39). But feminist theory also deconstructs language and signification, ana- lyzing not just representations but the manifest and latent mechanisms of repre- sentation. One the one hand, feminist criticism can inscribe the female body in the text and, on the other hand, show how that textual body is *fabricated*— in both senses of the world—as a fiction and as a construct. One can unveil Lolita's viewpoint and simultaneously stress its verisimilitude—as opposed to its *veracity:* "Is it possible," Nabokov asks, "to imagine in its full reality the life of another, to live it oneself and transfer it intact onto paper? I doubt it . . . it can only be the verisimilar, and not the verifiable truth, that the mind perceives. . . . What we call art is, in essence, truth's picture window: one has to know how to frame it, that's all."[36]

Framed between Ray's foreword and Nabokov's spurious afterword, Hum- bert's narrative fixes our attention on "love" as the vehicle for artistic immortality. Paradoxically, the more he mocks his own prose style, the more we notice its beauty and endorse the Humbertian aesthetic manifesto of "aesthetic bliss." By seeing how the framing of *Lolita* elides the issue of father-daughter incest, one shifts and transforms the questions, revealing how the father's sexuality is superimposed upon the daughter's body. The most eloquent testimony of the results comes from Lolita herself. In one of the few instances where she speaks in her own voice (which is as stark in its simplicity as Humbert's is baroque), she sends Humbert a brief letter from Gray Star: "I have gone through much sadness and hardship" (243).

The female subject need not disappear, despite poststructuralism's relativizing of relations between writer, reader, and critic, for the feminist critic can exploit that notion of relativity. Although Humbert's cunning aesthetic manifesto has been blithely endorsed by generations of critic, it is itself relative, which is why I have tried to defamiliarize it here. Since the foreword parodies case histories, we tend to forget that "representation *does* bear a relation to something which we can know previously existed."[37] Specifically, the incestuous father's tyranny is clinically verifiable in this novel. Nor does the subject's decentering invalidate the notion of agency: despite his insistence on *jouissance,* Humbert remains culpable. Deconstructive strategies, in fact, help to expose multiple frames of reference: the intertextual allusions to Dickens, Poe, and James (all dealing with the exploitation and death of children and childhood) undermine the purely aesthetic approach to the novel. Clinical studies of incest further expose Humbert's rhetorical ruses. By combining feminist with deconstructive strategies, one discovers that the novel Trilling heralded as the greatest love story of the twentieth century in fact indicts the ideology of love and exposes literature's complicity in perpetuating it. The answer to the question, "Is there a woman in this text?" is no. But there was a female, one whose body was the source of crimes and puns, framed unsettlingly between the horror of incest and aesthetic *jouissance,* between material reality and antimimesis, between pathos and parody. That body was not a woman's; like Lolita's stillborn baby, it was a girl's.

NOTES

[1] Vladimir Nabokov, *Lolita* (1955; reprinted New York: Berkley Books, 1977), p. 18; hereinafter cited parenthetically in the text.

[2] See Linda Kauffman, *Discourses of Desire* (Ithaca: Cornell University Press, 1986), pp. 44–45, 77–78, 130–40, 201, 204–7, 269–73.

[3] Johann Wolfgang von Goethe, *The Sorrows of Young Werther,* trans. Catherine Hutter (New York: New American Library, 1962), p. 26; hereinafter cited parenthetically in the text.

[4] Goethe, "Reflections on Werther," afterword in *The Sorrows of Young Werther,* pp. 139–40.

[5] For an account of Goethe's dismay at the public's identification with Werther, which culminated in a rash of suicides among young men, see ibid., pp. 130–53.

[6] Lionel Trilling, "The Last Lover: Vladimir Nabokov's *Lolita,*" *Encounter* 11 (October 1958): 9–19; hereinafter cited parenthetically in the text.

[7] Humbert's legal rights as guardian are never notarized, but he exercises those "rights" nonetheless, threatening Lolita with reform school if she reveals their sexual relationship, and taking control of her inheritance following her mother's death.

[8] The afterword, "On a book entitled *Lolita,*" dated 12 November 1956, is appended to every edition except the first, including over twenty-five translations. There are many precedents for discussing afterwords or appendices—some written many years later—as "integral" parts of novels: William Faulkner's *The Sound and the Fury* and *Absalom, Absalom!* come to mind. No afterword, however, can be relied upon as an answer to questions raised in a novel; instead, it makes the questions more problematic, as Nabokov's afterword to *Lolita* demonstrates.

[9] Thomas Molnar, "Matter-of-Fact Confession of a Non-Penitent," *Chronicles of Culture* 2 (January–February 1978): 11–13.

[10] Alfred Appel, Jr., "*Lolita:* The Springboard of Parody" in *Nabokov: The Man and His Work,* ed. L. S.

Dembo (Madison: Univ. of Wisconsin Press, 1967), p. 121; emphasis added; hereinafter cited parenthetically in the text.

[11] Judith Fetterly, *The Resisting Reader: A Feminist Approach to American Fiction* (Bloomington: Indiana Univ. Press, 1978), p. xii.

[12] Claude Lévi-Strauss, *The Elementary Structures of Kinship* (1949; reprinted Boston: Beacon, 1969), p. 115.

[13] Patrocinio P. Schweickart, "Reading Ourselves: Toward a Feminist Theory of Reading," in *Gender and Reading: Essays on Readers, Texts, and Contexts*, ed. Elizabeth A. Flynn and Patrocinio P. Schweickart (Baltimore: Johns Hopkins Univ. Press, 1985), pp. 31–62; hereinafter cited parenthetically in the text.

[14] Frederick W. Shilstone, "The Courtly Misogynist: Humbert Humbert in *Lolita*," *Studies in the Humanities* 8 (June 1980): 5–10.

[15] Appel, Jr., "An Interview with Vladimir Nabokov," in Dembo, *Nabokov*, pp. 19–44; emphasis added.

[16] Henry James, *The Art of the Novel*, intro. Richard P. Blackmur (New York: Scribner's, 1934), p. 172. For a discussion of the tale as an elegiac reaccentuation of sentimental fiction, see Kauffman, *Discourses of Desire*, chap. 6.

[17] Henry James to Dr. Louis Waldstein, 21 October 1898, in *The Turn of the Screw*, ed. Robert Kimbrough (New York: W. W. Norton, 1966), p. 110.

[18] For evidence that James's governess murders Miles, see Kauffman, *Discourses of Desire*, chap. 6.

[19] Edgar Allan Poe, "Lenore," in *Poetry and Tales* (New York: Library of America, 1984), p. 69.

[20] Vladimir Nabokov, *Lectures on Literature*, ed. Fredson Bowers, intro. John Updike (New York: Harcourt Brace Jovanovich, 1980), p. 83; hereinafter cited parenthetically in the text.

[21] See James R. Pinnells, "The Speech Ritual as an Element of Structure in Nabokov's *Lolita*," *Dalhousie Review* 60 (Winter 1980–81): 605–21. Pinnells points out that in the speech rituals in *Lolita*, two realities come in conflict: average reality and Humbert's solipsism. Lolita is seldom allowed to speak in her own voice, but when she does, she effectively shatters Humbert's fantasies and exposes his lies, distortions, and duplicity. The best example of Pinnells's thesis is the scene at the Enchanted Hunters Motel, when Humbert speaks euphemistically about fathers and daughters sharing hotel rooms: " 'Two people sharing one room, inevitably enter into a kind—how shall I say—a kind—' 'The word is incest,' said Lo" (110–11).

[22] Judith Lewis Herman, *Father-Daughter Incest* (Cambridge, Mass.: Harvard Univ. Press, 1981), p. 4.

[23] Carol Lynn Mithers, "Incest and the Law," *New York Times Magazine*, 21 October 1990, pp. 44, 53, 58, 62–63; see also Catharine A. MacKinnon, *Feminism Unmodified: Discourses on Life and Law* (Cambridge, Mass.: Harvard Univ. Press, 1987). MacKinnon argues that "one of two hundred of us, conservatively estimated, is sexually molested as a child by her father. When brothers, stepfathers, uncles, and friends of the family are included, some estimate that the rates rise to two out of five," p. 23. See also p. 197, below.

[24] Herman, chaps. 5–7.

[25] Ibid., chap. 5.

[26] Pinnells, pp. 612, 618.

[27] Harry K. Frankfurt, "Freedom of the Will and the Concept of a Person," in *Free Will*, ed. Gary Watson (New York: Oxford Univ. Press, 1982), pp. 81–95.

[28] See René Girard, *Deceit, Desire, and the Novel: Self and Other in Literary Structure*, trans. Yvonne Freccéro (Baltimore: Johns Hopkins Univ. Press, 1965).

[29] In *Totem and Taboo*, trans. James Strachey (London: Routledge and Kegan Paul, 1950), Freud states that

> anyone who has violated a taboo becomes taboo himself because he possesses the dangerous quality of tempting others to follow his example: why should he be allowed to do what is forbidden to others? Thus he is truly contagious in that every example encourages imitation, and for that reason he himself must be shunned.

> But a person who has not violated any taboo may yet be permanently or temporarily taboo because he is in a state which possesses the quality of arousing forbidden desires in others and of awakening a conflict of ambivalence in them.   (32)

[30] For feminist critiques of mimetic desire and male rivalry, see Michelle Richman, "Eroticism in the Patriarchal Order," *Diacritics* 6 (1976): 46–53; Mary Jacobus, "Is There a Woman in This Text?" *New Literary History* 14 (Autumn 1982): 117–42; and Toril Moi, "The Missing Mother: The Oedipal Rivalries of René Girard," *Diacritics* 12 (Summer 1982): 21–31.

[31] Edgar Allan Poe, "The Philosophy of Composition," in *Essays and Reviews* (New York: Library of America, 1984), p. 19.

[32] Clinical case studies help to explain Quilty's appeal for Lolita: incest victims tend to overvalue and idealize men, to seek out men who resemble their fathers (men who are older, or married, or indifferent to them), thereby compulsively reenacting the familiar pattern of exploitation and debasement. See Herman, chap. 2.

[33] Vladimir Nabokov, *Pale Fire* (1962; reprinted New York: Berkley Books, 1977), p. 12.

[34] On temporal differences between narrative focus and voice, see Gérard Genette, *Narrative Discourse: An Essay in Method*, trans. Jane E. Lewin (Ithaca: Cornell Univ. Press, 1980), pp. 180–83, 206–7, 255.

[35] Shoshana Felman, "Women and Madness: The Critical Phallacy," *Diacritics* 4 (Winter 1975): 2–10.

[36] Vladimir Nabokov-Sirine, "Pouchkine ou le vrai et le vraisemblable," *La Nouvelle Revue Française* 48 (1937): 362–78, trans. Dale Peterson in "Nabokov's Invitation: Literature as Execution," *PMLA* 96 (October 1981): 824–36.

[37] Michèle Barrett, "Ideology and the Culture Production of Gender," in *Feminist Criticism and Social Change: Sex, Class, and Race in Literature and Culture*, ed. Judith Newton and Deborah Rosenfelt (London: Methuen, 1985), p. 70.

Vladimir E. Alexandrov

LOLITA

The remarkable reception *Lolita* received after it was published in 1955—celebration, outrage, best-sellerdom—prompted Nabokov to come to its defense in an unusual afterword, "On a Book Entitled *Lolita*."[1] He explained that part of the reason the novel was widely misunderstood was that "none of my American friends have read my Russian books and thus every appraisal on the strength of my English ones is bound to be out of focus" (p. 318). This is an important admission by Nabokov about the continuity between the Russian and English parts of his oeuvre. Indeed, *Lolita* can best be seen as an ingenious variation on the themes and artistic practices that characterize all of his earlier works. In terms of the development of Nabokov's art, what is perhaps most striking about *Lolita* is the sudden increase in the distance between its surface features and its deeper concerns. Rather than portray an eccentric chess genius, or a gnostic captive, or a brilliant expatriate writer, Nabokov created a character obsessed with sexual perversity to explore love, passion, art, perception, fate, morality, and their ties to the otherworld.

Nabokov's own pronouncements support this inference. In the afterword, the eloquent justification he provides for any truly artistic novel's existence is also undoubtedly a statement about *Lolita:* "a work of fiction exists only insofar as it affords me what I shall bluntly call aesthetic bliss, that is a sense of being somehow, somewhere, connected with other states of being where art (curiosity, tenderness, kindness, ecstasy" is the norm" (pp. 316–17). References to "other states of being" and "ecstasy" in relation to art, as well as the ethical resonances of the words *tenderness* and *kindness,* evoke the implications of Nabokov's "otherworldly" theme.[2] Although Nabokov denies in the afterword that *Lolita* has any didactic intent (p. 316)—which clearly it does not, in the limited sense of being concerned with pointing an accusatory finger at sexual perversion in the United States, or at "modern man's" moral failing in general—in his private correspondence with Edmund Wilson he insisted that the novel is a "pure and austere work" and "a highly moral affair."[3] In an interview, he made this point equally strongly: "I don't think

From *Nabokov's Otherworld* (Princeton: Princeton University Press, 1991), pp. 160–86.

Lolita is a religious book, but I do think it is a moral one. And I do think that Humbert Humbert in his last stage is a moral man because he realizes that he loves *Lolita* [*sic*] like any woman should be loved. But it is too late, he has destroyed her childhood. There is certainly this kind of morality in it."[4] On other occasions he referred to *Lolita* as "the purest of all, the most abstract and carefully contrived" of his works; and "as my most difficult book—the book that treated of a theme which was so distant, so remote, from my own emotional life that it gave me a special pleasure to use my combinational talent to make it real."[5] The notoriety that in some quarters is still attached to *Lolita,* and which ironically led to its original popular success, results largely from misunderstandings caused by the deceptive surface features of the story.

Another source of confusion, particularly with regard to the central question of whether or not Humbert undergoes an authentic moral awakening (which Nabokov believed he did) is the double point of view that is inherent in a memoir, and is thus a function of the genre. Critics have claimed that Humbert's expressions of contrition and professions of love for the married Lolita are undermined by passages in which he allows his passion for her to eclipse all other feelings. It is essential to realize, however, that this feature of the text is not Nabokov's attempt to confuse or complicate the issue of ethics in the novel, but an inevitable conse-quence of the fact that Humbert's recollections of Lolita are both a record of his experiences as they happened, and the way he views them later, when he is recording them in prison. Separating the two points of view and the two time frames is a fundamental change in Humbert's attitude toward Lolita that occurs during the "friendly abyss" scene following her escape from him, and that Humbert includes near the end of his text (p. 309). Nabokov carefully plots this change in the novel's chronology, with the result that Humbert's guilt and purified love for Lolita emerge as a final, reconsidered view of her. But since his purpose is truth about his past—which he wants to explain to others and understand himself—he preserves as well his contemporaneous states of mind in all their sweep and mad passion without adulterating them through retroactive projection. Thus, whatever moral equivocation Humbert records is confined solely to his contemporaneous experi-ences with Lolita. A related, double point of view informs the image of Charlotte that Humbert creates. Even though she remains forever a philistine in his mind, his expressions of contrition are his final, and dominant attitude toward her.[6]

Although it would be misleading simply to translate Humbert's passion for little girls—what he calls "nympholepsy"—into the terms of Nabokov's aesthetics, art is intimately connected with Humbert's pursuits and thus with what lies at the novel's core.[7] On the obvious level that most readers have noted Humbert refers to himself as a "poet" (e.g., pp. 90, 133), both in relation to his perceptions of Lolita and of the world around him, and his attempts to render these in words in the long confession that constitutes the body of the novel (as well as in a number of interpolated smaller pieces, including verse). Humbert also raises implicit questions about the nature of his artistic gift by making a typically Nabokovian connection between it and ethics when he asserts "poets never kill" (p. 90), which, it should be noted, he writes *after* he murders Quilty. However, the fact that Nabokov grants his character's document a range of cunning narrative strategies, and numerous passages of great beauty, pathos, and humor (in addition to some of bathetically purple prose) suggests that Humbert's presumptions about his talent cannot be altogether dismissed.[8] In other words, Nabokov can be understood as having intentionally shared part of his own genius as a writer with a first-person narrator who in most other respects is deplorable.[9] This results in a fictional world that presents unusual complexities from the point of view of differentiating between truth and falsehood, right and wrong, parody and what can be taken literally.

One path through this tangle is provided by Humbert's attempt to define nymphets, which clearly lies at the heart of his compulsion to explain his life to himself as well as his readers. What has not been realized by commentators is that his formulations recall the specific terms of Nabokov's descriptions of cosmic synchronization and artistic inspiration in his earlier novels, in the "The Art of Literature and Commonsense," and in chapter II of *Speak, Memory,* which he wrote at approximately the same time as his early stages of work on *Lolita.*[10] The effect of this overlap between Nabokov's aesthetic concepts and Humbert's erotically charged speculations about nymphets is that the latter emerge as aestheticized—as a sort of potential artistic medium, subject, or construct about which Humbert thinks and with which he attempts to work. Humbert's theories confront pragmatics when he meets Lolita; and as his experiences with her prove, there are disastrous consequences to confusing love and erotics with aesthetics when the object of one's attention is an independent being and refuses to be malleable. Put more simple, Humbert's desire "to fix once for all the perilous magic of nymphets" (p. 136) proves to be realizable in words, but not in the flesh.[11]

The central, albeit abstract, instance of Humbert's aestheticization of love and passion is his description of the fundamental difference between nymphets and normal girls. He claims the latter "are incomparably more dependent on the *spatial world of synchronous phenomena* than on that *intangible island of entranced time* where Lolita plays with her likes" (italics added; p. 19). To speak of timelessness in connection with intense love or passion is of course a commonplace in writing on the subject from all times. But the synchronization of phenomena in space, especially when contrasted with a privileged moment in time, recalls nothing so much as Nabokov's discussions of "cosmic synchronization" or "inspiration." There are two crucial differences, however. The first is of course that Nabokov's subject is the provenance of verbal art, not the nature of nymphets or other human beings (although it is important to recall that he describes love in *Speak, Memory* in terms very similar to those he uses for cosmic synchronization). And the second is that Humbert severs into two incompatible realms what Nabokov describes as phases in a causal sequence or continuum: it is precisely the artist's recognition of linkages, or synchronization, among widely separated phenomena, that, when combined with memories, leads to a timeless, epiphanic moment of inspiration. Because of Humbert's distortions, the relationship between his formulations and Nabokov's ideas can be understood as *parodic*. Humbert's conception of nymphets thus illustrates what Nabokov once described in an interview as his practice of giving characters ideas that are "deliberately flawed."[12]

This inference is supported by other details in Humbert's analysis. His explanation that one has to be "an artist and a madman . . . to discern at once, by ineffable signs" a nymphet among other little girls (p. 19) parallels Nabokov's insistence on the importance of sensory data for the creation of art. (In practice, Humbert of course betrays this requirement.) When Humbert first meets Lolita, and recognizes in her, as he believes, his long lost Annabel, he experiences a timeless moment that is very like Nabokov's descriptions of the disappearance of time under the impact of memory or during artistic inspiration: "The twenty-five years I had lived . . . tapered to a palpitating point, and vanished"; "I find it most difficult to express with adequate force that flash, that shiver, that impact of passionate recognition" (p. 41). The result of Humbert's privileged perception of nymphets is a kind of insight into a transcendent realm that resembles the Nabokovian artistic epiphany. Humbert claims that in contrast to the sexual experiences of normal men with "terrestrial" women he had "caught glimpses of an incomparably more poignant bliss" (p. 20), one that is "*hors concours* . . . belongs to another class, another plane of sensitivity" (p. 168). He also speaks of the nymphets he encounters as if they were indelibly colored for him by the timelessness of epiphanic perceptions: he wants the young prostitute Monique to remain forever in his consciousness as she was "for a minute or two" (p. 25), and yearns for "the eternal Lolita as reflected in my blood," even when he realizes she will change with time (p. 67).

In the context of Nabokov's descriptions of cosmic synchronization, Humbert's severing the realm of normal little girls (a "spatial world of synchronous phenomena") from that of nymphets (an "island of entranced time") constitutes an implicit claim regarding his ability to achieve a form of transcendence without going through the preliminary step that anchors the experience in the material world. In short, Humbert is actually speaking of what is, in Nabokov's terms, an unwarranted leap into an empyrean. This is one of the most important conclusions to be drawn from the famous "couch scene," during which Humbert believes he transcends the quotidian plane of being—but only by solipsizing Lolita, that is, by *not* seeing her for what she is.

The fundamental error in Humbert's conceptual segregation of "nymphets" from little girls is amply confirmed by his own experiences. In one of the most important passages in the novel, when he finally and unequivocally acknowledges that his relations with Lolita were profoundly immoral, Humbert is standing on a cliff edge, looking out over a vast valley containing a town, and listening to children at play in the distance. The passage is filled with sound repetitions, and Humbert's perceptions are dominated by a sense of harmony and synaesthetic linkages between sights and sounds. In other words, we have the ingredients implied by the idea of a "spatial world of synchronous phenomena." And it is in this setting that Humbert comes to his momentous conclusion that the "hopelessly poignant thing" was not that Lolita had run away from him with Quilty but that her voice was missing from "that concord" rising from the valley floor (pp. 309–310). The entire proto-epiphanic image is thus an implicit rebuttal of Humbert's original idea that nymphets occupy a special realm of frozen time different from that of other girl children. But the implications of the passage reach even further, because by erasing the difference between Lolita and other girls Humbert is in effect abandoning the entire category of "nymphet," which, in retrospect, appears to have been nothing more than his aberrant fantasy. It is noteworthy that in his afterword to *Lolita* Nabokov includes this scene in his short list of the "nerves . . . secret points, the subliminal co-ordinates by means of which the book is plotted" (p. 318).

The privileged nature of Humbert's experience above the "friendly abyss" is also underscored by its position at the intersection of several important motifs in the novel. One of these is Humbert's constant concern with ethical questions, which is resolved in the scene; another involves his varying, but repeated impression of being on the edge of a figurative abyss during his travels with Lolita. A third and less obvious motif consists of scenes that are structured as antitheses to the feeling of harmony and unity he experiences on the cliff edge; in fact, what characterizes them is a striking disunity among their constituent elements. Humbert calls attention to this himself in a passage that is particularly important because it also includes something like an occult message that he does not appear to understand. While waiting for Lolita at a gasoline station, he describes the various unrelated objects he sees, and comments that the rhythm of the radio music coming out the door "was *not synchronized* with the heave and the flutter and other gestures of wind-animated vegetation"; then he adds: "The sound of Charlotte's last sob *incongruously* vibrated through me as, with her dress *athwart* the rhythm, Lolita *veered* from a totally *unexpected* direction" (italics added; pp. 213–14). On a simple level, Lolita had presumably again eluded Humbert's watchful eye for a few moments in order to communicate with Quilty, thus prefiguring her permanent escape shortly thereafter. But the reference to the incongruity of Charlotte's "last sob" in connection with the "unexpectedness" of Lolita's appearance can be read as Nabokov's allusion to Charlotte's final words to Humbert shortly before she is killed about how he will never see Lolita again (p. 98). The "sob" thus foreshadows Humbert's imminent loss of Lolita, and is "incongruous" only because he is unaware of what is in store for him (which contrasts with the true Nabokovian epiphany). The association of the sob with Humbert's fragmented perception suggests that the latter may be a fateful predisposition on his part—one that is intimately connected not only with his loss of Lolita, but also with how he perceives her. This interpretation is supported by the link between Humbert's holistic perception in the scene on the cliff edge (from which Lolita is absent) and his view of her as his victim. The "sob" also fits the pattern of other clairvoyant visions of Charlotte in or near death, which literally haunt Humbert during his life with Lolita.

Another passage suggesting that Humbert's experiences are parodies of cosmic synchronization is a diary entry he makes soon after meeting Lolita. He quotes her request to be taken swimming, which she delivers in a "voluptuous whisper," and then enumerates the following details: "The reflection of the afternoon sun, a dazzling white diamond with innumerable iridescent spikes quivered on the round back of a parked car. The leafage of a voluminous elm played its mellow shadows upon the clapboard wall of the house. Two poplars shivered and shook. You could make out the formless sounds of remote traffic; a child calling 'Nancy, Nan-cy!' In the house, Lolita had put on her favorite 'Little Carmen' record which I used to call 'Dwarf Conductors,' making her snort with mock derision at my mock wit" (p. 47). These details stand out in effective relief, but it is odd (in the context of Nabokov's style) that potential linkages among them, which clearly lie just beneath the surface, are never realized by Humbert: the quivering of the sun's reflection on the car is not unlike the play of shadows on the wall or the shivering of poplars; and these motions, in turn, have something of the randomness of the traffic sounds and a child's cries (which of course foreshadow the children's voices in the scene on the cliff edge, and which Humbert perceives altogether differently). Moreover, the reference to the record establishes obvious links with the orgasmic couch scene during which Humbert garbles the song in question. One would also think that the entire brief diary entry would be associated with the effect that Lolita's voluptuous whisper had on Humbert. However, the listed details are not erotically charged, and are free of timelessness or synchronization; in fact, time's passage is implied by the gap between Lolita's whisper and the record she plays. Given Humbert's still selfish, and therefore limited view of Lolita at this point in his story, it is possible to conclude that his method of seeing the rest of the world is similarly flawed. The importance of this conclusion is that it points to his particular limitation as an artist in terms of Nabokov's values. This also has a bearing on the nature of the memoir he produces, which on a textual level is filled with numerous linkages that he does not notice (in addition to those for which he does claim responsibility.)

The ethical implications of perception in Nabokov's terms are underscored in a scene that relates the effect Lolita's appearance has on Humbert to the way he perceives details. He is on the verge of seeing her again after a month's lapse, and wants to capture the moment "in all its trivial and fateful detail." The reader inevitably expects Humbert to be in a state of erotico-aesthetic inspiration. But the description that follows is strikingly unpoetic, and shows nothing of Humbert's conception of nymphets: "hag Holmes writing out a receipt, scratching her head, pulling a drawer out of her desk ... photographs of girl-children." Moreover, among the various items he notices in the camp office is "some gaudy moth or butterfly, still alive, safely pinned to the wall" (p. 112); in Nabokov's world, Humbert's uncertainty about the two major subdivisions of the order Lepidoptera is an obvious encoded sign of blindness. The anti-epiphanic description of the setting continues even after Lolita arrives, when "for a second" Humbert is struck by the impression that she is "less pretty than the mental imprint I had cherished for more than a month" (p. 113). (Humbert makes similar, "prosaic" observations about Lolita's adolescent philistinism and grubbiness later in the novel as well [e.g., pp. 150, 206].) In other words, Humbert at first sees her as something other than his quintessential nymphet, which, therefore, again puts into question whether or not nymphets exist outside his imagination, and only during aberrant moments at that.

This is reinforced by Humbert's acknowledgment that his impression regarding Lolita's looks carries with it a distinct sense of moral obligation to give this "orphan" a "healthy and happy childhood" (p. 113). Seeing Lolita for what she is thus elicits a "normal" human reaction from Humbert. This state lasts a very short time, however, before the "angelic line of conduct" is "erased," and Humbert sees her as "my Lolita again" (p. 113), which indicates that a secondary projection has obscured the initial perception. An additional element in this sequence that underscores the difference between Humbert's perception of Lolita and his conception of nymphets is his remark when the ethical imperative disappears that "time moves ahead of our fancies." This suggests that, paradoxically, Humbert sees Lolita as a *orphan* during a timeless fancy (what he also calls "a very narrow human interval between two tiger heartbeats"), which counters the notion of Lolita being a *nymphet* on an island of entranced time. In turn, this moment anticipates the scene on the cliff edge when Humbert acknowledges his guilt during a proto-epiphanic moment.

But what of Humbert's claims throughout his text regarding his unerring ability to discern a nymphet by means of subtle physical indices? Although in theory this resembles Nabokov's elevation of perceptual acuity to a primary aesthetic principle, Humbert's claims are in fact undermined by the varieties of flagrant blindness that he manifests, most notably with regard to Lolita's emotional and psychological constitution during the years of their travels. His claims are also undermined by another fundamental principle in his conception of how a nymphet can be perceived, which, moreover, appears to be yet another parodic evocation of Nabokov's aesthetics in *Speak, Memory*. Humbert's discussion of the conditions necessary to perceive a nymphet hinges on the issue of time, which he says "plays such a magic part in the matter." His point is that there must be a significant difference in age "between maiden and man to enable the latter to come under a nymphet's spell. It is a question of focal adjustment, of a certain distance that the inner eye thrills to surmount" (p. 19). Humbert's translation of time into space ("a certain distance") is a curious echo of his announcement at the outset of this entire discussion of nymphets that he has chosen to "substitute time terms for spatial ones" (p. 18). In fact, he does the opposite, because he refers to the ages of "nine" and "fourteen" in spatial terms: "as the boundaries—the mirrory beaches and rosy rocks—of an enchanted island haunted by those nymphets of mine." The result of this confusion is that time and space become interchangeable in Humbert's discussions of nymphets, with the unintentionally ironic consequence that his emphasis on temporal *difference* begins to sound like spatial *distance*. (This also further undermines his distinction between girls occupying a "spatial world" and nymphets who live on an "island of entranced time.") And distance cannot help but raise questions about the accuracy of perception. Indeed, there are several descriptive passages later in the novel that resemble dramatizations of Humbert's original formulation, and that suggests his distanced cognitive stance is an inducement to projection rather than accurate perception. In one he states: "it may well be that the very attraction immaturity has for me lies not so much in the limpidity of pure young forbidden fairy child beauty as in the security of a situation where infinite perfections fill the gap between the little given and the great promised"; and he goes on to admit that "I sometimes won the race between my fancy and nature's reality" (p. 266). In another passage about how he slowly and stealthily approaches Lolita before trying to touch her, Humbert states that he seems "to see her through the wrong end of a telescope" (p. 56), which means, of course, that she appears to be more distant than she in fact is, and that he is actively resisting seeing her as she is.

A discussion of related issues also appears in *Speak, Memory,* and develops out of Nabokov's marveling at such things as the beauty of magic lantern slides when not projected but held up to the light, and, conversely, the beauty of slides under the microscope. He concludes: "There is, it would seem, in the dimensional scale of the world a kind of delicate meeting place between imagination and knowledge, a point, arrived at by diminishing large things and enlarging small ones, that is intrinsically artistic" (pp. 166–67). The implication of this passage is that imagination, and, by extension, art can be valid only if rooted in precise knowledge, and that the blending of knowledge and imagination, or the transition between them, is not arbitrary but a function of specific circumstances. Thus knowledge and imagination are not only not incompatible, but are necessary complements for each other, which is an idea that Nabokov repeated often in other discursive writings as well. In these terms, Humbert's error is that he has not respected the "delicate meeting place" between fact and fancy in his perceptions of Lolita or other "nymphets" (Annabel was another matter because she was Humbert's coeval and loved him). A remark of Humbert's following his epochal visit to Lolita after she has become Mrs. Schiller confirms this inference and shows that he has come to understand his error in the same terms: "I reviewed my case. With the utmost simplicity and clarity I now saw myself and my love. Previous attempts seemed *out of focus* by comparison" (italics added; p. 284). In *Lolita,* Nabokov can thus be understood as having chosen to dramatize the failure of a character to respect the crucial dividing line between insight and solipsism, or sensory data and imagination, that other characters, such as Fyodor in *The Gift* or Sebastian Knight, succeed in maintaining.

Parody is not the only link between Humbert's and Nabokov's ideas; there are also some topics on which they simply agree. Two of the more obvious instances are their keen eye for varieties of American "poshlost'," including psychoanalysis, and their similar admiration for American scenic beauties. A more complicated link between them hinges on another aspect of time. Humbert describes an essay he had once published entitled "Mimir and Memory" that presents "a theory of perceptual time based on the circulation of the blood and conceptually depending ... on the mind's being conscious not only of matter but also its own self, thus creating a continuous spanning of two points (the storable future and the stored past)" (p. 262). What Humbert seems to mean by this is that the sense of time is a function of being alive (i.e., of the "circulation of the blood"), and thus is not a fact independent of human existence; moreover, both the individual's perceptions and his apprehension of time may be relative because both depend on the individual's consciousness.

The first thing to say about this is that Humbert's perceptions of Lolita (as well as other, earlier nymphets) flagrantly contradict his theory in the essay. Prior to his moral awakening on the cliff edge, Humbert's relations with Lolita hinge on his attempts to ignore or deny her individuality: as a nymphet she purportedly exists out of time, but Humbert in fact worries intermittently about what he will do once she outgrows this state. Thus, in the case of his relations with the most important person in his life, Humbert is not fully aware of what lies outside him and focuses primarily on what is within his consciousness. In short, no "continuous spanning of two points" actually takes place with regard to Lolita. Instead, Humbert recalls the specific "circulatory" imagery of the essay when he speaks of the "*eternal* Lolita as reflected in my *blood*" (italics added; p. 67). This immutability contradicts the process implied in his "theory of perceptual time."

Although Humbert's linking of time to the circulatory system might seem at first to be a joke or a pseudoprofundity, intended perhaps as a sign of his eccentricity, it is most interesting that Nabokov makes the same connection in *Speak, Memory* when he speaks of his little son's fondness for all fast, wheeled things, especially railway trains. (The deeply emotional tone of the entire chapter in which this description appears precludes any possibility that he may have been joking.) This leads to Nabokov's implication that time is a human projection onto the world, and that the child's love for velocity may be an adumbration of cosmic synchronization, since the outermost limit of the desire to maximize spatial enjoyment is omnipresence or omniscience in a moment of time (Fyodor in *The Gift* comes to very similar conclusions [354: 384].)

Humbert's "Mimir and Memory" can thus be seen as a reasonably faithful variation on Nabokov's own ideas. What significance does this have for understanding *Lolita?* First, it adds weight to the conclusion that Humbert is not simply a madman, and thus implies that other hidden "Nabokovian" themes, ideas, and practices in his long confession might have to be taken seriously when making sense of the novel as a whole. Secondly, Humbert's essay also has a bearing on how we can understand the status of Lolita in his life. Although the theory of perception in "Mimir and Memory" and Humbert's actual perception of Lolita as a nymphet are contradictory and incommensurable, she remains a central fact of his existence; another way of saying that is that she has an intrusive relationship to it, and is discordant within it. This may seem a paradoxical claim, given that Humbert spends much of his life anticipating or searching for Lolita following his abortive love for Annabel. But in fact, seeing Lolita as alien to at least a part of Humbert's consciousness underscores her fateful role in his life. He is, as can be demonstrated, driven toward her by forces that largely transcend his ken.

Another instance of Humbert's being given a distinctive Nabokovian trait is the narrative strategy he claims to have used in telling his story. When he finally extracts Quilty's name from Lolita, Humbert does not actually reveal it to the reader; instead, he makes an oblique allusion to a moment several years before when Jean Farlow almost spoke Quilty's name out loud. Humbert explains that his purpose in doing this is to let the reader experience the same kind of realization that he had when he heard the name: "Quietly the fusion took place, and everything fell into order, into the pattern of branches that I have woven throughout this memoir with the express and perverse purpose of rendering . . . that golden and monstrous peace through the satisfaction of logical recognition, which my most inimical reader should experience now" (p. 274). Nabokov has thus granted Humbert a form of artistic control that is modeled on his own (the importance of which is signaled at the conclusion of *Speak, Memory* by the reference to the game "Find What the Sailor Has Hidden"). The crucial difference between the two, however, is that Nabokov's formal method parallels the structure of cosmic synchronization. By contrast, the "golden and monstrous peace" to which Humbert refers in connection with his aesthetic structure recalls the conclusion of his falsely epiphanic ecstasy with Lolita in the couch scene ("that state of absolute security, confidence and reliance not found elsewhere in conscious life"[p. 62]) which, rather than being expansive and oriented toward making connections between the self and what lies outside it, is narrowly (indeed solipsistically) focused on what lies within the self.

Humbert's experience in the couch scene is a major thematic and structural node in the novel that is characterized by a hybridization of aesthetics and erotics: as he puts it, he feels "suspended on the brink of [a] voluptuous abyss (a nicety of physiological equipoise comparable to certain techniques in the arts)" (p. 62). (This image of the "abyss" has an obvious antiphonal relationship to the scene on the cliff edge when Humbert experiences his moral awakening, a fact of which he is of course unaware.) The result of this synthesis, as he freely admits, is that "what I had madly possessed was not she, but my creation, another, fanciful Lolita—perhaps, more real than Lolita; overlapping, encasing her; floating between me and her, and having no will, no consciousness—indeed, no life of her own" (p. 64). It is a measure of Humbert's occasional perspicacity that he is sufficiently aware of what he is doing to say that "Lolita had been safely solipsized"; the Russian translation makes the point even more bluntly: "Real'nost' Lolity byla blagopoluchno otmenena," which means, literally, "Lolita's reality was successfully canceled" (pp. 62: 49). There is thus considerable authorial irony implied by Humbert's assertion that because Lolita was supposedly unaware of what he was doing he "had stolen the honey of a spasm without impairing the morals of a minor" (p. 64). That Humbert would be concerned with ethical considerations is to his credit in Nabokov's terms, but his actual blindness with regard to Lolita in this and numerous other scenes is a clear sign of his moral failing. Indeed, Humbert's congratulating himself because Lolita had noticed nothing is itself undermined by how he describes her during the act and immediately afterward: "a sudden shrill note in her voice," "she wiggled and squirmed, and threw her head back, and her teeth rested on her glistening underlip as she half-turned away," "she stood and blinked, cheeks aflame, hair awry" (p. 63). Later in the novel, in what may be a reference to the same scene, Lolita accuses Humbert of trying to violate her when he was still her mother's roomer (p. 207). Humbert's misperception of Lolita even betrays his love for Annabel, which, as he admits, is the mainspring of his life and all his subsequent passion. The distinctive feature of the "frenzy of mutual possession" that he experienced with Annabel is that it "might have been assuaged only by our actually imbibing and assimilating every particle of each other's soul and flesh" (p. 14). With Lolita, by contrast, there is neither mutual attraction, nor any concern on Humbert's part with anything like her soul.

The scene on the couch also contains several details the sole purpose of which appears to be to call into question Humbert's entire theory of nymphets. For example, at the outset, Lolita and Humbert grab an apple and a magazine out of each other's hands, which leads him to comment: "pity no film had recorded the curious pattern, the monogrammatic linkage of our simultaneous or overlapping moves" (p. 60). Humbert's emphasis on the patterning and simultaneity of their actions recalls what he had said earlier about normal girls being dependent on the world of synchronous phenomena in contrast to nymphets (and constitutes a sharp contrast to Quilty's pornographic film project that Lolita rejects). Thus the implication of Humbert's perception of Lolita in terms of spatial synchronization is either that Lolita is a normal girl, or that nymphets do not exist. The other detail with a comparable function is that Humbert enters into an isolated, timeless state of bless when Lolita is on his lap. Since she is unaware of his state, his generalization about nymphets and islands of timelessness seems more a remark about his own peculiar consciousness and solipsistic projections than about Lolita or other hypothetical nymphets.

In order to grasp fully the nature of Nabokov's deceptive complication of ethics in the novel, it is important to realize that a number of Humbert's perceptions of Lolita transcend his habitual purblindness. The most striking illustration is his celebration of her playing tennis in Colorado. He does not see her as a nymphet at this point, but as a participant in a game comparable to the theatrical exercises she also enjoys. In Humbert's view, her form is so perfect he has "the teasing delirious feeling of teetering on the very brink of unearthly order and splendor" (p. 232). Although this image might seem to be yet another variant of his specious claims about nymphets and the realm they inhabit, the reference to the "brink" suggests a veiled connection with the cliff edge where Humbert undergoes his moral epiphany. In fact, on an abstract level, the two passages share the same cardinal feature—Humbert's acknowledgment of the difference between what Lolita actually is, and his own view of her as a nymphet or other aestheticized being: "Her tennis was the highest point to which *I can imagine* a young creature bringing the art of make-believe, although I daresay, *for her it was* the very geometry of basic reality (italics added; p. 233). The scene is also distinguished by the fact that Humbert pays close attention to all the specifics of Lolita's gestures and behavior during the game, rather than allowing projections to intervene (pp. 232–36). Humbert even unwittingly registers a typically Nabokovian authorial intrusion into the entire sequence, which sanctions is as being especially noteworthy, when he comments: "An inquisitive butterfly passed, dipping, between us" (p. 236).

A more intriguing imprimatur for Humbert's sensation that he is close to something literally "unearthly" is that the description of Lolita's game is followed by the fulfillment of a prophetic vision he had some time earlier. He is called away from Lolita's side on the tennis court by a telephone call that proves to be a ruse. When he returns, he sees her playing with three other people—Quilty and two of his friends, as the reader, but not Humbert, concludes. This incident is noteworthy not only because it provides additional evidence for Quilty's shadowing Humbert and Lolita prior to spiriting her away, but also because Humbert actually foresaw a variant of the scene during one of Lolita's previous tennis games in Arizona. He was returning with drinks he had brought for her and another girl with whom she had been playing (which is itself part of a fatidic pattern, since it foreshadows his return to the tennis court in the episode with Quilty), and feels "a sudden void" in his chest when he sees that the court is empty:

> I stooped to set down the glasses on a bench and for some reason, with a kind of icy vividness, saw Charlotte's face in death, and I glanced around, and noticed Lo in white shorts receding ... in the company of a tall man who carried two tennis rackets. I sprang after them, but as I was crashing through the shrubbery, I saw, in an alternate vision, as if life's course constantly branched, Lo, in slacks, and her companion, in shorts ... beating bushes with their rackets in listless search for their last lost ball.   (P. 165)

As a number of commentators have noted, Humbert's vision of a man with Lolita is of course a prefiguration of Quilty.[13] But it should be noted that the image of "Charlotte's face in death" can also be linked directly to Humbert's imminent loss because of her warning to him before she died that he would never see Lolita again (p. 98). Charlotte's prediction is borne out not only by Lolita's eventual escape, but also by the fact that Lolita the nymphet no longer exists either in Humbert's imagination or in reality when he finally meets her again as Mrs. Richard Schiller. The prophetic character of Humbert's vision is also confirmed by the detail that he foresees Lolita leaving in "white shorts," whereas in actuality she is wearing "slacks" while playing with her friend in Arizona (p. 165). When Quilty intrudes into the tennis game in Colorado, Lolita is indeed wearing "white wide little-boy shorts" (pp. 232–33).

The significance of the links between the two passages dealing with tennis is twofold. Humbert emerges as being caught in a sequence of events of which he is only partially aware, and of which Quilty is a function rather than a cause. The second tennis scene's role as a confirmation of a clairvoyant vision makes it stand out in the novel and suggests that its other implications are also especially important. And in contrast to his problematic segregation of nymphets on a timeless island, Humbert does manage to glimpse Lolita as transcending his habitual reality—but only when he focuses on her, and temporarily eschews the category of nymphet. Humbert's experience in this instance thus approaches an unadulterated Nabokovian moment of inspiration.

In his afterword to *Lolita*, Nabokov describes the "initial shiver of inspiration" that eventually became the novel as having been "somehow prompted by a newspaper story about an ape in the Jardin des Plantes, who, after months of coaxing by a scientist, produced the first drawing ever charcoaled by an animal: the sketch showed the bars of the poor creature's cage" (p. 313). Whether or not this is a faithful account of the origin of the novel is less important than the clear hint the anecdote provides about the novel's central problem, which can be put into the form of a question: what can an imprisoned creature see other than the means of its imprisonment?[14] This is, in effect, a formulation of the problem that preoccupied Nabokov throughout his oeuvre. It is surely no mere coincidence that Humbert suggests the most obvious parallel between the anecdote and the novel when he refers to his "aging ape eyes" at the moment he first sees Lolita (p. 41; later, Quilty calls Humbert "you ape, you," p. 300). In part, this is of course an allusion to the "bestial" nature of his passion, and thus reflects his ambivalence toward it. But because the context for the phrase is the link between his memories of Annabel's nudity and what he imagines is concealed beneath the garment Lolita is wearing when he first sees her, the reader concludes that Humbert's perceptions of Lolita and Annabel are inextricably tied. This point is also amply and overtly confirmed as early as the novel's eighth line—"there might have been no Lolita at all had I not loved . . . a certain initial girl-child"—and by Humbert's references to Lolita as "my Riviera love" and "the same child" (p. 41). Thus, Annabel emerges as an analogue to the bars on the ape's cage in the anecdote, and Humbert's perception of Lolita is like the ape's drawing of the bars of its cage. In other words, Humbert cannot help perceiving the nymphets who constitute the world in which he is trapped because of Annabel.

It is another sign of Humbert's intermittent perspicacity that he invokes the concept of fate when he ponders his fixation on nymphets in general and Lolita in particular. He raises a crucial question for understanding the novel when he asks if it was during the summer with Annabel "that the rift in my life began; or was my excessive desire for that child only the first evidence of an inherent singularity?" (p. 15). Neither he, nor the novel can answer his question unequivocally. But a comparison of Humbert's short-lived affair with Annabel to analogous moments in Nabokov's earlier works suggests that their meeting was somehow foreordained. Firstly, all of Humbert's descriptions stress that the attraction between them was not only physical but also spiritual (e.g., pp. 14, 16). Secondly, the details he provides to prove this point imply that their spiritual link was underlain by experiences that touched upon the otherworldly: "Long after her death I felt her thoughts floating through mine. Long before we met we had the same dreams. We compared notes. We found strange affinities. The same June of the same year (1919) a stray canary had fluttered into her house and mine, in two widely separated countries" (p. 16). These are precisely the kinds of seminal details that a purely metaliterary reading of the novel cannot explain (except by stressing metaliterary patterning beyond all credibility), and which, therefore, militate against it. (A different but not unrelated textual detail that adds to the slight flavor of the extramundane in aspects of Humbert's childhood is that his aunt, appropriately named Sybil, predicted correctly that she would die soon after his sixteenth birthday [p. 12].)

The Platonic conception of love implied in Humbert's description of his tie to

Annabel can be found in Nabokov's early poetry, in the case of Luzhin and his fiancée, Cincinnatus and his idealized image of a soul mate, and Fyodor and Zina. The sense of spiritual affinity that Humbert has with Annabel after her death is also like V.'s with Sebastian after his death. And the seemingly trivial detail about the canaries that Humbert mentions is actually no different in kind from what Nabokov describes when he speaks of fateful patterning in *Speak, Memory,* whose significance is unrelated to its content. All this lends weight to the argument in favor of taking what Humbert says about his love for Annabel at face value—as an extraordinary experience that literally marked him for life: "We loved each other with a premature love, marked by a fierceness that so often destroys adult lives. I was a strong lad and survived; but the poison was in the wound" (p. 20). In terms of the hierarchy of values Humbert establishes in the novel, his love for Annabel raises him to her level—to "that same enchanted island of time" she occupies. Humbert's search for nymphets is thus a (futile) attempt to reexperience what he knew through Annabel, which appears to have been an authentic spiritual affinity for a specific girl, marked by a plane of being transcending the earthly.

This larger context for Humbert's existence is not limited to his childhood. From the start, the word *fate,* and what it implies, is a leitmotif of his narrative about Lolita (e.g., pp. 16, 23, 62, 68, 105, 118, 175); he goes to the extent of personifying it as "Aubrey McFate" (p. 58), and invoking "angels" as the agents behind it (p. 169). Moreover, Humbert's conception of "destiny" is like Nabokov's in that it is essentially backward- rather than forward-looking: Humbert understands that memory can use "certain obscure indications" to discern patterns in the past, and that these should not be read as foreshadowings of the future (p. 213). He is also aware of the limitations to which memory and interpretation are subject: "It is just possible that had I gone to a strong hypnotist he might have extracted from me and arrayed in a logical pattern certain chance memories that I have threaded through my book with considerably more ostentation than they present themselves with to my mind even now when I know what to seek in the past" (p. 257). This admission cannot but prompt the reader to search for the connections and meanings that elude Humbert.

Humbert's own hermeneutic efforts yield both insight and varying degrees of error or uncertainty regarding events that appear to have been portentous. On the one hand, he marvels at the coincidence of finding a book in his prison library that contains a series of references to people and events in his life (pp. 33–34). On the other, there is no indication that he ever recognizes the significance of Lolita's saying during a thunderstorm, "I am not a lady and do not like lightning" (pp. 222: 201), which parodies the title of one of Quilty's plays that is mentioned in the book: *The Lady Who Loved Lightning.* Moreover, Lolita's remark is also an echo of the accidental death of Humbert's mother, which he laconically summarizes as "picnic, lightning" (p. 12). It is worth noting that Nabokov made a significant change in this scene when he translated the novel into Russian: he added Humbert's comment that Lolita "stranno vyrazilas'" when she utters her phrase about lightning, which means, literally, "expressed herself in a strange manner," or "put it oddly." This inevitably calls the reader's attention to the hidden meaning of her words in a way that the English original does not, and at the same time implies that Humbert could not have noticed it.

Humbert also wonders at the coincidence that Lolita is in fact on a hike at her camp after he had asserted that she was, for the benefit of the Farlows (pp. 102, 108). This event is accompanied by the additional curious detail that the pay telephone he uses to call the camp returns all the coins he had deposited, causing him to wonder if this is not a signal from McFate (p. 109). The reader familiar with *The Real Life of Sebastian Knight* may be tempted to answer this question on the basis of the similarity between the telephone's returning Humbert's money and Silbermann's returning V.'s. In both instances, the sudden gifts are contrary to expected norms, and can be correlated with the hints that both recipients' quests are touched by the otherworld.

Humbert seems to be at least partially aware of the rather fantastic series of coincidences that leads to his landing at Charlotte's and eventually becoming Lolita's guardian: the McCoo house, in which he had been planning to stay, burns down upon his arrival in Ramsdale (p. 37), and he has to be put up somewhere else. (In the Russian translation of the scene where Lolita is telling Humbert about her life after she had run away from him and how Quilty's ranch burned down, Nabokov adds the following remark to Humbert's lines: "Chto zh, u Mak-Ku bylo tozhe pokhozhee imia, i tozhe sgorel dom" [p. 257], which means, "Well, McCoo had a similar name, and his house also burned down." This enlarges the network of patterning in the novel by exploiting the echo between Quilty's nickname in the Russian version, "Ku" as in "Koo," and the McCoos, and between the latter and Humbert's personified "McFate." Similarly, Boyd has pointed out that Nabokov strove to augment the theme of fate in Humbert's life when he wrote his screenplay of *Lolita* "as compensation for the loss of Humbert's reflections on the theme— which only shows how essential Nabokov felt it to be to any treatment of the *Lolita* story—or to make explicit the motivation implicit in the novel.")[15] Humbert is thus handed over to Charlotte as a boarder, but the only reason he manages to marry her, and stay near Lolita, is that the old spinster Miss Phalen, who was supposed to take care of Humbert and Lolita while Charlotte sought employment in a city, happens to fall and break her hip "on the very day" Humbert arrives (p. 58). Charlotte's death is also multifariously fatidic: it saves Humbert from having to leave Lolita because his passion for her has been discovered; it is a realization of the murder that he himself contemplates; and it is caused by the neighbor's dog that he mentions as attacking his car when he is first being driven to Charlotte's house (p. 38).

What prevents these overt coincidences from becoming merely a metaliterary parody of fate is that they are anchored to the "reality" of *Lolita*'s fictional world by the much subtler patterning in Humbert's life of which he is *unaware*. An important example is Humbert's observation that his pursuer left clues that were "tuned" to his "mind and manner." Humbert goes so far as to conclude that "the tone" of Quilty's brain "had affinities with my own" (p. 251). What Humbert does not appear to notice, however, is that this is a trait he also shared with Annabel, whose thoughts he "felt," and with whom he had other "strange affinities" (p. 16). This coincidence adds to the portentousness of Quilty's role in helping Lolita escape Humbert, which can be seen as a variation on Humbert's loss of Annabel, and a foreshadowing of his permanent loss of Lolita when she becomes Mrs. Richard Schiller. In light of this, Humbert's calling Quilty his "brother" (p. 249) is much more ironic than might have seemed at first. Commentators tend to interpret this reference in terms of the Romantic literary theme of "the double," a concept whose relevance to Nabokov's works is questionable, and which he rejected in interviews. Humbert's use of the word can actually be explained more simply as an instance of his ironic play with Quilty's claim about being Lolita's "uncle" when he signs her out of the hospital (p. 248). Since Humbert on occasion thinks of Lolita as his daughter, her "uncle" is potentially his "brother." The hint of a covert tie based on unspecified "affinities" linking Annabel, Humbert, and Quilty is more intriguing than the obvious connections among Humbert, Quilty, and Lolita because it points to a misperception on Humbert's part about the nature of the mesh in which he is caught. (The two triangles cannot be equated because the nature of Humbert's tie to Annabel is fundamentally different from that to Lolita.) Humbert understands that Lolita's illness "was somehow the development of a theme—that it had the same taste and tone as the series of linked impressions which had puzzled and tormented me during our journey; I imagined that secret agent, or secret lover, or prankster, or hallucination, or whatever he was, prowling around the hospital" (p. 243). What he does not recognize, however, is that Quilty (although not exclusively a "nympholept") is not a random pursuer but a significant part of the same pattern that begins with Annabel and centers on her. Quilty's connection to Humbert's fate is further strengthened by the fact that he connives with Lolita at the very time when she is sufficiently ill to require hospitalization; he becomes, as it were, part of the illness that wrests Lolita from Humbert. And although Lolita recovers, her escape from Humbert via the hospital is as permanent as his loss of Annabel, who "died of *typhus* in Corfu" (italics added, p. 15).

Many other details fall into patterns which Humbert does not recognize either during the time frame of his experiences, or when he is setting them down in prison. An important example is the scene at Hourglass Lake when Charlotte says "waterproof," and Jean Farlow mentions that she once saw "two children, male and female, at sunset, right here, making love. Their shadows were giants" (p. 91). Humbert's sole concern as narrator at this point is to preserve the "reality" of the scene by not supplying Quilty's name after Jean almost mentions it. But the reader cannot help noticing the symbolic significance of what Jean describes: that the shadow of Humbert and Annabel—the novel's original children on a beach—in fact falls across Humbert's entire narrative; that the shadow's association with what Charlotte likes to think of as her private beach anticipates the recapitulatory nature of Humbert's involvement with Lolita; and that the shadow's contiguity with an allusion to Quilty once again links him to Annabel as much as to Lolita.

Before going on to other important hidden patterns in *Lolita*, it is worth pausing on the question of the relation between them and the reliability of parts of Humbert's narrative. Despite his claims about his prodigious memory, it may seen implausible that he could have remembered so many details, but did not openly integrate them into his story. A related consideration is that Humbert admits to intentionally hiding networks of details in his narrative on occasion, as in the case of the word *waterproof.* It is thus possible to conclude, as many readers have, that Nabokov made Humbert an untrustworthy narrator in order to foreground the fictionality of his memoir, and by extension of all literature and life stories. Given that the bulk of *Lolita* is told in the first person, there is no way of totally disproving Humbert's supposed untrustworthiness. But there are compelling arguments that can be made against it. A dominant theme in the novel is Humbert's blindness about what is most important to him—Lolita. If he can fail to comprehend what he is doing to her for much of his narrative, he can certainly fail to notice subtle patterns that suggest he is trapped in a course of action that is not of his own devising. Nabokov has Humbert acknowledge as much when he says that a hypnotist could have extracted significant patterns from his memory, which suggests that Humbert realizes that he has seen and remembered details whose significance he cannot fathom. There is also the pressure of the context of Nabokov's other writings. Although his earlier and later novels cannot dictate a specific reading of *Lolita,* they can help to buttress a choice between alternative readings that are suggested by the text of the novel itself.

One of the most important hidden networks of recurring details in Humbert's life consists of two strands linking Lolita and her mother that center on meteorological and water imagery. Early in the novel, he describes Charlotte's eyes as "sea green" (p. 39). This association is resurrected when he briefly falls asleep near Lolita in The Enchanted Hunters and dreams that "Charlotte was a mermaid in a greenish tank" (p. 134). What could have motivated Nabokov to plant this connection in the novel? A possible answer is the significance of water and beaches in Humbert's life: on the one hand, he met and loved Annabel on the Riviera; on the other, he contemplated drowning Charlotte in Hourglass Lake in order to possess Lolita. Charlotte's association with the sea and a mermaid can thus be read in several ways: as ironic, because Humbert describes her in the scene at the lake as "a very mediocre mermaid" (p. 88), and as a "clumsy seal" (p. 89); as Charlotte's being linked to the theme of Annabel, which she clearly is through her daughter; and, what is most intriguing, as a suggestion that Charlotte may be at home in water, or, in other words, that she might not have died had Humbert actually tried to drown her (and not because Jean Farlow was concealed nearby, or because someone else might have come to the rescue), and, therefore, that her death in the car accident might not have been final.

There are in fact hints in *Lolita* that Humbert is accompanied by Charlotte's occult presence after she dies.[16] These first appear in connection with the thunderclap that reverberates immediately after Jean Farlow tells Humbert, "kiss your daughter for me" (p. 106). On a "realistic" level, the thunder derives form the "black thunderhead" Humbert had just described as looming over the town (p. 105).[17] But

on a symbolic level, given the words Jean utters, the thunder is a melodramatically
portentous sign that recalls the striking of the midnight hour when little Luzhin first
demonstrates his chess prowess openly: the thunder marks a turning point in
Humbert's life similar to Luzhin's by underscoring the falsehood he told Jean, which
is instrumental in his obtaining control over Lolita. The fact that the sign is obvious
tends to camouflage its true import, because one is tempted to dismiss it as a mere
gothic flourish on Humbert's (or Nabokov's) part. However, another, subtler manifestation of the approaching storm enters into this network of associations together with Charlotte. Humbert looks at her house before leaving it, and notes the
following details: "The shades—thrifty, practical bamboo shades—were already
down. On porches or in the house their rich textures lend modern drama. The
house of heaven must seem pretty bare after that. A raindrop fell on my knuckles"
(pp. 105: 91). Nabokov's Russian translation makes it clear that the second sentence
in this passage is a quotation from an advertisement on which Charlotte had relied
while decorating. Thus, Humbert's reference to "the house of heaven" can be taken
as a clear allusion to the different circumstances in which Charlotte finds herself
after death. What changes this from being merely a turn of phrase on Humbert's
part is the sentence about the "raindrop" that falls on his hand. On one level, this
is still a manifestation of the same thunder cloud. But the detail has greater significance that emerges from an additional complex of associations scattered across the
early parts of the novel. The first of these is revealed when Humbert is registering
at The Enchanted Hunters with Lolita. After receiving the key with the obviously
significant number "342," he happens to notice that Lolita is leaving a dog that she
had stopped to pet in the lobby, which he interprets as a foreshadowing of how she
will eventually leave him (and which is part of the novel's concealed "dog motif.")
He then writes: "a raindrop fell on Charlotte's grave" (p. 120). In its immediate
context this is an odd detail to mention, even though it recalls the raindrop that falls
onto Humbert's hand earlier in the novel. The incongruity of the raindrop's appearance while Humbert is registering militates against its being his subtle way of
signaling that his guilty conscience does not allow him to forget Charlotte; after all,
he is quite willing to express contrition openly on a number of occasions. The
necessary explanation for the raindrop is suggested by the scene of Humbert
buying clothing for Lolita prior to going to her camp: "I moved about fish-like, in a
glaucous aquarium. I sensed strange thoughts form in the minds of the languid ladies
that escorted me from counter to counter, from rock ledge to seaweed, and the
belts and the bracelets I chose seemed to fall from siren hands [in Russian, 'iz
rusaloch'ikh ruk,' 'from mermaid hands'] into transparent water" (pp. 110: 95). Thus
Lolita (and Humbert) become associated with marine imagery that had been used
for her mother, a link that is further augmented by the substitution of "mermaid"
for "siren" in the Russian translation. (Later, Humbert describes Lolita's approach to
the gifts he bought her as "the lentor of one walking under water or in a flight
dream" [p. 122]; he also speaks of her as "a little curved fish" in her mother's
stomach [p. 78], buys The Little Mermaid for her [p. 176], and himself sheds
"merman tears]" [p. 257]. Moreover, Annabel is evoked in this context by Hum-

bert's reference to being able to sense the salesclerks' "thought forms.") But Charlotte herself is not forgotten, because a few lines later Humbert remarks that "somehow, in connection with that quiet poetical afternoon of fastidious shopping, I recalled the hotel or inn with the seductive name of The Enchanted Hunters which Charlotte happened to mention shortly before my liberation" (p. 110). As a result of this remark, the raindrop that inexplicably falls on Charlotte's grave is revealed to be part of a network of allusions that subtly remind the reader of her and her prophecy at crucial pints in Humbert's affair with Lolita. It is of course at The Enchanted Hunters that Humbert's loss of Lolita begins because that is where Quilty sees her. Thus Charlotte's spirit appears to abet this event by prompting Humbert to go to that hotel. In the context of *The Gift* and *The Real Life of Sebastian Knight,* where there are hints that the dead may attend the quick, as well as in keeping with the otherworldly aura established by Humbert's description of the spiritual links between him and Annabel, the series of rain and water images can be interpreted as hints that Charlotte's spirit is a constituent element of Humbert's fate.[18] (Similar hints appear when Humbert rings Mrs. Richard Schiller's doorbell and hears a dog barking [p. 271], which recalls the moment of Charlotte's death and her prophecy [pp. 99, 100]; when Lolita lights a cigarette, and Charlotte appears to rise from her grave [p. 277]; and when Humbert murders Quilty, which makes him think of Charlotte "sick in bed" [p. 306].)

Some chains of details in Humbert's narrative recur so often, and change so little, that they become leitmotifs. One such strand is that of sunglasses, which first appear "lost" by somebody on the beach where Humbert tries to possess Annabel (p. 15), and then reappear as "dark glasses" on one of the men in the procuress's apartment that Humbert visits in search of a nymphet (p. 26; they also appear on pp. 41, 56, 85). The most obvious meaning of this motif, in addition to its import as a formal recurrence in Humbert's life, is of course that dark glasses obscure vision, which is obviously related to Humbert's blindness when pursuing nymphets. (Sunglasses have a similar function in Nabokov's short story "Sovershenstvo," "Perfection.")

Another leitmotif in the novel is centered on the color red and colors related to it. In a note to Appel, Nabokov objected to the latter's tracing "red" imagery in the novel because the practice tended to make the color symbolic and thus to substitute "a dead general idea for a live specific impression"; moreover, Nabokov explained, distinctions between "visual shades" ("a ruby" and "a pink rose") are as important for him as differences between colors.[19] Nabokov's warning is entirely unexceptionable when understood as his annoyance with readers who do not pay due attention to details, or who approach works in terms of preconceived ideas. His remarks are thus not directed against the possibility that systems of correspondences could be identified in a particular work that derive from the specific associations that colors are given in the work. This is in fact what we find in *Lolita.* For example, Humbert and Annabel have their last tryst "in the violet shadow of some red rocks ['rozovykh skal,' literally 'rose cliffs' in Nabokov's translation];" (pp. 15: 5); and Humbert imagines nymphets on an island whose boundaries include "rosy rocks" ("aleiushchie skaly," which in Russian denotes cliffs of a color related to bright red; pp. 18: 8). It is clear that Humbert's nymphets begin with Annabel, and the related setting and colors simply confirm this on another level. Nabokov's modifications of colors in his translation actually serve to increase the correspondence. Similarly, it would be a mistake not to note that a wind blows out of Charlotte's "red" candles when Humbert is sitting with her on the veranda (p. 67), because Quilty's first concealed appearance is in the "rubious convertible" that makes room for Humbert and Lolita when they arrive at The Enchanted Hunters (p. 119), because Quilty says "sleep is a rose" to Humbert when the latter unwittingly sits next to him on the hotel porch (p. 129), and because Quilty strikes "a light" in the same scene that fails to illuminate his face, probably because the wind blows it out (p. 129). It is possible "the dark-red private plane" that flies over Hourglass Lake when Humbert is there with Charlotte (p. 88) is also an evocation of Quilty's role in the novel (although not necessarily of his presence in the sky), especially since Humbert will eventually murder him rather than drown Charlotte. (On the other hand, Nabokov removed the color description of the plane from this scene in his screenplay of the novel, which suggests either that he may not have intended it to be an allusion to Quilty, or that he made a concession to black-and-white cinematography. Nabokov also changed the scene by having Humbert refer to the plane as a "guardian angel," and by indicating in the scenic directions that "a butterfly passes in shorebound flight." These details serve to underscore the moral dimension of Humbert's contemplated crime.)[20] Nabokov in fact increases the significance of the family of colors related to "red" and associated with Quilty by adding a phrase to the Russian translation of the scene when Lolita plays tennis with Quilty about how his tennis balls have "domodel'nye otmetiny krovavogo tsveta" (literally: "homemade, blood-colored marks") on them, a detail that is absent altogether from the English original (pp. 237: 216). And finally, when Humbert is on his way to kill Quilty, he notices an "airplane ... gemmed by Rubinov" (p. 284). Nabokov does not translate the jeweler's surname in either the original or the Russian version of the novel. In fact, the name can be read as a genitive formation from the Russian word for "ruby" ("rubin"), a gloss that is probably not entirely over the heads of readers without Russian. Thus this detail establishes a neat, and fateful symmetry with the red plane above Hourglass Lake when Humbert is thinking of murdering Charlotte.[21]

Given the numbers of readers who view *Lolita* as an immoral or amoral work, it is indeed ironic that Nabokov allows Humbert to make one of the most overt connections among ethics, aesthetics, and metaphysics that can be found in any of his novels. This is the entire content of a page-long chapter in which Humbert describes how he had once gone to a Catholic priest because he "hoped to deduce from my sense of sin the existence of a Supreme being" (p. 284). Humbert's ethics turn out to be much more severe than those of the Church: he states that "I was unable to transcend the simple human fact that whatever spiritual solace I might find, whatever lithophanic eternities might be provided for me, nothing could make my Lolita forget the foul lust I had inflicted upon her." Thus Humbert rejects personal salvation because he is convinced that there can be no forgiveness for his crime. All he can allow himself as "treatment of my misery" is "the melancholy and very local palliative of articulate art."

The ethical stance to which Humbert subscribes is encapsulated in a quotation from an unnamed "old poet" (whom Nabokov invented, as the Russian translation implies): "The moral sense of mortals is the duty / We have to pay on mortal sense of beauty" (pp. 285: 263). In other words, an individual's perception of something or someone as beautiful automatically awakens an ethical faculty in that person; this emerges as a function of being alive, or "mortal." [22] It is significant in terms of the novel's development that Humbert makes this point shortly after he describes his meeting with Lolita in her avatar as Mrs. Schiller. She is no longer a nymphet, and by his previous standards, Humbert should have lost all interest in her. Instead, he abandons his entire erotico-aesthetic set of criteria: "I insist the world know how much I loved my Lolita, *this* Lolita, pale and polluted, and big with another's child, but still grey-eyed, still sooty-lashed, still auburn and almond, still Carmencita, still mine" (p. 280). The fact that he says he loves her now more than "anything I had seen or imagined on earth" (p. 279) is an additional sign that he has abandoned "nymphet" as a category. In other words, when he sees Lolita as she really is, he finds her more beautiful than when he perceived her solipsistically; and a full awareness of her physical and spiritual constitution during the present moment makes him realize his crime toward her in the past. The importance of this kind of network of connections among perception, beauty, and ethics for understanding *Lolita* is that it is identical to Nabokov's own as he describes it in "The Art of Literature and Commonsense." Moreover, Humbert's twice repeated emphasis on "mortal" experience in the couplet he quotes evokes the metaphysical task he had set himself—of deducing "the existence of a Supreme Being ['Vysshego Sudii,' literally, 'Supreme Judge']" from his "sense of sin." He does not indicate directly whether or not he succeeded in arriving at the faith he sought. But his intuition that it does matter "in the infinite run" (p. 285) that he sinned against Lolita anchors his ethical stance in something beyond the mortal realm.[23] (Humbert thus stops short of rejecting God or His world because of the unjustifiable suffering of an innocent child. In this he differs from Ivan in Dostoevsky's *The Brothers Karamazov*, whose concern with comparable issues inevitably comes to mind in connection with *Lolita*.) We thus return to the theme of Humbert's existence being colored by experiences that transcend the earthly, which was first sounded in connection with Annabel, and then repeated in the form of fatidic patterning that fills his life. The vagueness of Humbert's intuitions, which do not extend as far as a literal belief in God, does not betray Nabokov's own intimations about the role of the "otherworld" in his existence.

This short chapter, together with the scene of Humbert's moral epiphany on the cliff edge, defines a crucial change in Humbert's existence and the entire novel's direction. But it is important to remember that the ethical stance Humbert assumes in it is clearly foreshadowed throughout the earlier parts of his narrative, and is intimately interwoven with them. Humbert refers to Lolita as "my sin, my soul" in the novel's first line, thus raising the theme of ethics, as well as weaving it into the rhythmical and alliterative texture of the novel. Elsewhere, ambivalence is the hallmark of Humbert's view of what he has been doing to Lolita. His passion and lust for her are on the surface throughout. But concurrently, and showing through them, we find that he was consistently, if intermittently, filled with an acute aware-ness of his sin. Representative examples include his reference to "the cesspoolful of rotting monsters" behind his smile (p. 46), his intention to "protect the purity of that twelve-year-old child" (p. 65), and his moment of hesitation before entering the room where Lolita is asleep in The Enchanted Hunters, when he says, before inserting the key into the lock, "one could still—" (pp. 129: 113; the Russian version is even more explicit: "Mozhno bylo eshche spastis'," literally, "One could still save oneself"). As Humbert indicates himself, blindness explains his behavior toward Lolita. In an especially revealing passage, he describes how Lolita is weeping in his arms after "the operation was over." Her reason is that he "had just retracted some silly promise she had forced me to make in a moment of blind impatient passion, and there she was sprawling and sobbing, and pinching my caressing hand, and I was laughing happily, and the atrocious, unbelievable, unbearable, and, I suspect, eternal horror that I know *now* was still but a dot of blackness in the blue of my bliss" (p. 171; similar moments appear on pp. 137, 139, 142).

Humbert's blindness also underlies an ethically based generalization about nymphets that he uses a number of times in the novel. He says that their "true nature" is "demoniac" (p. 18), that a nymphet is a "little deadly demon" (p. 19), or a "demon child" (p. 22), and that "nymphean evil breath[ed] through every pore" of Lolita (p. 127), who is actually "some immortal daemon disguised as a female child" (p. 141), and that a "devil" was behind his initial dealings with Lolita when he was still a roomer in her mother's house (pp. 57, 58). How can Humbert's allusion to one of the commonest religious explanations for the existence of evil be rec-onciled with the novel? Or is it simply Humbert's turn of phrase? The answer is suggested retroactively, when, after making some purchases, Humbert returns to the motel where he had stopped with Lolita, and notices "a red hood [that] protruded in somewhat codpiece fashion" from one of the garages (p. 215). Humbert does not recognize that this is of course Quilty's car, as both the color and the sexual connotation of its description indicate. When he enters the room, however, Humbert sees Lolita "dreamily brim[ming] with a diabolical glow that had no relation to me whatever" (p. 216). The reader concludes that Lolita has just been left by Quilty, and even Humbert suspects "her infidelity," although he does not know with whom (p. 217). Lolita has a similar mien later in the novel when she is recovering in the hospital. Humbert has unwittingly just seen an envelope that must have contained a letter from Quilty, and it is presumably under its influence that Lolita is lying in bed, as Humbert puts it, "innocently beaming at me or nothing" (p. 245). These two passages contain a nexus of details implying that Humbert's conception of nymphets as diabolical is yet another function of his blindness, and is thus a solipsistic projection rather than a true perception. It is Lolita's *indifference* to him, her being caught up in concerns that are totally unrelated to him, that Humbert perceives as "nymphean evil." Humbert's abandoning the category of nymphet as a specious fiction of course also supports the view that his "demons" are nonexistent. The conception of evil that emerges from *Lolita* is thus comparable to that described in "The Art of Literature and Commonsense"—it is the absence of good, even in the limited sense of empathy or attentive sympathy, rather than a "noxious presence."

At the conclusion of the novel, Humbert addresses Lolita rhetorically and explains that his reason for wanting to live a few months longer than Quilty is "to make you live in the minds of later generations. I am thinking of aurochs and angels, the secret of durable pigments, prophetic sonnets, the refuge of art. And this is the only immortality you and I may share, my Lolita" (p. 310). His implicit inclusion of his narrative in the category of "art" (which is in keeping with his earlier references to himself as a "poet"), together with his mentioning "angels" and "immortality," inevitably evokes his couplet about the "moral sense in mortals" being "the duty" they "have to pay on mortal sense of beauty." This connection implies that ethics have a textual dimension, because if Humbert's narrative is art, and therefore beautiful (the attempt to capture Lolita's beauty in language) there is a "moral sense" attached to it. This bridge implies another—that memory has an ethical dimension as well, which follows from the fact that the mode of existence of art ("durable pigments," "prophetic sonnets"), as well as other things both "real" and not ("aurochs," which are extinct, and "angels," who belong to imagination or metaphysics), is to "live in the minds of . . . generations." This conclusion inevitably draws the reader into the novel's, and Nabokov's, value system: if beauty is a function of accurate perception, then the careless reader is immortal. The final implication of the novel's conclusion has to do with metaphysics. Humbert speaks of the "refuge of art" being the "only immortality" that he can share with Lolita. This does not mean, however, that art is the only immortality that exists. Humbert's couplet in fact suggests that his ethical sense is a sign of some absolute that validates human behavior. In these terms, therefore, the emphasis in the novel's concluding sentence can be seen as falling on the *kind* of immortality that the *sinner* can share with his *victim,* which leaves open the possibility that Lolita occupies another space altogether.

NOTES

Works by Nabokov cited in the text and notes:

The Annotated Lolita. Edited, with a preface, introduction, and notes by Alfred Appel, Jr. New York: McGraw-Hill, 1970.
"Foreword." In his *Despair.* New York: Putnam's, 1965. 7–10.
The Gift. Translated by Michael Scammell in collaboration with the author. 1963. Reprint. New York: Wideview/Perigee, n.d.
Lolita: A Screenplay. New York: McGraw-Hill, 1974.
The Nabokov-Wilson Letters: Correspondence between Vladimir Nabokov and Edmund Wilson, 1940–1971. Edited, annotated, and introduced by Simon Karlinsky. New York: Harper and Row, 1979.

Speak, Memory: An Autobiography Revisited. New York: Putnam's, 1966.
Strong Opinions. New York: McGraw-Hill, 1973.

[1] All page references are to *The Annotated Lolita* and will be given in the text. Where given, references to Nabokov's Russian translation of the novel (*Lolita,* translated by Vladimir Nabokov [New York: Phaedra, 1967]) will be in the form (English: Russian). Some of the changes Nabokov made when translating the novel are discussed by Jane Grayson, *Nabokov Translated* (Oxford: Oxford University Press, 1977), 255, and by Gennady Barabtarlo, "Onus Probandi: On the Russian *Lolita,*" *Russian Review* 47, no. 3 (1988): 237–52.

[2] Lucy Maddox, *Nabokov's Novels in English* (Athens: University of Georgia Press, 1983), 74–78, makes a similar point and draws parallels with Proust, Keats, and Poe, all of whom are alluded to in the novel.

[3] *The Nabokov-Wilson Letters,* 296, 298. David Rampton, *Vladimir Nabokov: A Critical Study of the Novels* (Cambridge: Cambridge University Press, 1984), 103–7, argues against seeing *Lolita* as pornographic, and provides an excellent analysis of Nabokov's style from this point of view.

[4] Quoted by Rampton, 202 n. 34.

[5] *Strong Opinions,* 47, 15; see ibid., 23, for Nabokov's sympathy for Lolita. Nabokov's remark in his afterword to the novel (316) that "*Lolita* has no moral in tow" should clearly be read as a denial that there is anything in the work that is not fully integrated into its theme and form. It is also noteworthy that Nabokov saw Humbert as someone who had partially redeemed himself ("Foreword" to *Despair,* 9).

[6] Rampton, 107–9, 115, discusses the issue of the reader's ethical response to the work, but sees it as more equivocal than I do. A good, brief overview of trends in criticism of *Lolita* is in Pekka Tammi, *Problems of Nabokov's Poetics: A Narratological Analysis* (Helsinki: Suomalainen Tiedeakatemia, 1985), 276–79. Tammi also stresses the importance of distinguishing between Humbert as character and Humbert as self-conscious narrator of his experiences (281–86). However, not all features of Humbert's narrative can be ascribed to him; a higher agency of which he is not fully aware is also implied in the novel. For a discussion of the novel's subtle rhetoric, see Nomi Tamir-Ghez, "The Art of Persuasion in Nabokov's *Lolita,*" *Poetics Today* 1, nos. 1–2 (1979): 65–84.

[7] A related argument has been advanced by Douglas Fowler, *Reading Nabokov* (Ithaca: Cornell University Press, 1974), 172; and Appel, "Introduction," *The Annotated Lolita,* lvi. Tammi, 275, concludes after an ingenious examination of the evidence about the audience for whom Humbert intends his narrative, that he comes close to seeing it "as a literary work in its own right."

[8] Tammi, 279ff., argues convincingly that Humbert's own narrative strategies derive from detective fiction, and that he is not, therefore, as unselfconscious a narrator as some critics have thought.

[9] Fowler, 1948–51, clearly overstates the case when he claims that Humbert is one of Nabokov's "favorites." This assessment is due in part to Fowler's misreading the scene at Hourglass Lake when Humbert contemplates drowning Charlotte: since Jean Farlow is concealed nearby, Humbert is hardly presented with the opportunity for a "perfect crime." On the other hand, Fowler is correct to stress the role of fate in Humbert's existence, and the important effect it has on limiting his guilt.

[10] "The Art of Literature and Commonsense" was delivered around 1951. Chapter 11 of *Speak, Memory,* which deals with "cosmic synchronization" and related matters, was first published in the September 1949 issue of *Partisan Review* (see *Speak, Memory,* 10). Nabokov states that he began to compose *Lolita* in approximately 1949 (after writing a related story in Russian some ten years earlier, which was published posthumously in English translation as *The Enchanter*) and completed the manuscript in 1954 (see "On a Book Entitled *Lolita,*" *The Annotated Lolita,* 314).

[11] A similar conclusion has been reached by a number of critics: see, for example, Michael Bell, "*Lolita* and Pure Art," *Essays in Criticism* 24, no. 2 (1974): 169–84, and Robert T. Levine, "'My Ultraviolet Darling': The Loss of Lolita's Childhood," *Modern Fiction Studies* 25, no. 3 (1979): 471–79, who also discusses the related issue of the impossibility for Humbert to live in a timeless world with Lolita. *Laughter in the Dark* (1938) resembles Lolita in the way the villain Axel Rex views and treats all other human beings in terms of aesthetic criteria. However, the omniscient narrative structure of this novel allows Nabokov to condemn Rex overtly.

[12] *Strong Opinions,* 147.

[13] For example, Appel, *The Annotated Lolita,* 409 n. 237/2; other patterning related to tennis is described by Appel in *Nabokov's Dark Cinema* (New York: Oxford University Press, 1979), 150.

[14] Andrew Field, *VN: The Art and Life of Vladimir Nabokov* (New York: Crown, 1986), 316–17, reports that he found no such story in French newspapers of the day, and concludes it was probably "one of Nabokov's false trails." He also discussed the story in *Nabokov: His Life in Art* (Boston: Little, Brown, 1967), 323–24. Appel traces prison imagery in his introduction and notes to *The Annotated Lolita,* xx–xxi, lii, 438.

[15] Brian Boyd, *Nabokov's Ada: The Place of Consciousness* (Ann Arbor: Ardis, 1985), 238 n. 14. Boyd assumes (57) that free will as well as chance plays a role in Humbert's life, and gives such examples as "had not Humbert been tempted by the thought of lodging with Ginny McCoo, he would never have come to Ramsdale," and "had not Humbert by chance spotted Lolita, he would not have stayed at 342 Lawn Street." However, given that Humbert wonders if he is not predisposed toward nymphets, it is inevitable that he would be tempted to investigate a little girl in the person of Ginny (whose surname echoes Quilty's nickname, moreover, and thus acquires additional resonance). And the fact that Humbert spots Lolita sunning herself in a scene that is clearly a parodic evocation of Annabel by the sea, makes the "chance" nature of the sighting more than suspect. In general, the dominance of fate and patterning in Nabokov's fictions makes it virtually impossible to prove the absence of determinism from any concatenation of events.

[16] W. W. Rowe, *Nabokov's Spectral Dimension* (Ann Arbor: Ardis, 1981), 67–73, also investigates this possibility, and traces some of the related meteorological imagery.

[17] Carl R. Proffer, *Keys to* Lolita (Bloomington: Indiana University Press, 1968), 127, points out that the thunderhead is also linked to the church that Charlotte attended during Humbert's couch scenes with Lolita, which increases its portent.

[18] Boyd, *Nabokov's Ada*, 182–83, 187, 192, 194, 277, points out that aquatic and mermaid imagery in *Ada* suggests that Lucette's spirit may have influenced Van and Ada after she commits suicide.

[19] Quoted by Appel, *The Annotated Lolita*, 362 n. 58/1.

[20] *Lolita, A Screenplay*, 81.

[21] Another dimension of concealed patterning is literary allusions; useful studies that identify these include Appel's annotations in *The Annotated Lolita*, and Proffer, *Keys to* Lolita, 3–53.

[22] Tammi, 286, reads this passage in the light of his basically metaliterary view that Nabokov is often concerned with demonstrating "the superiority of literary structuring [to private allusion] as the dominant theme of [his] novels."

[23] The novel's ethics are thus less nihilistic than a number of interpreters have claimed: for example, Martin Green, "Tolstoy and Nabokov: The Morality of *Lolita*," in *Vladimir Nabokov's* Lolita, edited by Harold Bloom (New York: Chelsea House, 1987), 13–33.

CONTRIBUTORS

HAROLD BLOOM is Sterling Professor of the Humanities at Yale University and Henry W. and Albert A. Berg Professor of English at the New York University Graduate School. He is a 1985 MacArthur Foundation recipient, served as the Charles Eliot Norton Professor of Poetry at Harvard University (1987–88), and is the author of nineteen books, the most recent being *The Book of J* (1990). Currently he is editing the Chelsea House series Modern Critical Views and The Critical Cosmos, and other Chelsea House series in literary criticism.

GABRIEL JOSIPOVICI is a prolific and respected British novelist, critic, and playwright. Among his critical works are *The World and the Book* (1971), *The Lessons of Modernism* (1977), *Writing and the Body* (1982), and *The Book of God: A Response to the Bible* (1988). His recent novels include *Contre-Jour: A Triptych after Pierre Bonnard* (1986) and *In the Fertile Land* (1987). In 1990 appeared *Steps: Selected Fiction and Drama*.

STEVEN SWANN JONES is Professor of English at California State University, Los Angeles. He has compiled *Folklore and Literature in the United States: An Annotated Bibliography of Studies of Folklore in American Literature* (1984) and has written *The New Comparative Method: Structural and Symbolic Analysis of the Allomotifs of "Snow White"* (1990).

LUCY B. MADDOX is Professor of English at Georgetown University. She is the author of *Nabokov's Novels in English* (1983).

RICHARD H. BULLOCK is Associate Professor of English at Wright State University (Dayton, OH). He is coeditor, with John Trimbur, of *The Politics of Writing Instruction: Postsecondary* (1991).

JEFFREY BERMAN, Professor of English at SUNY–Albany, is author of *Joseph Conrad: Writing as Rescue* (1977), *The Talking Cure: Literary Representations of Psychoanalysis* (1985), and *Narcissism and the Novel* (1990). He is also general editor of a new series of books on literature and psychoanalysis to be published by New York University Press.

JOHN HAEGERT is Professor of Modern Literature and Critical Theory at the University of Evansville (Evansville, IN). He has written articles on D. H. Lawrence, John Fowles, Herman Melville, and Frank Conroy.

TREVOR McNEELY is the author of articles on Hopkins, Emerson, Hemingway, and Shakespeare's *Othello*. He is Professor of English at Brandon University (Brandon, Manitoba).

LINDA KAUFFMAN is Professor of English at the University of Maryland (College Park, MD). She has written *Discourses of Desire: Gender, Genre, and Epistolary Fictions* (1986) and *Special Delivery: Epistolary Modes in Modern Fiction* (1992) and has edited *Feminism and Institutions: Dialogues on Feminist Theory* (1989) and *Gender and Theory: Dialogues on Feminist Theory* (1989).

VLADIMIR E. ALEXANDROV is Professor of Russian Literature at Yale University. He is the author of *Andrei Bely: The Major Symbolist Fiction* (1985) and *Nabokov's Otherworld* (1991).

BIBLIOGRAPHY

Adams, Robert Martin. "Vladimir Nabokov." In *Afterjoyce: Studies in Fiction After* Ulysses. New York: Oxford University Press, 1977, pp. 146–61.

Aldridge, A. Owen. "*Lolita* and *Les Liaisons dangereuses*." *Wisconsin Studies in Contemporary Literature* 2, No. 3 (Fall 1961): 20–26.

Amis, Kingsley. "She Was a Child and I Was a Child." *Spectator,* 6 November 1959, pp. 635–36.

Anderson, William. "Time and Memory in *Lolita*." *Centennial Review* 24 (1980): 360–83.

Appel, Alfred, Jr. "*Lolita:* The Springboard of Parody." *Contemporary Literature* 8 (1967): 204–41.

———. *Nabokov's Dark Cinema.* New York: Oxford University Press, 1974.

———. "The Road to *Lolita,* or the Americanization of an Emigré." *Journal of Modern Literature* 4 (1974–75): 3–31.

Bader, Julia. *Crystal Land: Artifice in Nabokov's English Novels.* Berkeley: University of California Press, 1972.

Banta, Martha. "Benjamin, Edgar, Humbert, and Jay." *Yale Review* 60 (1970–71): 532–49.

Bell, Michael. "*Lolita* and Pure Art." *Essays in Criticism* 24 (1974): 169–84.

Bloom, Harold. *Vladimir Nabokov's* Lolita. New York: Chelsea House, 1987.

Brand, Dana. "The Interaction of Aestheticism and American Consumer Culture in Nabokov's *Lolita*." *Modern Language Studies* 17, No. 2 (Spring 1967): 14–21.

Brown, Clarence. "A Little Girl Migrates." *New Republic,* 20 January 1968, pp. 19–20.

Bruss, Elizabeth W. "Vladimir Nabokov: Illusions of Reality and the Reality of Illusions." In *Autobiographical Acts: The Changing Situation of a Literary Genre.* Baltimore: Johns Hopkins University Press, 1976, pp. 127–62.

Butler, Steven H. "*Lolita* and the Modern Experience of Beauty." *Studies in the Novel* 18 (1986): 427–37.

Campbell, Felicia Florine. "A Princedom by the Sea." *Lock Haven Review* No. 10 (1968): 39–46.

Ciancio, Ralph A. "Nabokov and the Verbal Mode of the Grotesque." *Contemporary Literature* 18 (1977): 509–33.

Clancy, Laurie. *The Novels of Vladimir Nabokov.* New York: St. Martin's Press, 1984.

Cummins, George M. "Nabokov's Russian *Lolita*." *Slavic and East European Journal* 21 (1977): 354–65.

Danzig, Allan. "Lolita and the Lechers." *Satire Newsletter* 2, No. 1 (Fall 1964): 57–63.

Dennison, Sally. "Vladimir Nabokov: The Work of Art as a Dirty Book." In *[Alternative] Literary Publishing: Five Modern Histories.* Iowa City: University of Iowa Press, 1984, pp. 157–89.

Dillard, R. H. W. "Not Text, but Texture: The Novels of Vladimir Nabokov." *Hollins Critic* 3, No. 3 (June 1966): 1–12.

Dupee, F. W. "*Lolita* in America." *Encounter* 12, No. 2 (February 1959): 30–35.

———. "A Preface to *Lolita*." *Anchor Review* No. 2 (1957): 1–13.

———, et al. *L'Affaire* Lolita: *Défense de l'écrivain.* Paris: Olympia Press, 1957.

Dyer, Gary R. "Humbert Humbert's Use of Catullus 58 in *Lolita*." *Twentieth Century Literature* 34 (1988): 1–15.

Field, Andrew. *Nabokov: His Life in Art.* Boston: Little, Brown, 1967.

Fowler, Douglas. *Reading Nabokov.* Ithaca, NY: Cornell University Press, 1974.

Gamel, Mary-Kay. "You Can Always Count on a Murderer for a Fancy Prose Style; or, The Net and the Pin." *Pacific Coast Philology* 18, Nos. 1–2 (November 1983): 100–107.

Giblett, Rodney. "Writing Sexuality, Reading Pleasure." *Paragraph* 12 (1989): 229–38.

Grabes, H. *Fictitious Biographies: Vladimir Nabokov's English Novels.* The Hague: Mouton, 1977.

Green, Geoffrey. *Freud and Nabokov.* Lincoln: University of Nebraska Press, 1988.

Green, Martin. "The Morality of *Lolita.*" *Kenyon Review* 28 (1966): 352–77.

Harold, Brent. "*Lolita:* Nabokov's Critique of Aloofness." *Papers on Language and Literature* 11 (1975): 71–82.

Harris, Harold J. "*Lolita* and the Sly Foreword." *Mad River Review* 1, No. 2 (Spring–Summer 1965): 29–38.

Hiatt, L. R. "Nabokov's *Lolita:* A 'Freudian' Cryptic Crossword." *American Imago* 24 (1967): 360–70.

Hicks, Granville. "*Lolita* and Her Problems." *Saturday Review,* 16 August 1958, pp. 12, 38.

Hinchcliff, Arnold P. "Belinda in America." *Studi Americani* 6 (1961): 339–47.

Hughes, D. J. "Reality and the Hero: *Lolita* and *Henderson the Rain King.*" *Modern Fiction Studies* 6 (1960): 345–64.

Hyde, G. M. *Vladimir Nabokov: America's Russian Novelist.* London: Marion Boyars, 1977.

Jong, Erica. "Time Has Been Kind to the Nymphet: *Lolita* 30 Years Later." *New York Times Book Review,* 5 June 1988, pp. 3, 46–47.

Joyce, James. "Lolita in Humberland." *Studies in the Novel* 6 (1974): 339–48.

Karges, Joann. *Nabokov's Lepidoptera: Genres and Genera.* Ann Arbor: Ardis, 1985.

Lee, L. L. *Vladimir Nabokov.* Boston: Twayne, 1976.

Levine, Robert T. "*Lolita* and the Originality of Style." *Essays in Literature* 4 (1977): 110–21.

McDonald, James L. "John Ray, Jr., Critic and Artist: The Foreword to *Lolita.*" *Studies in the Novel* 5 (1973): 352–57.

Maddox, Lucy. *Nabokov's Novels in English.* Athens: University of Georgia Press, 1983.

Masinton, Charles G. "What *Lolita* Is Really About." *New Mexico Humanities Review* No. 31 (1989): 71–76.

Mayer, Priscilla. "Nabokov's *Lolita* and Pushkin's *Onegin:* McAdam, McEve and McFate." In *The Achievements of Vladimir Nabokov,* edited by George Gibian and Stephen Jan Parker. Ithaca, NY: Center for International Studies, Cornell University, 1984, pp. 179–211.

Megerle, Brenda. "The Tantalization of *Lolita.*" *Studies in the Novel* 11 (1979): 338–48.

Mitchell, Charles. "Mythic Seriousness in *Lolita.*" *Texas Studies in Literature and Language* 5 (1963–64): 329–43.

Morton, Donald E. *Vladimir Nabokov.* New York: Ungar, 1974.

Nabokov, Vladimir. *The Annotated Lolita.* Edited by Alfred Appel, Jr. New York: McGraw-Hill, 1970.

Nelson, Gerald B. "*Lolita.*" In *Ten Versions of America.* New York: Knopf, 1972, pp. 185–201.

Nemerov, Howard. "The Morality of Art." *Kenyon Review* 19 (1957): 313–21.

Olsen, Lance. "A Janus-Text: Realism, Fantasy, and Nabokov's *Lolita.*" *Modern Fiction Studies* 32 (1986): 115–26.

Packman, David. *Vladimir Nabokov: The Structure of Literary Desire.* Columbia: University of Missouri Press, 1982.

Parker, Stephen Jan. *Understanding Vladimir Nabokov.* Columbia: University of South Carolina Press, 1987.

Pearce, Richard. "Nabokov's Black (Hole) Humor: *Lolita* and *Pale Fire.*" In *Comic Relief: Humor in Contemporary American Literature*, edited by Sarah Blacher Cohen. Urbana: University of Illinois Press, 1978, pp. 28–44.

———. "The World Upside Down II: William Burroughs's *Naked Lunch* and Nabokov's *Lolita.*" In *Stages of the Clown: Perspectives on Modern Fiction from Dostoyevsky to Beckett.* Carbondale: Southern Illinois University Press, 1970, pp. 84–101.

Phillips, Elizabeth. "The Hocus-Pocus of *Lolita.*" *Literature and Psychology* 10 (1960): 97–101.

Pifer, Ellen. *Nabokov and the Novel.* Cambridge, MA: Harvard University Press, 1980.

Pinnells, James R. "The Speech Ritual as an Element of Structure in Nabokov's *Lolita.*" *Dalhousie Review* 60 (1980–81): 605–21.

Prioleau, Elizabeth. "Humbert Humbert *Through the Looking Glass.*" *Twentieth Century Literature* 21 (1975): 428–37.

Pritchett, V. S. *"Lolita." New Statesman,* 10 January 1959, p. 38.

Proffer, Carl R. *Keys to* Lolita. Bloomington: Indiana University Press, 1968.

Quennell, Peter, ed. *Vladimir Nabokov: His Life, His Work, His World: A Tribute.* New York: Morrow, 1980.

Rackin, Donald. "The Moral Rhetoric of Nabokov's *Lolita.*" *Four Quarters* 22, No. 3 (Spring 1973): 3–19.

Rampton, David. *Vladimir Nabokov: A Critical Study of the Novels.* Cambridge: Cambridge University Press, 1984.

Rivers, J. E., and Charles Nicol, ed. *Nabokov's Fifth Arc: Nabokov and Others on His Life's Work.* Austin: University of Texas Press, 1982.

Rowe, W. W. *Nabokov's Deceptive World.* New York: New York University Press, 1971.

———. *Nabokov's Spectral Dimension.* Ann Arbor, MI: Ardis, 1981.

Rubinstein, E. "Approaching *Lolita.*" *Minnesota Review* 6 (1966): 361–67.

Rubman, Lewis H. "Creatures and Creators in *Lolita* and 'Death and the Compass.'" *Modern Fiction Studies* 19 (1973): 433–52.

Scheid, Mark. "Epistemological Structures in *Lolita.*" *Rice University Studies* 61 (1975): 127–40.

Schickel, Richard. "A Review of a Novel You Can't Buy." *Reporter,* 28 November 1957, pp. 45–47.

Shilstone, Frederick W. "The Courtly Misogynist: Humbert Humbert in *Lolita.*" *Studies in the Humanities* 8, No. 1 (June 1980): 5–10.

Shute, J. P. "Nabokov and Freud: The Play of Power." *Modern Fiction Studies* 30 (1984): 637–50.

Stark, John O. "Vladimir Nabokov." In *The Literature of Exhaustion: Borges, Nabokov, and Barth.* Durham, NC: Duke University Press, 1974, pp. 62–117.

Stegner, Page. *Escape into Aesthetics: The Art of Vladimir Nabokov.* New York: Dial Press, 1966.

Tamir-Ghez, Nomi. "The Art of Persuasion in Nabokov's *Lolita.*" *Poetics Today* 1, Nos. 1–2 (Autumn 1979): 65–83.

Tekiner, Christina. "Time in *Lolita.*" *Modern Fiction Studies* 25 (1979): 463–69.

Toker, Leona. *Nabokov: The Mystery of Literary Structures.* Ithaca, NY: Cornell University Press, 1989.

Uphaus, Robert W. "Nabokov's Kunstlerroman: Portrait of the Artist as a Dying Man." *Twentieth Century Literature* 13 (1967): 104–10.

Veeder, William. "Technique as Recovery: *Lolita* and *Mother Night.*" In *Vonnegut in*

America, edited by Jerome Klinkowitz and Donald L. Lawler. New York: Delacorte Press/Seymour Lawrence, 1977, pp. 97–132.

Vesterman, William. "Why Humbert Shoots Quilty." *Essays in Literature* 5 (1978): 85–93.

Wallace, Ronald. "No Harm in Smiling: Vladimir Nabokov's *Lolita.*" In *The Last Laugh: Form and Affirmation in the Contemporary American Novel.* Columbia: University of Missouri Press, 1979, pp. 65–89.

Winston, Mathew. "*Lolita* and the Dangers of Fiction." *Twentieth Century Literature* 21 (1975): 421–27.

Zall, Paul M. "Lolita and Gulliver." *Satire Newsletter* 3, No. 1 (Fall 1965): 33–37.

[Unsigned.] "Lolita's Creator—Author Nabokov, a 'Cosmic Joker.'" *Newsweek,* 25 June 1962, pp. 51–54.

ACKNOWLEDGMENTS

"On a Book Entitled *Lolita*" by Vladimir Nabokov from *Anchor Review* 2 (1957), © 1957 by Doubleday & Company, Inc. Reprinted by permission.

"A Lance into Cotton Wool" by Frank S. Meyer from *National Review*, November 22, 1958, © 1958 by National Weekly, Inc. Reprinted by permission of *National Review*.

"Lolita Lepidoptera" by Diana Butler from *New World Writing* 16 (1960), © 1960 by J. B. Lippincott Co. Reprinted by permission of HarperCollins Publishers, Inc.

"*Lolita*, or Scandal" by Denis de Rougemont from *Love Declared: Essays on the Myths of Love* by Denis de Rougemont, translated by Richard Howard, © 1961 by Editions Albin Michel, © 1963 by Random House, Inc., Reprinted by permission of Random House, Inc.

"*Dolorès Disparue*" by David L. Jones from *Symposium* 20, No. 2 (Summer 1966), © 1966 by *Symposium*. Reprinted by permission.

Vladimir Nabokov by Julian Moynahan, © 1971 by the University of Minnesota. Reprinted by permission of University of Minnesota Press.

"The Devil and Lolita" by Garry Wills from *New York Review of Books*, February 21, 1974, © 1974 by NYREV, Inc. Reprinted by permission.

"*Lolita* as Bildungsroman" by James Twitchell from *Genre* 7, No. 3 (September 1974), © 1974 by The University of Oklahoma. Reprinted by permission of *Genre*.

" 'My Ultraviolet Darling': The Loss of Lolita's Childhood" by Robert T. Levine from *Modern Fiction Studies* 25, No. 3 (Autumn 1979), © 1979 by the Purdue Research Foundation. Reprinted by permission of the Purdue Research Foundation.

"Io's Metamorphosis: A Classical Subtext for *Lolita*" by Susan Elizabeh Sweeney from *Classical and Modern Literature* 6, No. 2 (Winter 1986), © 1986 by CML, Inc. Reprinted by permission of *Classical and Modern Literature* and the author.

"Rereading *Lolita*, Reconsidering Nabokov's Relationship with Dostoevskij" by Katherine Tiernan O'Connor from *Slavic and East European Journal* 33, No. 1 (Spring 1989), © 1988 by AATSEEL of the U.S., Inc. Reprinted by permission.

"*Lolita*: Parody and the Pursuit of Beauty" by Gabriel Josipovici from *The World and the Book: A Study of Modern Fiction* by Gabriel Josipovici, © 1971 by Gabriel Josipovici. Reprinted by permission of Stanford University Press and The Macmillan Press Ltd.

"Folk Characterization in *Lolita*" (originally titled "The Enchanted Hunters: Nabokov's Use of Folk Characterization in *Lolita*") by Steven Swann Jones from *Western Folklore* 39, No. 4 (October 1980), © 1980 by the California Folklore Society. Reprinted by permission of the California Folklore Society.

"Necrophilia in *Lolita*" by Lucy B. Maddox from *Centennial Review* 26, No. 4 (Fall 1982), © 1982 by *The Centennial Review*. Reprinted by permission of *The Centennial Review* and the author.

"Humbert the Character, Humbert the Writer" (originally titled "Humbert the Character, Humbert the Writer: Artifice, Reality, and Art in *Lolita*") by Richard H. Bullock from *Philological Quarterly* 63, No. 2 (Spring 1984), © 1984 by The University of Iowa. Reprinted by permission of *Philological Quarterly* and the author.

"Nabokov and the Viennese Witch Doctor" by Jeffrey Berman from *The Talking Cure: Literary Representations of Psychoanalysis* by Jeffrey Berman, © 1985 by New York University. Reprinted by permission of New York University Press.

"The Americanization of Humbert Humbert" (originally titled "Artist in Exile: 'The Americanization of Humbert Humbert") by John Haegert from *ELH* 52, No. 3 (Fall 1985), © 1985 by The Johns Hopkins University Press. Reprinted by permission of The Johns Hopkins University Press.

" 'Lo' and Behold: Solving the *Lolita* Riddle" by Trevor McNeely from *Studies in the Novel* 21, No. 2 (Summer 1989), © 1989 by the University of North Texas. Reprinted by permission of *Studies in the Novel*.

"Framing Lolita: Is There a Woman in the Text?" by Linda Kauffman from *Special Delivery: Epistolary Modes in Modern Fiction* by Linda Kauffman, © 1992 by The University of Chicago Press. An earlier version was published in *Refiguring the Father: New Feminist Readings of Patriarchy*, edited by Patricia Yaeger and Beth Kowaleski-Wallace, © 1989 by the Board of Trustees, Southern Illinois University. Reprinted by permission of the author and Southern Illinois University Press.

"*Lolita*" by Vladimir E. Alexandrov from *Nabokov's Otherworld* by Vladimir E. Alexandrov, © 1991 by Princeton University Press. Reprinted by permission of Princeton University Press.

INDEX

A la recherche du temps perdu (Proust), 25
Abélard, Pierre, 150
Ada, 108
Albertine (*A la recherche du temps perdu*), 25–30, 64
Albinus (*Laughter in the Dark*), 29, 55, 57, 63–64
Aldanov, Mark, 5
Alice in Wonderland (Carroll), 20, 147–48
All the King's Men (Warren), 2
Ambassadors, The (James), 24
Amerigo, Prince (*The Golden Bowl*), 24
Annabel. *See* Leigh, Annabel
"Annabel Lee" (Poe), 14, 24, 30, 80, 82–83, 139
Antony (*Antony and Cleopatra*), 18
Appel, Alfred, Jr., 68, 72–75, 101, 121, 136, 141, 143, 154, 163, 187
Argus (*Metamorphoses*), 45–47
"Art of Literature and Commonsense, The," 171, 189, 191, 192n.10

Baal, 76
Bacon, Sir Francis, 117
Bader, Julia, 101–2
Beatrice (*The Divine Comedy*), 3, 10, 19, 30, 65
Bédier, Joseph, 19
Beebe, Maurice, 99–100
Bend Sinister, 22, 58–60
Béroul, 19
Blake, William, 68
Bleak House (Dickens), 158–59
Boone, Daniel, 128
Bovary, Emma (*Madame Bovary*), 88
Boyd, Brian, 183, 193n.15
Brooks, Van Wyck, 128, 130
Brothers Karamazov, The (Dostoevsky), 189
Burden, Jack (*All the King's Men*), 2
Burney, Fanny, 35

Candy (Southern), 35
"Cap o'Rushes," 73
Carmen (*Carmen*), 30

Carroll, Lewis (pseud. of C. L. Dodgson), 20, 147
Catholicism, 19, 57, 188
Charybdis (*Odyssey*), 76
Christianity, 73, 77
"Cinderella," 72
Circe (*Odyssey*), 74–75
Clarissa (Richardson), 35
Clemm, Virginia, 30
Cleopatra (*Antony and Cleopatra*), 18
Clifton, Gladys M., 114
Colette (childhood friend of Nabokov), 22
Compson, Caddy (*The Sound and the Fury*), 1–2, 35
Crime and Punishment (Dostoevsky), 33

Dahl, Mona, 149
Dante Alighieri, 3, 10, 19, 30, 65, 147
Daphne (*Metamorphoses*), 47–48
Dark, Juanita, 6
Darkbloom, Vivian, 42
Dedalus, Stephen (*A Portrait of the Artist as a Young Man*), 100
Defoe, Daniel, 35
Delalande, Pierre, 53
Despair, 50
Dickens, Charles, 11, 158–59
Dilsey (*The Sound and the Fury*), 1
Dodgson, C. L. *See* Carroll, Lewis
Don Quixote (*Don Quixote*), 88
Dostoevsky, Fyodor, 27, 33, 49–51, 146, 189
Double, The (Rank), 114

Eliot, George, 36
Eliot, T. S., 146
Emmie (*Invitation to a Beheading*), 22

Fanny Hill. See *Memoirs of a Woman of Pleasure*
Farlow, Jean, 177, 184–85
Faulkner, William, 1, 83, 166n.8
Felman, Shoshana, 165
Fetterly, Judith, 155
Fiedler, Leslie A., 137, 148n.6

Field, Andrew, 91, 97–98, 102, 109, 114
Flaubert, Gustave, 8, 88
Fliess, Wilhelm, 108
Fowler, Douglas, 98, 192nn.7, 9
Frankfurt, Harry K., 162
Franklin, Benjamin, 128
Freud, Sigmund, 2–3, 7, 10, 20, 88, 105–19, 155, 167n.29
Fromm, Erich, 116

Gift, The, 176–77, 187
Girard, René, 163
Goethe, Johann Wolfgang von, 19, 150–51, 164
Gold, Herbert, 49
Golden Bowl, The (James), 24
Great Gatsby, The (Fitzgerald), 31, 131
Green, Martin, 139

Handmaid's Tale, The (Atwood), 157
Harold, Brent, 99, 101
Hawthorne, Nathaniel, 120
Haze, Charlotte, 24, 31, 43–44, 46, 58, 69–70, 83–86, 91–93, 109, 124–26, 130, 145, 149–50, 161, 164, 173, 180, 183–88
Haze, Dolores. See *Lolita*
Hegel, G. W. F., 68
Héloïse, 150
Herman, Judith Lewis, 159
Heroides (Ovid), 150
Hogarth, William, 21
Holmes, Charlie, 41–42, 58, 69, 144–45
Home, Rachel, 6
Humbert, Humbert: as artist, 57, 61–67, 87–104, 112, 121–22, 130, 143–44, 150–52, 170–91; as émigré, 122–32; as folk character, 73–75; and homosexuality, 114–15; intellect of, 11; as Jupiter, 45–47; language of, 18, 61–62, 79–82, 149–50; his love for Lolita, 1–3, 9–10, 18–21, 30, 33–34, 38, 56–57, 112–15; morality of, 16, 28, 44, 49–51, 188–91; as murderer, 2, 29, 41; name of, 23; sexuality of, 12, 15, 38, 40, 54–56, 85–86, 112–14, 156, 160–61, 178–79
Humbertson, Jack, 97
"Hunter, The," 74

In the American Grain (Williams), 128
Interpretation of Dreams, The (Freud), 107, 109
Invitation to a Beheading, 22, 53, 60
Io (*Metamorphoses*), 45–49
Isolde (or Iseult), 13, 21

James, Henry, 23, 141, 157–58
Jones, John, 67n.4
Juliet (*Romeo and Juliet*), 10
Jung, C. G., 100–101
Juno (*Metamorphoses*), 45
Jupiter (*Metamorphoses*), 45–47
Juvenal (D. Julius Juvenalis), 13

Kafka, Franz, 51
Keats, John, 57, 64, 67n.4
Khodasevich, Vladislav, 111
Kierkegaard, Søren, 136
Kinbote, Charles (*Pale Fire*), 60, 102, 111, 116, 164
Kohut, Heinz, 116
Krafft-Ebing, Richard von, 144
Kühn, Sophie von, 19

Lamia (Keats), 64
Laughter in the Dark, 29, 55, 57, 59, 63–64
Lauter, Paul, 42, 44
Lawrence, D. H., 32, 120
Leigh, Annabel, 17, 20, 24–25, 31, 39–40, 54, 70, 76, 80–82, 91–93, 108, 110, 123, 125, 127, 129, 156, 163, 172, 176–79, 181–82, 184–85, 187–88
"Lenore" (Poe), 158
Lévi-Strauss, Claude, 155
Lewis, Sinclair, 10
"Ligeia" (Poe), 82–83
Lincoln, Abraham, 135
"Little Red Riding Hood," 74–75, 116
Lolita: and American culture, 8, 10, 31–32, 58, 120–33, 135; as *Bildungsroman*, 35–39; as epistolary novel, 149–51; and fairy tales, 68–78; and feminism, 149–68; and irony, 18, 23–24, 53–54, 105–6; and language, 9, 135–36; and literary criticism, 134–43; morality of, 7–8, 136–48, 152–54, 169–70, 188–91; Nabokov on, 5–9, 22–23, 103, 120, 134–35, 169–70; origin of,

5–6, 22–23; and pornography, 7,
9–10, 20, 33; and psychiatry, 105–
19; as satire, 12–14, 126–27; and
Tristan, 19–21
Lolita: as butterfly, 16–17; character of,
2, 9, 12, 18–19, 24, 111–12, 145–
46; death of, 77; as Dolores Haze,
17–18, 23–24, 31–32, 36, 39, 43,
45, 74–75, 85, 91, 93, 95, 99,
107, 110–12, 114, 156–57, 160;
her feelings toward Humbert, 21–
22, 33–34, 161; as folk character,
70–73; as Io, 45–49; maturation
of, 35–39; name of, 23; sexuality
of, 25–28, 95, 114, 144–45, 162,
165; as victim, 3, 18, 28, 40–45,
50, 114, 153–66

McCarthy, Joseph, 106
McFate, Aubrey, 32–33, 41, 162,
182–83
"Maiden without Hands, The," 71, 73
Marble Faun, The (Hawthorne), 24
Margot (*Laughter in the Dark*), 58, 64
Mariette (*Bend Sinister*), 22
Marlowe, Christopher, 30
Memoirs of a Woman of Pleasure
(Cleland), 9, 35
Mercury (*Metamorphoses*), 45–47
Merivale, Patricia, 100
Merrill, Robert, 138, 143
Metamorphoses (Ovid), 45–49
"Metamorphosis, The" (Kafka), 51
Mignon (*Wilhelm Meister's Apprentice-
ship*), 19
Mithers, Carol Lynn, 161
Modest Proposal, A (Swift), 12
Moll Flanders (Defoe), 35
Molnar, Thomas, 154–55, 158
Monique, 40, 172
Moynahan, Julian, 44
Murdoch, Iris, 2
Musil, Robert, 21
Myth of the Birth of the Hero, The
(Rank), 113

New Republic, 13–14
Novalis (pseud. of Friedrich von Hard-
enberg), 19

Odysseus (*Odyssey*), 74–75
Odyssey (Homer), 74

Oedipus complex, 107, 109, 113,
115–16
"On a Book Entitled *Lolita,*" 53, 169
Ovid (P. Ovidius Naso), 45–49, 65

Paduk (*Bend Sinister*), 58
Pale Fire, 60, 102, 107, 111, 116, 121,
153, 164
Pamela (Richardson), 35
Paris Soir, 50
Petrarch (Francesco Petrarca), 19, 65,
147
Phillips, Elizabeth, 105
Playboy, 134
Pnin, 107–8
Poe, Edgar Allan, 2, 14, 19–20, 24,
30, 79–80, 82–83, 88, 109, 120,
127, 139–41, 148n.12, 151, 158,
163
"Poetic Principle, The" (Poe), 139
*Portrait of the Artist as a Young Man,
A* (Joyce), 100
Possessed, The (Dostoevsky), 146
Proteus, 46
Proust, Marcel, 2, 24–30, 63
Pygmalion, 112

Quilty, Clare: character of, 15, 33, 60–
61, 63, 90, 95–96, 100, 149, 155;
as folk character, 73–75; as homosexual, 114; and Humbert, 30, 41,
44, 57, 60–62, 83, 98–99, 102,
109, 114–15, 125–26, 130, 162–
64, 177, 180–81, 183, 188, 191;
and Lolita, 2, 15, 26–27, 60–61,
86, 95–96, 116, 172–73, 179–80,
183–84, 190; murder of, 29–31,
33, 41, 46, 61, 84–85, 98–99,
101, 110, 131, 145, 150, 165, 171,
187; as playwright, 42, 46, 60, 95–
96, 182; sexuality of, 15, 30, 109,
179

Rambeau, James R., 110
Rank, Otto, 107, 113–14
Raskolnikov (*Crime and Punishment*),
33
Ray, John, Jr., 5, 8, 54, 87–88, 101,
105–6, 108, 121, 140, 151–53,
157, 160–61, 165
Real Life of Sebastian Knight, The, 183,
187

Rex, Axel (*Laughter in the Dark*), 59, 62–64
Richardson, Samuel, 23, 35
Rita, 92, 97, 101, 157
Romanticism, 2–3, 57, 64–65, 67n.4, 151
Romeo (*Romeo and Juliet*), 10
"Rose for Emily, A" (Faulkner), 83
Roth, Phyllis, 115
Roxanna (Defoe), 35
"Rumpelstiltskin," 73

Sade, Donatien Alphonse François, marquis de, 7
Schiller, Richard F., 72–73, 83, 97, 110, 116, 139
Schweickart, Patrocinio, 156, 165
Scylla (*Odyssey*), 76
Shklovsky, Victor, 149
Skinner, B. F., 107
"Sleeping Beauty," 71–72
"Snow White," 69–74, 76
Sophocles, 43
Sorrows of Young Werther, The (Goethe), 162
Sound and the Fury, The (Faulkner), 1
"Sovershenstvo," 187
Speak, Memory, 171, 175–78, 182
"Special Type of Choice of Object Made by Men, A" (Freud), 112–13
Spillane, Mickey, 15
Stavrogin (*The Possessed*), 51; 146
Stegner, Page, 98, 101, 136
Steinberg, Saul, 37
Stowe, Harriet Beecher, 23
Strong Opinions, 111
Svidrigajlov (*Crime and Punishment*), 49–51
Swann, M. (*A la recherche du temps perdu*), 2

Swift, Jonathan, 12–13, 58–59
Swine, Mr., 75
Syrinx (*Metamorphoses*), 45, 47–48

Tale of a Tub, A (Swift), 59
Tammi, Pekka, 192nn.6–8
Thackeray, William Makepeace, 35
Thoreau, Henry David, 162
Tolstoy, Leo, 139
Trilling, Lionel, 13–14, 18, 42, 137, 148n.6, 152–55, 158
Tristan (*Tristan and Isolde*), 13, 19–21
Tristan and Isolde (Gottfried von Strassburg), 20–21
Turn of the Screw, The (James), 157–58, 162

"Ultima Thule," 107

Valeria, 28, 83, 86, 91–93, 110, 115, 145, 157
Valéry, Paul, 66
Vanity Fair (Thackeray), 35

Wagner, Richard, 21
Warren, Robert Penn, 2
Werther (*The Sorrows of Young Werther*), 150–51
Wharton, Edith, 35
What Is Art? (Tolstoy), 139
Wilde, Oscar, 139–40
"William Wilson" (Poe), 163
Williams, William Carlos, 128, 130
Williams, Carol T., 99
Wilson, Edmund, 169
Wine of the Puritans, The (Brooks), 128

Zoo (Shklovsky), 149, 154